Wow—I read the book on the plane last night—it's the book I've always wanted to write. You'll want to keep it close at hand. It is an eminently readable dissertation on best practices, application architectures, and organizational metamorphoses that every e-business IT manager needs to know.

—Anne Thomas Manes, Director Business Strategy,
Sun Microsystems

I was delighted to see a book that talks to the people who need to get us where we are going. Not overly technical and a healthy change from the overly generalized genre of business IT books published.

—Gregory Maciag, President and CEO, ACORD

This is really a terrific book! In the current rush of books on e-commerce, the treatment is generally too high-level to be of any value, or too low-level to help manage the difficult transition from business to e-business. This book finally bridges the gap, with hands-on details for the manager who has to somehow transition 40 years worth of computing detritus supporting a bricks-and-mortar operation to an online business melding the walk-in customer with the surf-in customer. Congratulations to one and all.

—Richard Mark Soley, Ph.D., Chairman and CEO,
Object Management Group, Inc.

A powerful yet easily understandable strategic blueprint for successful transition to e-business augmented with liberal examples showing the application of technology for business advantage. A must read for those tasked with managing the migration to e-business.

—Paul Allen, Principal Component Strategist,
Computer Associates

The software architectures that have evolved over the last decade to drive the Internet and the "knowledge economy" are truly complex—they are today's rocket science. The authors have produced a cogent, readable explanation of state-of-the-art thinking about modern e-business software: a useful framework for corporate decision makers. The book gives high-level perspectives and practical guidance for rethinking business processes and retooling applications development to support business in the modern, totally wired age. The inclusion of several case studies is particularly helpful.

—Avron Barr and Shirley Tessler,
Stanford Computer Industry Project

Developing E-Business Systems & Architectures

A Manager's Guide

Developing E-Business Systems & Architectures

A Manager's Guide

Paul Harmon

Michael Rosen

Michael Guttman

MORGAN KAUFMANN PUBLISHERS

AN IMPRINT OF ACADEMIC PRESS

A Harcourt Science and Technology Company

SAN FRANCISCO   SAN DIEGO   NEW YORK   BOSTON
LONDON   SYDNEY   TOKYO

Acquisitions Editor	Tim Cox
Publishing Services Manager	Scott Norton
Senior Production Editor	Edward Wade
Production Assistant	Mei Levenson
Editorial Assistant	Stacie Pierce
Cover Design	Ross Carron Design
Cover Image	© Stone/Robert Frerck
Text Design	Side By Side Studios/Mark Ong
Technical Illustration and Composition	Technologies 'N Typography
Copyeditor	Ken DellaPenta
Proofreader	Jennifer McClain
Indexer	Ty Koontz
Printer	Courier Corporation

Designations used by companies to distinguish their products are often claimed as trademarks or registered trademarks. In all instances where Morgan Kaufmann Publishers is aware of a claim, the product names appear in initial capital or all capital letters. Readers, however, should contact the appropriate companies for more complete information regarding trademarks and registration.

ACADEMIC PRESS
A Harcourt Science and Technology Company
525 B Street, Suite 1900, San Diego, CA 92101-4495, USA
http://www.academicpress.com

Academic Press
Harcourt Place, 32 Jamestown Road, London, NW1 7BY, United Kingdom
http://www.academicpress.com

Morgan Kaufmann Publishers
340 Pine Street, Sixth Floor, San Francisco, CA 94104-3205, USA
http://www.mkp.com

05 04 03 02 01   5 4 3 2 1

Library of Congress Cataloging-in-Publication Data is available for this book.

ISBN 1-55860-665-3

This book is printed on acid-free paper.

Foreword

by Ed Yourdon

Since the late 1990s, *e-business* has been the hottest buzzword in corporations throughout the United States and in most advanced countries around the world. Not only do senior executives see the Internet and the Web as mechanisms for attracting new customers and entering new markets, they also see it as the basis for new competitive threats—from existing competitors in their existing marketplace, from established firms in distant geographical regions, and from upstart competitors who would never have been taken seriously before the arrival of the Web.

As a result, the publishing industry has been churning out e-business books for desperate executives, advising them on the risks and potentials of the new e-business world. At the same time, we have seen a larger number of books aimed at the technical developers who work at the "bits-and-bytes" level—for example, books on Java, HTML, XML, and the technical details of Web servers. But there has been a vacuum in the middle, in the area where senior IT architects and middle-level operational managers are struggling to turn the vision statement of senior management into reality.

But while there may have been a lack of high-level "how-to" books, there certainly has not been a lack of activity. Consultants like Paul Harmon, Mike Rosen, and Michael Guttman have spent the past several years—all the way back to the early and mid-1990s, before the Internet/Web buzzwords had even been established—working with companies who are transforming themselves into e-businesses. In some cases, this means working with managers of end user departments, or P&L business units, to reengineer their business practices to take advantage of the Internet/Web. And in many other cases, it means working with IT managers who are responsible for designing and developing new e-business applications, while also integrating those applications with the vast legacy systems that still run the "back office" part of the organization.

Based on several years of this kind of hands-on experience, Harmon, Rosen, and Guttman have written a book that will serve as a road map for today's generation of business and IT managers engaged in the e-business "transformation" of their existing organizations. Interestingly, the authors do not view this transformation as an optional exercise: They firmly believe that any major company wishing to survive the current decade will find it imperative to transform itself into an e-business operation. To paraphrase Jack Welch, the fabled head of General Electric, e-business is priority 1, and 2, and 3 for major businesses today.

Obviously, this must begin with the formulation of an e-business strategy. The authors devote an early chapter to this topic, but it's not really the core of the book. Nor should it be; as mentioned earlier, there is already a plethora of books from Harvard Business School professors about the details of e-business strategy formulation. Unfortunately, most of these books don't answer the question asked by the IT managers and operational business managers: "Fine, we understand the vision statement, but how do we actually *do* it?"

"Doing it," as the authors point out, begins with the reengineering of business processes. The very mention of reengineering will discourage some readers, especially those who remember unsuccessful reengineering efforts from the early 1990s. But the reality is that today's businesses—no matter how lean and mean they may be, no matter how "customer-focused" they may think they are—will be *forced* to reengineer their business processes to take advantage of Internet technology. Not only that, but businesses must reorganize their IT operations, because e-business necessitates fundamental changes in the way companies develop software systems.

The heart of *Developing E-Business Systems & Architectures* focuses on the *technology* associated with creating an e-business operation. The authors provide an overview of components and the range of component technologies used in e-business development. They explain why a successful e-business implementation should be based on an enterprise component architecture, and they describe how to implement such an architecture. And since all of these technologies must be created by people, and organizational groups, they conclude this part of their discussion with a detailed plan for how an IT organization can transform itself into a new organization capable of carrying out component-based development.

Harmon, Rosen, and Guttman acknowledge that they have not written a "handbook" for developing e-business systems, and that they haven't provided a lot of detail about various aspects of the effort. But some of those detailed handbooks already exist, and the authors intend to write new ones of their own. The main point to realize, though, is that without a road map, a detailed handbook will distract the reader into focusing on tactical problems, while leaving strategic issues unsolved. The road map must come first, and *Developing E-Business Systems & Architectures* does an excellent job of providing that road map.

Contents

Foreword
 by Ed Yourdon ix
Preface xvii

1. **The E-Business Challenge** 1
 Toys R Us 2
 Charles Schwab 8
 Citigroup and World Banking 10
 Automakers and Their Parts Suppliers 13
 Summary 18

2. **Developing an E-Business Strategy** 21
 Defining a Strategy 23
 Porter's Model of Competition 25
 Industries, Products, and Value Propositions 29
 Strategies for Competing 30
 An E-Business Strategy 32
 Developing Your Strategy 33
 The Classic Model of Competition 38
 Summary 44

3. **Redesigning Business Processes for E-Business** 47
 Transitioning to an E-Business 48
 Business Process Reengineering 50

BPR for E-Business   58
Converting to an E-Business   60
The New Role of the Customer   64
Changing Business Processes for the Web   68
Summary   81

4. **E-Business Applications**   83
The Challenges of the E-Business Environment   84
Enterprise Application Requirements   94
Types of E-Business Applications   101
Summary   108

5. **Components**   109
What Is a Business Component?   111
Client Components   118
Server Components   125
Container Viewpoint   127
Application Servers as Containers   129
Business Viewpoint   132
Packaging Viewpoint   134
Server Component Models   136
Abstract and Implementation Component
Models   139
Summary   140

6. **An Enterprise Component Architecture**   141
What Is an Architecture?   142
A Component Architecture   144
The Architecture Development Process   148
The Technical Architecture   152
Summary   167

7. **Implementing a Component Architecture**   169
The Component Factory   170
The Component Model   172

Interface Design Considerations 173
Other Component Design Considerations 176
State Management 179
Transaction Models 180
Component Usage Models 183
Fundamental Interface Design Patterns 185
Application Scenarios 188
Summary 195

8. **Managing the Transition to an E-Business** 197
Types of Transitions 199
An Overview 201
A Transition Plan 204
Phase 1: Initiation 207
Phase 2: Pilot Application Development 214
Phase 3: Organizational Conversion 220
Phase 4: Continuation 223
Summary 223

9. **Retooling for the Internet Age** 227
The Business Challenge 232
Changing Software Strategies 233
A Journey of a Thousand Miles 235
Flipping Channels 236
Expanding the Transition 239
The Home Stretch 242
Summary 243

Afterword, Surviving the Transition 245

Glossary 249

Notes and References 259

Bibliography 263

Index 267

Preface

A manager would had to have been living in a cave during the past two years not to have heard about how the Internet or Web is changing business and how corporations are struggling to adapt to the challenges poised by e-commerce. There are articles in every magazine and newspaper describing the battles raging between older, established companies and new e-business upstarts. Everyone is aware of the venture money available for new Internet startups and the high market valuations many of the new Internet companies have achieved. Most software consultants are quick to offer some kind of advice on how companies should proceed.

This book is not simply another book on the Internet or a book designed to encourage readers to think about how their companies might prosper by embracing e-commerce. We assume our readers already know about these subjects.

Instead, this book was written to aid executives in companies that are considering or already engaged in transforming their companies into e-businesses, and especially for information technology (IT) managers with responsibilities for designing and developing new corporate software systems. We focus on how a company can transform itself into an e-business, and specifically on how business models will need to be revised and business processes redesigned. We also describe how computer architectures and software development practices will need to change, and how a company should approach planning for such a transition.

We have spent the last decade, individually and as employees of Genesis Development Corporation, helping large companies transition to Internet-based, enterprise-oriented systems. In some cases this has involved working with companies to redesign their business processes. In other cases it has involved helping companies create new software architectures and install new software infrastructures. It has often involved training business analysts and software developers to perform their jobs in new ways. And, in most cases, the consulting that we have provided has been done in conjunction with a company or departmental transition plan that we helped the organization develop. In other words, we specialize in helping companies transition to new business processes, new architectures, and new software development processes. At the same time, we help companies actually create the new e-business applications that will position them to survive in the Internet era.

New companies starting from scratch, or existing companies that simply want to build a Web site, can proceed without a detailed plan. Large corporations that have already invested vast sums of money in existing enterprise applications, in hardware, infrastructure technologies, and employees, however, can't simply change the way they do business overnight. The software techniques and skills required for successful Web-oriented development are different than those most companies are currently using. Corporate IT groups will need to learn new development techniques, new methodologies, and new ways of tying everything together into an integrated architecture if their transition to e-commerce is to be successful.

This book is not a handbook. It doesn't go into great detail about any specific aspect of the overall transition, architecture, or technology being described. What this book does do is provide managers with an overview of the major concepts and a road map that will help them develop a plan for what needs to be done. It highlights the issues that need to be addressed, considers the major options companies face, and offers some suggestions about how successful companies have made the transition.

The Argument of This Book

Very briefly, the argument of this book is as follows: Every major company that wants to survive the coming decade has got to convert itself into an e-business company. When we speak of an "e-business company," we don't refer to a company that simply has a Web site or some modest e-business applications. Instead, we mean a company that has significantly reorganized its business processes and software systems to support major e-commerce applications—a company that has reengineered itself to conduct its business via the Internet and the Web.

Before an existing company can transition from where it is today, it must undertake several steps. (See Figure I.1.) First, it must develop an e-business strategy—a conscious plan about how the company is going to compete, what its goals will be, and what policies it will follow to achieve those goals.

Next, it must do two things more or less simultaneously. It must decide how to redesign its existing business processes, or create new business processes to generate the products and services it intends to create to implement its e-business strategy.

At the same time, the company must decide how it will redesign its information technology (or information systems) architecture and development organization to assure that IT will be able to support the company's e-business strategy.

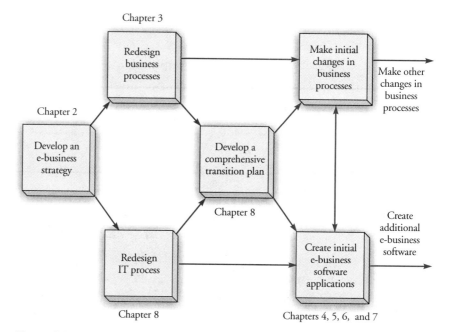

Figure P.1 An overview of an e-business transition plan.

Although we provide an overview of some of the important considerations that managers will face when approaching e-business strategy development and business process redesign, the main focus of this book is on the changes that companies will need to make in their IT organization to assure that they can support e-business initiatives. Most managers understand that IT will be a key player in their company's e-business transition effort. After all, e-business is business conducted over the Internet, so it obviously requires that IT develop Internet-oriented software applications. But what we want to emphasize in this book is that it will require a lot more than that. Very few corporate IT organizations are currently organized to support major Internet initiatives. They lack a corporate software architecture that can support rapid Internet development. Existing architectures are too inflexible to support technologies used for distributed Internet-oriented application development. Most IT groups also lack an infrastructure that can facilitate the integration of lots of existing legacy applications that will need to be linked into the new Internet applications. Large-scale Internet applications are usually distributed, component-based applications. Most IT groups don't have enough developers trained in these software development techniques.

In a nutshell, any company that wants to reengineer itself to function as an e-business has to begin by reengineering its IT organization. Obviously no organization can afford to put everything else on hold while it redesigns its software architecture, infrastructure, and IT development group. Instead, a successful organization will develop an e-business transition plan that manages to accomplish its business process redesign and its IT redesign simultaneously. Moreover, rather than trying to do it all at once, the organization will develop a plan that allows it to undertake the transition in phases. This book will provide readers with advice on how to accomplish this vital task.

An Overview of the Book

Figure P.1 not only provides an overview of the process we will consider but suggests where some of the information can be found in this book. To make the organization of the book even more explicit, here is what we will discuss in each of the chapters.

Chapter 1, The E-Business Challenge, introduces some case studies that illustrate the problems that companies face as they attempt to transition to enterprise e-business companies. We begin with these examples simply to ground our subsequent discussion in some concrete and well-known examples of actual transition efforts.

Chapter 2, Developing an E-Business Strategy, provides readers with a high-level discussion of business strategies and of the kinds of changes that the Internet revolution will force on company planners.

Chapter 3, Redesigning Business Processes for E-Business, builds on Chapter 2 and discusses how companies will be forced to reengineer their existing business processes to make them more appropriate for e-business. In Chapter 3 we emphasize that any company that plans to succeed in transitioning to an e-business must change the way it develops software systems. Rather than go into that subject next, however, we will delay a detailed discussion of the IT change process until we have established the reasons and the dimensions of the change required of IT. Hence, instead of going from the redesign of business processes to the redesign of IT, we go to a generic discussion of how e-business software applications are different from conventional applications.

Chapter 4, E-Business Applications, discusses the business and technical challenges facing e-business and how successful Internet and Web applications must differ from conventional software applications. Chapters 5, 6, and 7 elaborate on the technical and architectural differences between conventional and e-business applications and provide the reader with specifics about the technologies that IT developers will need to master.

Chapter 5, Components, provides an overview of the nature of components and the range of component technologies used in e-business development. Components will be the underlying technology used to build successful e-business applications. This chapter provides an overview of the existing component technologies and how they can be used to address the business challenges laid out in Chapter 4.

Chapter 6, An Enterprise Component Architecture, explains the importance of component-architecture-centered design, the basic principles of component architectures, and how a good architecture helps solves business reengineering and enterprise application developmental requirements. We describe a high-level software architecture for e-business systems that has been successfully implemented in a variety of applications.

Chapter 7, Implementing a Component Architecture, continues the discussion initiated in Chapter 6 and goes into more detail on the critical technical decisions that must be made in component designs. This chapter covers the important problems that designers and architects face when they use components and offers some high-level solutions.

Chapter 8, Managing the Transition to an E-Business, returns to the point we arrived at earlier when we argued that the IT group would need to be changed in order to support enterprise e-business development. In effect, this chapter presents a detailed plan for how an IT organization can transition to component-based development. It solves the dilemma organizations face when they are asked to make a major transition while simultaneously creating major new e-business applications in a very short time.

Chapter 9, Retooling for the Internet Age, describes how a specific company, *enhansiv,* transitioned from conventional development to component-based development, following a change strategy similar to the one described in Chapter 8.

The Afterword, Surviving the Transition, sums up the argument of the entire book and offers a final bit of encouragement to readers.

Since this is an introductory book, in general we have tried to avoid technical details and footnotes. We have included a Notes and References section, organized by chapter, at the end of the book.

Acknowledgments

Paul Harmon writes a monthly newsletter, *Component Development Strategies,* and works with a related consulting group, the Cutter

Consortium. Much of the background research that was done for this book was done in the process of working on articles or reports for the newsletter or for Cutter Consortium. In addition to the people at various companies who have provided insights, Paul wants to thank the people at Cutter who have contributed directly or indirectly to this effort, including Ed Yourdon, Karen Coburn, Anne Mullaney, and Jill Rose.

Mike Rosen is chief enterprise architect and Mike Guttman is chief technology officer at Genesis Development Corporation, an IONA Technologies company. Genesis is a worldwide consulting services group that provides enterprise component solutions. Most of the senior consultants at Genesis are working on projects similar in scope to those described in this book. These senior consultants regularly meet to discuss problems and approaches to dealing with them. In effect, this book represents the combined wisdom and daily practices of the analysts, architects, designers, and consultants at Genesis. Thus, we wish to acknowledge the insights and advice received from all of the senior members of the Genesis staff.

In addition, we would like to acknowledge some of the key customers who had the insight to move forward with an enterprise architecture and transition program, thus contributing to the accumulated wisdom of this book: IMA; the Hartford Insurance Co.; VIAG Interkom, AG; MetLife Insurance; Infostrada; AIG International, Inc.; and UBS.

All three authors would like to thank Celia Wolf and Carolyn Potts, who initially helped get this book project under way, and the people at Morgan Kaufmann, who have supported the development and edited and overseen the publication of this book. Our special thanks go to Diane Cerra, Tim Cox, Edward Wade, Stacie Pierce, and Technologies 'N Typography, who provided expert composition and illustration services.

chapter 1

The E-Business Challenge

In this first chapter, we want to briefly review what a few compa-

nies are doing to adapt to the Internet challenge. These examples

will provide managers with some concrete examples of the complex

problems they will face as they try to help their companies develop

a response to the e-business challenge. At the same time, we will

use these examples to raise some of the themes that we develop

throughout the remainder of this book.

*Examples of
companies adapting
to the Internet
challenge*

None of these companies is standing still, of course, so each of these stories is really only a snapshot of a company, as it was in mid-2000. Each of these companies will continue to make adjustments in hopes of evolving the best possible response to the e-business challenge. Their struggles to date, however, suggest some of the problems and opportunities that may arise at the companies of those who read this book.

Toys R Us

*Toys R Us—a
successful company*

In 1997, Toys R Us was the leader in its market and owned toy stores throughout the world. A conventional business analysis, at that time, would have suggested that Toys R Us had a strong hold on its market. It had a well-established name brand and a good reputation. More importantly, any company that wanted to enter the toys market would have faced the huge expense involved in trying to duplicate the Toys R Us distribution system. The new company would have needed to build a large number of toy stores and warehouses to even gain a foothold in the market. Given the cost and the well-established position that Toys R Us had already established, few companies would have considered trying to challenge Toys R Us.

*eToys challenges
Toys R Us*

Today, that logic has been turned on its head. eToys is a new Web-based company that sells toys over the Internet. eToys doesn't have toy stores, salespeople, or even a delivery system. It takes orders over the Web and then uses an established shipping company like Federal Express to deliver the toys to the customer. eToys began offering toys over the Web in 1998. Its sales went from $25,000 in 1998 to $25 million in 1999. Even so, eToys was still only selling a fraction of the toys sold by Toys R Us. Nevertheless, Toys R Us began to feel the heat as its profits dropped.

Once eToys demonstrated that you don't need toy stores to sell toys, Toys R Us's assets—its toy stores, salespeople, warehouses, and trucks—suddenly became a liability. Overnight the costs of buildings, lights, and the employees in all those toy stores became costs that kept Toys R Us from matching the low prices that eToys can offer.

To make matters worse, if Toys R Us seeks to compete by also selling toys over the Web, it will, in effect, be competing with itself and taking sales away from the toy stores that Toys R Us owns, further reducing the profitability of its toy stores. Few large companies relish the idea of destroying their own assets. Lots of managers will fight to maintain the toy store operation, arguing rightly that it still provides most of the company's current income. This is exactly the kind of dilemma that Barnes & Noble and Merrill Lynch faced when they were challenged by Internet rivals. Indeed, this kind of dilemma currently faces thousands of companies throughout the world.

If the new Web companies were valued to reflect their actual sales or profits, the established firm could simply buy them and close them down, or run them in such a way that they didn't compete with the company's established business. This has happened in dozens of cases over the past hundred years. Today, however, the willingness of the stock market to buy shares of new Internet companies, which aren't even showing a profit in most cases, changes the entire equation. eToys' $25 million in sales in 1999 amounted to the sales of two of Toys R Us's 1486 toy stores. The market, however, which valued Toys R Us at $5.6 billion in mid-1999, decided that eToys was worth $7.8 billion! (These valuations refer to the companies' market capitalization, which is the number of company shares times the current price per share.) Clearly, in spite of its vastly greater sales, Toys R Us was not in the position to buy eToys. In fact, eToys in mid-1999 had all the cash it needed to

The stock market made eToys a rival overnight

compete with Toys R Us, and it could even consider trying to buy Toys R Us, if it wanted.

You can think of the huge market capitalizations being assigned to Internet startups in different ways. You could simply blame it on what Federal Reserve Chairman Greenspan has called an "irrational exuberance." You could blame it on an Internet bubble that began to deflate in March 2000. Or you could say that the market truly and correctly believes that, in the long run, eToys will pay better dividends than Toys R Us. The latter may be hard to believe, considering how much eToys would need to earn to justify its current capitalization, but if you truly believe that businesses are going through a major transition and that by the end of the coming decade the dominant players will be very different from those that dominate today, then perhaps such a valuation is worth the risk. In the meantime, however, it means that established companies are faced with startups that are financially able to do just about anything they want. Moreover, the startups have the latest computer systems, tailored for Internet commerce. The new companies are totally focused on e-commerce and don't have any managers or departmental groups who are arguing that they should continue to pursue older business models.

Anyone who has been involved in a major corporate reengineering effort knows how hard it is to get large corporations to modify their business practices. Having been through such a process, it's easier to understand why many would bet on the new company rather than on the possibility that the established company will change direction in time.

If a new company like eToys wants to build a Web site to sell products to consumers, it hires architects and developers acquainted with the latest software techniques. The developers feel comfortable with objects, components, and distributed systems design. They use Java and Enterprise JavaBeans and the latest application servers to quickly build a powerful, scalable Internet commerce application, and they design their applications for growth and change. They are motivated to work quickly because they are being offered stock in a company that might well make them rich overnight.

An established company like Toys R Us, on the other hand, begins with legacy applications and its existing software developers, just as it has stores, salespeople, and its existing marketing and distribution systems. The established company has all the resistance to change that conservative organizational cultures normally create. And, as we have already suggested, it faces the horrible dilemma of creating new systems that will compete with its existing systems. Only powerful and truly focused CEOs will be able to turn such organizations around in the time allowed.

Established companies have legacy systems and older developers

In early 1999 Toys R Us announced that it had allotted $80 million to create its own Internet toy store. The press release glowed with quotes from Toys R Us managers, describing their commitment to rise to the challenge. Toys R Us adopted the currently popular strategy: It created an "independent" subsidiary, Toysrus.com, to implement its electronic toy store. More interestingly, it got Benchmark Capital, a prominent venture capital firm, to join it as a partner and financial backer.

Toys R Us created an independent e-subsidiary, Toysrus.com

In the summer of 1999, Bob Moog, the initial CEO of Toysrus.com, resigned, reportedly after disputes with Toys R Us management. The disputes were said to concern independence and staffing policies. Apparently Moog had wanted to treat the venture as a "startup," pay higher salaries, and give key employees blocks of stock. Without that, Moog apparently argued, he simply couldn't attract the programming talent he needed to compete with other Silicon Valley Internet startups, like eToys.

The problems continued. Toys R Us ended its relationship with Benchmark Capital because of disagreements over how to run Toysrus.com. In the fall of 1999, Toys R Us attributed a 25% decline in its second quarter earnings to the $4 million in expenses

At first, Toysrus.com ran into trouble

that its Internet subsidiary had incurred. At the same time, Toys R Us announced that its e-commerce effort remained a high priority and announced the appointment of a new CEO. Meanwhile, Toys R Us reported sales of $2.2 billion for the quarter, up 9% over the same quarter in 1998.

During this same period, Internet stock indexes had fallen by almost half. In spite of that, in the fall of 1999, Toys R Us had a market capitalization of $3.7 billion, while eToys had a market capitalization of $5.4 billion.

By Christmas 1999 Toysrus.com was doing better

During the 1999 Christmas season, both eToys and Toys R Us sold lots of toys over the Web. By the end of the 1999 season, in spite of increased sales, neither company had made any profits on its Web sales operations. Meanwhile, slowly but surely, Toysrus.com was beginning to learn how to make money. In March 2000, there was a sharp drop in the value of most e-business companies. By June 2000, Toys R Us still had a market capitalization of $3.5 billion, but eToys' capitalization had dropped to approximately $660 million. At about the same time, Toysrus.com announced a deal with Nickelodeon to make their toys available on their Web site, suggesting that other toy companies recognized that Toys R Us seemed to have mastered online sales.

Established companies must reconceptualize how they do business

We recount this story not to remark on the toy retailing business as such, but simply to underline themes that we will be considering throughout this book. It's very hard for established companies to change. Moreover, the Internet is the most difficult challenge companies have faced since computers became available. Success on the Internet is going to require companies to entirely reconceptualize how they do business. It isn't simply a matter of introducing new software or creating a Web site. The change requires that companies reengineer their basic business practices. This, in turn, will require fundamental changes in how tasks are performed and how employees are compensated.

For many companies, the most wretched part of the change process involves the fact that they are forced to compete with themselves. They are forced to take money out of currently successful operations and invest it in new operations that will, if they succeed, degrade the value of the currently successful operations. In effect, Toys R Us is being forced to turn its major assets—its existing toy stores and the people who work in them—into a liability. In the long run, if Toysrus.com can use the toy stores as a way to distribute toys, they may turn out to be an asset again, or they may remain a liability that Toys R Us will eventually have to phase out. Every instinct of every manager involved in the current toy store operation will be to maintain an asset that is currently generating over $2 billion dollars! If there were turf fights within the company before, they have surely escalated in the past two years.

Established companies must overcome resistance to change

In this specific example, it sounds like one major fight was centered around the fact that the "independent" subsidiary was going to pay its developers much more than developers at the parent company and also give greater incentives. You can imagine how the Toys R Us software development managers complained. It would mean that their best people would leave to go to the subsidiary. It would create hurt feelings and result in the loss of existing Toys R Us developers. The software development managers certainly had a point. Senior management apparently bought the argument. But in doing so, it convinced the venture capital firm that the management of Toys R Us was incapable of making the kinds of changes that would be required to succeed as an e-business. And, of course, it confirmed those who had sold their stock in Toys R Us and bought stock in eToys. It also brought into question the idea that a company can quickly enter the Internet market by simply creating a subsidiary. The strategy obviously won't work if the subsidiary is simply treated as part of the parent firm.

Toys R Us took two years to meet the challenge

At the moment, it sounds like Toys R Us has begun to make a successful transition, but only after a long and rending struggle. There's hope that large, established companies can succeed in the long run, but only if they are willing to take big risks and suffer through cultural changes that will create severe tension for months or years.

Charles Schwab

Schwab moved faster

Luckily for the established companies, there are a few examples of companies, like Charles Schwab, that show that established companies can react quickly and decisively to the Internet challenge. In Schwab's case, a smaller broker has succeeded in attracting so many investors to e-trading that its giant rival Merrill Lynch, having argued for two years that it wouldn't do e-trading, reversed itself and is currently engaged in a desperate catch-up effort to deal with the "Internet threat" it now perceives. At the same time, Schwab's success and popularity has limited the success of the various startups that have tried to offer online trading, and Schwab seems destined to dominate its market for the foreseeable future.

Schwab demonstrated that an established company, if it reacted quickly enough, could leverage its resources and effectively preempt new e-commerce startups from taking away its existing business. In order to succeed with this strategy, of course, Schwab had to undertake very bold action. That meant that its CEO and senior managers had to agree to make major changes in the way the company did business and then effect those changes virtually overnight. It meant that Schwab needed to redesign business practices that relied on telephoned orders, and shift to Internet orders. This, in turn, meant that it had to redesign its brokerage software systems so that information that was previously available to telephone brokers could be displayed to customers on Web sites.

Schwab had some significant advantages over more staid brokerages. For years it had specialized in selling trading services at a discount. The people a customer spoke to on the phone when they called Schwab didn't recommend stock; they simply took the order. Hence there wasn't a large commissioned broker structure to tear down. Similarly, Schwab had experimented in offering stock over the Internet. In pre-Web days the Schwab Internet option never amounted to much, but at least Schwab's IT folks were aware of the problems of providing information and taking orders over the Internet. The Web made it possible to create a graphical user interface that made it much easier for customers to examine their options and enter a trade, but the back-end processing was similar to what Schwab had already explored with its earlier Internet offering.

Schwab had always been innovative

Perhaps as important as all this, Schwab is ultimately managed by Charles Schwab, a CEO who is very active in managing the company and has always been interested in using technology. Clearly Charles Schwab backed the company's move into Web sales, and that certainly made it possible for Schwab to move quickly.

Schwab's CEO was behind the change

Schwab has an impressive IT organization. Nevertheless, when it decided to move to Web trading, it hired IBM's systems integration group and let IBM push Schwab in the direction of the latest hardware and software. Schwab's e-commerce systems are built in Java and are linked to IBM mainframes where most of the data is kept. As of June 2000, Schwab had 7 million active accounts, and 80% of its customers' trades were via the Internet.

Schwab used outside developers

While other established brokers are still struggling to catch up with Schwab, Schwab is investing heavily to stay ahead. It has had occasional problems with its online systems and has now com-

Schwab is moving ahead into wireless trading

pletely duplicated its online hardware and software systems to assure that its systems stay up 24 hours a day, 7 days a week. At the same time, Schwab, anticipating that online trading will soon move from PCs to cell phones and wireless digital devices, has invested in wireless systems and has just begun supporting Palm IIIx and VIIx organizers. It plans to add RIM pagers and Internet-enabled mobile phones in the near future.

Schwab illustrates that a large corporation can anticipate the market and succeed on the Web. It did this as a result of having a CEO who backed the effort and an IT group that moved very quickly, relying on consultants to assure they used the latest techniques.

Citigroup and World Banking

Citigroup wants 1 billion online customers

The cover story of *InfoWeek* in March 1999 described Citigroup's e-business plans. Citigroup, which is a combination of a bank, a brokerage firm, and an insurance group, hopes to provide services to 1 billion customers by the end of the coming decade. (That's one out of every six people in the world!) It admits it might not achieve its goal, but the strategy is clear: Citigroup wants to be a worldwide financial services firm, and it wants to do it by providing services to its customers via the Web.

Citigroup is selling U.S. dollar accounts

Compared with other companies selling products, Citigroup is in an enviable position, since it's selling financial services. Some products sell better in some countries and cultures and worse in others. It's hard to imagine, however, that lots of people throughout the world wouldn't find it pleasant to convert some of their income each month into dollars, which could be stored in a U.S. bank, assuming the various details can be handled efficiently. In a similar way, wealthy people throughout the world would probably like to be able to invest some of their funds in the U.S. stock market. In other words, Citi has a product with great appeal. The question is devising an Internet system that can reach and facilitate online banking throughout the world.

Citibank has some experience in this kind of thing. In the 1970s, Citi established a beachhead in California, which had previously been dominated by very powerful local banks like Bank of America, Wells Fargo, and Security Pacific. Since banking laws in the 1970s didn't allow banks from other states to operate branches outside the state in which they were incorporated (New York in the case of Citibank), Citi had the problem of creating a system that could function without branch offices. Luckily for Citi, bank card machines were just becoming popular. Citi joined with a number of national networks that would honor each other's bank cards at their automated teller machines (ATMs). Then they mailed letters to the wealthiest people in California and suggested they bank with Citi. The offer included a credit card and a bank card. Using the credit card, with a high credit limit, individuals could make loans to themselves. Using the ATM card, individuals could get money whenever they needed it – more conveniently than by going to a branch, in most cases. And, of course, Citi offered a toll-free, 24-hour number that individuals could use to talk with a Citi banker if they needed to. Citi didn't get a lot of customers in California using this approach, but they got some of the most profitable and showed that, as early as the 1970s, an aggressive organization could organize banking without depending on buildings and tellers.

Citi has always been innovative and aggressive

Obviously, using Internet and Web technology, Citigroup now hopes to extend this kind of service to a worldwide customer base. If they succeed, we suspect that Citigroup will be hailed as one of the first truly global companies. There are certainly international companies today that operate in large numbers of countries. Auto manufacturers are good examples. Most, however, think of their market as comprising millions of customers, not billions. Moreover, with a few exceptions, they depend on local distribution and

Using the Web, Citi wants customers worldwide

sales organizations to actually reach their customers. What Citigroup is proposing to do is to provide millions of customers with a single point of contact. In the process, they would be eliminating thousands of middlemen of all kinds. And ultimately, they will be eliminating branch banks throughout the world. That will upset local bankers, who will urge their governments to write laws limiting the possibilities. Thus, progress won't be quick or certain. In the long run, however, it should make it possible to significantly reduce the cost of banking, insurance, and trading to millions of individual customers. That, in turn, will mean that those same customers will have more money to spend on other things, and that should lead to a significant rise in the worldwide living standard.

Citi will face huge challenges

On the other hand, only a very brave IT manager would eagerly embrace the idea of building a computer system that could respond effectively to a billion people signing on to find out what their account balance is or their stock portfolio is worth this morning. The underlying systems may be the same, but lots of different interface screens will need to be designed to make access easy for people of widely different cultures.

A time for bold thinking

Luckily for the readers of this book, this kind and magnitude of change is still a few years off. It is, however, the type of change that the largest and most ambitious companies are now considering. Thus, it's important to know that, once a company starts to explore the use of the Web for e-commerce, it isn't simply planning a one-time change. In fact, it's entering a tornado that is going to keep spinning and accelerating for the next two decades. Halfway measures and cautious experiments probably won't do much good. This is a time for bold initiatives.

In the spring of 2000, John Reed, one of Citigroup's two CEOs, announced his retirement. Reed had a background in IT and had been the main force behind Citi's rapid move into e-commerce. Reed had insisted that most of Citi's e-business initiatives be concentrated in a subsidiary, eCiti, to assure that they could move forward quickly. It has recently been announced that many eCiti functions will be given back to various Citigroup operating groups. It will be interesting to see if Citi's e-buisness initiatives will continue to be pushed as they have been in the past.

Automakers and Their Parts Suppliers

Most major auto companies are engaged in efforts to transition to e-business. Ford, GM, and DaimlerChrysler have each announced efforts to sell cars via Web sites. Each has major e-commerce initiatives under way. Toyota, which currently has a capitalization that makes it worth more than both Ford and GM, has a popular Japanese Web site, gazoo.com, which sells a wide variety of products and services, including cars. Both Ford and GM have set up their e-business groups inside the regular companies, assuming that the entire company would benefit from their knowledge of how to use the Internet.

Automakers are trying to transition to e-business

A recent study by Goldman Sachs suggests that the Web and Internet will eventually save consumers about $695 per car. Goldman Sachs estimated the savings as shown in Figure 1.1.

In addition to selling cars online, all of the major auto companies have been working on online parts marketplaces or exchanges. A buyer would post a buy order on an exchange, and any parts dealer or other supplier that saw the buy order could respond with a bid. The buyer would respond by accepting the best bid. In effect, an auto parts exchange is a special approach to supply chain integration. More common supply chain models have simply linked one company's manufacturing line with suppliers, so that whenever inventory drops, orders are generated. What the automakers are proposing is a more generic and dynamic solution.

Automakers want online parts marketplaces

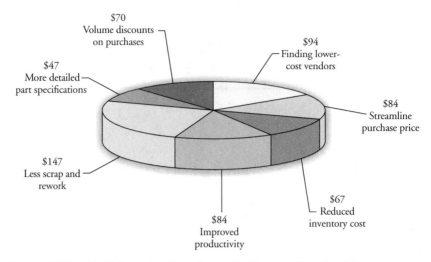

$70
Volume discounts
on purchases

$94
Finding lower-
cost vendors

$47
More detailed
part specifications

$84
Streamline
purchase price

$147
Less scrap and
rework

$67
Reduced
inventory cost

$84
Improved
productivity

Figure 1.1 How the Internet cuts auto costs. *Source:* Gary Lapidus, *E-Automotive Report,* Goldman Sachs Investment Research.

Auto industry analysts suggest that Ford and GM are moving rapidly toward the day when they can create custom cars for customers within two to three days. It turns out that it's cheaper, in the long run, for GM and Ford to create cars only after they have sold them online. There are significant costs to changing the manufacturing line to create cars on demand, but the approach saves so much in inventory and distribution costs that it would be worthwhile. The exchanges are one step in that direction. If cars are to be created on demand, the car manufacturers need a way to get parts quickly to respond to changing orders. The parts suppliers who can keep up will be the winners, and those that can't will simply drop by the wayside.

E-markets are very popular

Exchanges are very popular, and several dozen have already been launched. Among the most valuable is a chemical exchange and an iron and steel exchange that have been in business for over two years. New exchanges have been announced for banking, education, and in various retail markets.

Ford announced AutoXchange

Initially, Ford and General Motors each announced an independent exchange effort. Both companies hoped to have their exchanges up and running in early 2000. Ford, for example, announced plans to conduct purchasing transactions with most of its 30,000 parts suppliers via its AutoXchange system. In other words, Ford planned on spending $80 billion via its exchange. At the same time, any parts suppliers that are part of the Ford network will also be able to buy and sell parts to other companies on the network. Ford is partnering with Oracle and forecasts savings of 10–20% for exchange members.

General Motors' goal was to procure all its parts over its own exchange, TradeXchange, by the end of 2001. GM claims that its system will cut purchase order costs from $100 an order to about $10 an order. GM will be the major owner of the exchange and charge a fee for each transaction. GM is partnering with Commerce One. Federal Express will handle the logistics for GM's exchange. (Commerce One has just announced that it will acquire CommerceBid, an auction services vendor, to acquire technology for its joint venture with GM.)

GM announced TradeXchange

A company like TRW, which sells $11 billion worth of parts to both Ford and GM, will need to participate in both exchanges. Bill McCreary, the CIO of Pilkington Holdings, a supplier of auto glass for both GM and Ford, suggests that there will be a lot of "aggressive reengineering" going on as parts companies prepare to take part in the GM- and Ford-led ventures.

Large parts dealers must join multiple exchanges

Since the GM and Ford announcements in late 1999, things have gotten quite a bit more complex. First it was announced that GM, Ford, Mazda, and DaimlerChrysler AG would develop a joint exchange, pooling their resources and making it possible for any auto company to buy parts from any supplier. It was estimated that the joint exchange would cost $200 million and would result in an exchange in which $50 billion in transactions took place.

A proposed joint parts exchange

Since that announcement, there have been reports that the U.S. government is worried about the monopoly aspects of the deal.

Concerns about competition

There have also been rumors that some of the software companies that had agreed to work with the leading auto companies were unhappy trying to work together on the project. Several of the software vendors are intensely competitive and had hoped to acquire proprietary knowledge from the effort. Now, the senior partners are, in effect, asking them to all cooperate in a common system.

Huge application integration problems

At the same time, everyone involved in the project has begun to face up to the problems involved in trying to link three huge automotive companies with their various back office systems with thousands of trading partners. These companies already have some EDI systems set up before the Internet to link specific companies, and the companies don't want to rip them out. So any solution is going to have to find a way to integrate thousands of different software systems into a common network. It isn't clear that any of the initial proposals would have worked—this is rather new technology, after all. As the number of players has grown and as software vendors have been asked to blend their proprietary approaches together, things have not gotten simpler.

Other proposed auto parts exchange systems

Nor have things stood still. There has been talk about other auto manufacturers setting up a rival system, and the parts suppliers have also discussed setting up their own system. These various discussions tend to ultimately depend on who will make a profit. Originally, GM and Ford each estimated their systems would save the parts vendors money because they would avoid paperwork. In fact, however, the increased competition will probably press down on the margins of the parts suppliers. At the same time, each parts supplier will need to invest significant money in developing the software systems needed to interact with one or more of the proposed exchanges.

An exchange will take time to complete

A recent study by Merrill Lynch suggested that the first of the systems will require at least another year to complete because of the complex contractual problems involved in the collaboration of

competitors. The same report suggested that the exchange probably wouldn't improve the profit margins of the parts suppliers, but
that it would reduce the costs of parts acquisition to the auto manufacturers and that a good part of the savings would get passed on
to customers (see Figure 1.1).

The automakers' exchange initiative is an example of a "second-
generation" e-business system. These companies aren't simply trying to use their Web sites to promote their products or to sell cars
(although they do both of those things). They are laying a new infrastructure that will totally change the way they do business. Instead of ordering parts in advance, they are laying the groundwork
for acquiring parts as needed. More importantly, instead of simply
acquiring parts, when needed, at some predetermined price, they
are creating a market that will allow parts companies to bid on
each new order as it is placed. This, in turn, will reduce prices by
allowing the parts suppliers to constantly adjust their bids in response to their own supplies, their competitors' bids, and various
other factors. In effect, the parts supply business is about to become as dynamic as the stock market.

An exchange is very complex

Obviously the automakers will have to be very precise about the
quality they require, and they will have to build in feedback loops
that quickly detect any defective parts and cut any suppliers who
provide below-standard parts out of the system. This is equivalent
to brokerage systems that continually monitor the creditworthiness
of their customers and prevent unworthy customers from ordering
stocks they can't afford.

An exchange will involve more than parts purchases

Meanwhile, what of the parts suppliers? It's one thing for the
management of a company like Schwab to evaluate the market and
decide they can make money by selling stocks and bonds online.
It's another for a parts supplier to suddenly find that to stay in
business it must quickly modify all of its IT systems to participate
in parts auctions. Old bidding models and large parts runs are

Parts suppliers must become e-businesses to survive

suddenly things of the past, and the parts supplier finds that it must totally reengineer its business processes and software systems. This shift from deciding to create a Web system for a customer to being forced to create a Web system to continue to do business with a major customer is what led us to call this a "second-generation" e-business application. As the whole Internet phenomenon continues to grow, secondary and tertiary effects like this will become common. Every company, indeed, soon will have to be an Internet company if it wants to survive.

Summary

These examples illustrate the problems

In this short introduction, we've looked at the problems and the opportunities faced by several companies. We could have considered any of dozens of other cases. Some would have emphasized how new e-business upstarts are redefining industries and challenging the currently dominant players. Others would have emphasized how established players are succeeding in developing an Internet presence that will protect their franchise, or even striking out in new directions in an effort to dominate entirely new markets. Still other stories would have suggested that success on the Internet can be achieved by hiring new programmers and creating new Internet applications from scratch. Some would have suggested how existing companies succeeded in retraining their own programmers and leveraged their existing applications to create new products for customers that their newer rivals couldn't match.

There's no magic formula for success

Our conclusion isn't simple. It isn't that everyone has to convert their company into an e-business overnight, although most companies will want to begin the transition as soon as possible. We certainly don't think there's a magic formula that will guarantee success in the new business environment that the Web is creating.

Instead, there is going to be a lot of competition, and old and new companies are going to be challenged in ways that they haven't been in the past. The laurel of success, however, will go to the companies that are well managed and that know how to organize themselves to meet the new challenges. In some cases the companies will be new and their managers will create new businesses that replace older, established giants. In other cases the survivors will be established companies whose managers face the challenge and change their companies in needed ways.

The challenge isn't simply a computer or a technological challenge. Certainly the Internet and the growing use of the Web are driving the changes that are occurring. Similarly, companies that meet the challenge are going to have to rely heavily on their software and computer systems people to create the new applications that the company will need to succeed on the Internet. But the creation of new software applications is only a part of what is needed.

Companies must create new software

Successful companies will need to begin by reconceptualizing the nature of their businesses. They will need to consider how they will change their existing business processes to take advantage of the opportunities that the Internet and the Web will create. They must have the will to destroy old business processes in order to adjust. They will have to retrain employees and redefine their jobs. Moreover, it isn't simply the salespeople or the store managers who will need to change. New approaches to software development will be required. New approaches that link marketing analysts and Web page designers will have to be created. New software infrastructures will need to be created.

Reconceptualizing the business is more important

The e-business challenge is ultimately a management challenge. Managers of successful companies will need to do what they have always done. They will need to survey the changing environment and then modify their company strategies to accommodate a changing world. Changed strategies will require changed business

E-business is a management challenge

processes and new software systems developed via new techniques. Resistance to change is always significant, and resistance to major changes can be horrific. If most large companies transition to e-business, it will only be because farsighted managers determine it must happen and then apply the pressure sufficient to overcome resistance.

The examples we have cited above suggest that this is already happening. This book was written to help managers analyze the changes and determine what needs to be done.

Developing an E-Business Strategy

The first thing that most senior managers consider when they begin to think about how they might transition their companies into e-business is how such a change would alter their company's overall strategy. Given the key role of strategy in modern business, we'll begin by providing an overview of how the e-business revolution impacts corporate strategy.

Business strategy defines a company's goals

The concept of a business strategy has been around for decades, and the models and process used to develop a company strategy are taught at every business school. Developing and updating a company's business strategy is one of the key responsibilities of a company's executive officers. A business strategy defines how a company is going to compete, what its goals will be, and what policies it will support to achieve those goals. Many managers refer to a company's strategy as the company's *business model.*

To develop a business strategy, senior executives need to consider the strengths and weaknesses of their own company and its competitors. They also need to consider trends, threats, and opportunities within the industry in which they compete, and within the broader social, political, technological, and economic environments in which the company lives.

Different schools of business strategy

There are different schools of business strategy. Some advocate a formal process that approaches the modeling process very systematically, while others propose less formal processes. A few argue that the world is changing so fast that companies must depend on the instincts of their senior executives in order to move rapidly. In effect, such companies evolve new positions on the fly.

Michael E. Porter, business strategy theorist

The formal approach to business strategy analysis and development is often associated with the Harvard Business School. In this brief summary we'll begin by describing a formal approach that is derived from Harvard professor Michael E. Porter's book, *Competitive Strategy.* Published in 1980 and now in its 60th printing, *Competitive Strategy* has been the best-selling strategy textbook throughout the past decade. Leaving aside whether Porter's approach is the best one, it is a well-known approach, and it will allow us to use some models that are already established among those familiar with management literature.

Porter defines business strategy as "a broad formula for how a business is going to compete, what its goals should be, and what policies will be needed to carry out these goals."

Defining a Strategy

Figure 2.1 provides an overview of the process that Porter recommends for strategy formation. It begins with an analysis of where the company is now—what its current strategy is—and the assumptions that the company managers currently make about the company's current position, strengths and weaknesses, competitors, and industry trends. Most large companies also have a formal strategy and have already gone through this exercise. Most large

Phase 1: Determine the company's current position

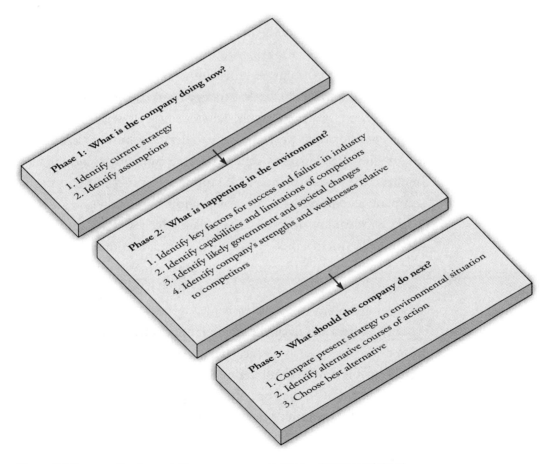

Figure 2.1 Process for formulating a company strategy. *Source:* Michael Porter, *Competitive Strategy.*

companies have managers who are assigned to constantly monitor the company's strategy.

Phase 2: Consider environmental conditions

In the second phase of Porter's strategy process (the middle box in Figure 2.1), the team developing the strategy considers what is happening in the environment. In effect, the team ignores the assumptions the company makes at the moment and gathers intelligence that will allow them to formulate a current statement of environmental constraints and opportunities facing all the companies in their industry. The team examines trends in the industry the company is in and reviews the capabilities and limitations of competitors. It also reviews likely changes in society and government policy that might affect the business. When the team has finished its current review, it reconsiders the company's strengths and weaknesses, relative to the current environmental conditions.

Phase 3: Determine the company's new strategy

During the third phase, the strategy team compares the company's existing strategy with the latest analysis of what's happening in the environment. Next, the team generates a number of scenarios, or alternate courses of action, that the company could pursue. In effect, the company imagines a number of situations that the company could find itself in a few months or years hence, and works backward to imagine what policies, technologies, and organizational changes would be required, during the intermediate period, to reach each situation. Finally, the company management team selects one alternative and begins to make the changes necessary to implement the company's new strategy.

Porter's process assumes a calm business environment

Porter offers lots of qualifications about the need for constant review and change as necessary, but, overall, Porter's model was designed for the relatively calmer business environment that existed 10 years ago. Given the constant pressures to change and innovate that we've all experienced during the last three decades, it may be hard to think of the 1980s as a calm period, but everything really is relative. When you contrast the way companies approached strategy development just 10 years ago with the kinds of changes occurring now as companies try to adjust to the world of the Internet, the 1980s were relatively sedate. Perhaps the best way to illustrate this is to look at Porter's general model of competition.

Porter's Model of Competition

Porter emphasizes that "the essence of formulating competitive strategy is relating a company to its environment." One of the best-known diagrams in Porter's *Competitive Strategy* is illustrated, with minor modifications, in Figure 2.2. Porter's diagram, which pulls together lots of information about how managers conceptualize the competition when they formulate strategy, is popularly referred to as the "five forces model."

Porter's five forces model of competition

Porter identifies five changes in the competitive environment that can force a company to adjust its business strategy. The heart of business competition, of course, is a set of rival companies that

Companies compete with others in the same industry

Figure 2.2 Forces driving industry competition. *Source:* Michael Porter, *Competitive Strategy.*

comprise an industry. The company and its competitors are repre-sented by the circle at the center of Figure 2.2. As rival companies make moves, the company must respond. Similarly, the company may opt to make changes itself, in order to place its rivals at a dis-advantage. Porter spends several chapters analyzing the ways com-panies compete within an industry, and we'll return to that in a moment.

Four types of change in the environment

Beyond the rivalry between the companies that make up the in-dustry, there are changes in the environment that can potentially affect all the companies in an industry. Porter classifies these changes into four groups: buyers, suppliers, potential new compa-nies that might enter the field, and the threat that new products or services will become desirable substitutes for the company's prod-ucts and services.

Buyers seek lower prices

Buyers, or customers, will tend to want to acquire the com-pany's products or services as inexpensively as possible. Some fac-tors give the seller an advantage: If the product is scarce, if the company is the only source of the product, or the only local source of the product, or if the company is already selling the product more cheaply than its competitors, the seller will tend to have better control of its prices. The inverse of factors like these gives the customer more bargaining power and tends to force the com-pany to reduce its prices. If there are lots of suppliers competing with each other, or if it's easy for customers to shop around, prices will tend to fall.

Suppliers seek higher prices

In a similar way, suppliers would always like to sell their prod-ucts or services for more. If the suppliers are the only source of a needed product, if they can deliver it more quickly than their ri-vals, or if there is lots of demand for a relatively scarce product, then suppliers will tend to have more bargaining power and will increase their prices. Conversely, if the suppliers' product is widely available, or available more cheaply from someone else, the buyer

will tend to have the upper hand and will try to force the supplier's
price down.

Companies in every industry also need to watch to see that no
potential substitutes establish themselves. At a minimum, a substitute product can drive down the company's prices. In the worst
case, a new product can render the company's current products obsolete. The manufacturers of buggy whips were driven into bankruptcy when internal combustion automobiles replaced horse-
drawn carriages in the early years of the 20th century. Similarly, the
availability of plastic products has forced the manufacturers of
metal, glass, and wood products to reposition their products in various ways.

*The threat of
substitute products
or technologies*

Finally, there is the threat that new companies will enter an industry and thereby increase the competition. More companies pursuing the same customers and trying to purchase the same raw materials tends to give both the suppliers and the customers more
bargaining power, driving up the cost of goods and lowering the
company's profit margins.

*New companies
enter the market*

Historically, there are a number of factors that tend to function
as barriers to the entry of new firms. If success in a given industry
requires a large capital investment, then potential entrants must
have a lot of money to even consider trying to enter the industry.
The capital investment could take different forms. In some cases, a
new entrant might need to build large factories and buy expensive
machinery. The cost of setting up a new computer chip plant, for
example, runs to billions of dollars, and only a very large company
could consider entering the chip manufacturing field. In other
cases, the existing companies in an industry may spend huge
amounts on advertising and have well-known brand names. Any
new company would be forced to spend at least as much to even
get its product noticed. Similarly, access to established distribution
channels, proprietary knowledge possessed by existing firms, or

*Barriers to the entry
of new companies*

government policies can all serve as barriers to new companies that might consider entering an established industry.

Globalization results in increased competition

Historically, in most mature industries, the barriers to entry were so great that the leading firms had a secure hold on their positions and new entries were very rare. In the past two decades the growing move toward globalization has resulted in growing competition among firms that were formerly isolated by geography. Thus, prior to the 1960s, the three large auto companies in the United States completely controlled the U.S. auto market. Starting in the 1960s, and growing throughout the next two decades, foreign auto companies began to compete for U.S. buyers and U.S. auto companies began to compete for foreign auto buyers. In the mid-1980s, a U.S. consumer could choose between cars sold by over a dozen firms. The late 1990s has witnessed a sharp contraction in the auto market, as the largest automakers have acquired their rivals and reduced the number of rivals in the market. A key to understanding this whole process, however, is to understand that these auto companies were more or less equivalent in size and had always been potential rivals, except that they were functioning in geographically isolated markets. As companies became more international, these companies found themselves competing with each other. They all had similar strategies, and the most successful have gradually reduced the competition by acquiring their less successful rivals. In other words, globalization created challenges, but it didn't radically change the basic business strategies that were applied by the various firms engaged in international competition.

A good strategy considers all five factors

In effect, when a strategy team studies the environment, it surveys all of these factors. They check to see what competitors are doing, if potential new companies seem likely to enter the field, or if substitute products are likely to be offered. And they check on factors that might change the future bargaining power that buyers or sellers are likely to exert.

Industries, Products, and Value Propositions

Obviously Porter's model assumes that the companies in the circle in the middle of Figure 2.2 have a good idea of the scope of the industry they are in and the products and services that define the industry. Companies are sometimes surprised when they find that the nature of the industry has changed and that companies that were not formerly their competitors are suddenly taking away their customers. This usually occurs because the managers at a company were thinking too narrowly or too concretely about what their company was selling.

Your real competitors

To avoid this trap, sophisticated managers need to think more abstractly about what products and services their industry provides. A "value proposition" refers to the value that a product or service provides to customers. Managers should always strive to be sure that they know what business (industry) their company is really in. That's done by being sure they know what value their company is providing to its customers.

Value propositions

Thus, for example, a bookseller might think they are in the business of providing customers with books. In fact, however, they are probably in the business of providing customers with information or entertainment. Once this is recognized, then it becomes obvious that a bookseller's rivals are not only other bookstores, but magazine stores, TV, and the Web. In other words, a company's rivals aren't simply the other companies that manufacture similar products, but all those who provide the same general value to customers. Clearly Time-Warner-AOL realize this and have combined companies that sell books, TV movies, magazines, and Web content in order to better serve their customers. Similarly, movies that are coordinated with books or comics also exploit the fact that they are providing a similar value to the same group of customers.

Booksellers sell information and entertainment, not books

If customers ever decide they like reading texts on computer screens in some "automated book device," then the book industry is in serious trouble. In this situation it will be obvious that the real value being provided is information and that the information could be downloaded from a computer just as well as printed in a book format. Many magazines are already producing online versions that allow customers to read and download articles in electronic form.

Managers must evaluate the value they deliver

Good managers must always work to be sure they really understand what customer needs they are satisfying. It's only by knowing the value they provide customers that they can truly understand the industry they are in and who their potential rivals are. A good strategy is focused on providing value to customers, not narrowly defined in terms of a specific product or service.

Start your strategic analysis with the customers

In spite of the need to focus on providing value to customers, historically, in designing their strategies, most companies begin with an analysis of their core competencies. In other words, they begin by focusing on the products or services they currently produce. They move from products to ways of specializing them and then to sales channels till they finally reach their various targeted groups of customers. Most e-business strategists suggest that companies approach their analysis in reverse. The new importance of the customer, and the new ways that products can be configured for the Web, suggests that companies should begin by considering what Web customers like and what they will buy over the Web, and then progress to what product the company might offer that would satisfy the new Web customers.

Strategies for Competing

Porter's three generic strategies

Earlier, we mentioned that Porter places a lot of emphasis on the ways existing companies can compete within an existing industry.

Porter describes competition in most traditional industries when he says that most companies follow one of three generic strategies: cost leadership, differentiation, and niche specialization.

Cost Leadership

The cost leader is the company that can offer the product at the cheapest price. In most industries, price can be driven down by economies of scale, by the control of suppliers and channels, and by experience that allows a company to do things more efficiently. Thus, in most industries, large companies dominate, manufacture products in huge volume, and sell them more cheaply than their smaller rivals.

Cost leaders offer low prices

Differentiation

If a company can't sell its products for the cheapest price, an alternative is to offer the best or the more desirable products. Customers are often willing to pay a premium for a better product, which allows companies to specialize in producing a better product to compete with those selling a cheaper, but less desirable product.

Differentiators offer premium features for premium prices

Niche Specialization

Niche specialists focus on specific buyers, specific segments of the market, or buyers in particular geographical markets and often only offer a subset of the products typically sold in the industry. In effect, they represent an extreme version of differentiation, and they can charge a premium for their products, since the products have special features beneficial to the consumers in the niche.

Niche specialists focus on limited market segments

Examples

The classic example of a company that achieved cost leadership in an industry was Ford Motor Company. The founder, Henry Ford, created a mass market for automobiles by driving the price of a car down to the point where the average man could afford one. To do

Porter's strategies applied to the auto industry

this, Ford limited the product to one model in one color and set up a production line to produce large numbers of cars very efficiently. In the early years of the 20th century, Ford completely dominated auto production in the United States.

As the U.S. economy grew after World War I, however, General Motors was able to pull ahead of Ford, not by producing cars as cheaply, but by producing cars that were nearly as cheap and that offered a variety of features that differentiated them. Thus, GM offered several different models in a variety of colors with a variety of optional extras.

Examples of niche specialists in the automobile industry are companies that manufacture only taxicabs or limousines.

Within any specific industry there are usually some special circumstances that allow for other forms of specialization or that determine what kinds of differentiation and what kinds of niche specialization will be effective.

Companies stick with winning strategies

Obviously, a student working for an MBA learns a lot more about strategy. For our purposes, however, this brief overview should be sufficient. In essence, business managers are taught to evaluate a number of factors and arrive at a strategy that will be compatible with the company's strengths and weaknesses and that will result in a reasonable profit. Historically, companies have developed a strategy and, once they have succeeded, continued to rely on that strategy, with only minor refinements, for years.

An E-Business Strategy

Companies must revise their strategies for e-business

Most managers realize that a major business transition is taking place. As customers begin to buy via the Internet and companies rush to use the Internet to create new operational efficiencies, most companies are seeking to update their business strategies. Some believe the various processes by which business strategies are devel-

oped will need to change. Today's business environment is suddenly much more dynamic. New value propositions are being promoted by new companies, and new technologies are being used to give companies competitive advantage. Consultants argue about whether it's a matter of applying the classic models, while taking the Internet into account, or a matter of developing altogether new approaches to business strategy. We're not prepared to answer these questions in any definitive way, but we do want to try to summarize some of the types of answers that are being advanced.

Developing Your Strategy

Today's business strategist needs to be much more flexible than in the past. It's no longer a matter of going through a multiday exercise and arriving at a strategy that will then remain valid for several years. Instead, the strategy development process needs to be much more dynamic. Most e-business strategists try to identify a point midway between the more formal and static model described by Porter and the very informal model that many companies seem to have adopted to deal with the rapidly changing business environment.

Strategies must be flexible

Very informal and dynamic approaches tend to degenerate from strategy into tactics. For example, to counter a perceived threat, a company may develop specific applications to deal with specific problems. One company creates a Web site, simply to have some kind of response to show its board. Another decides to sell its current products via a portal without really rethinking the nature of its products to determine if they provide value to Web customers. The problem with all these informal responses is that they usually lack any real insight into the overall strategy the company should be pursuing. They are exactly the kind of responses that strategists are

Strategies must be more than reactions

supposed to avoid. In most cases they are pursued simply because the changes taking place are so extensive and unprecedented, and the nature of the changes are so poorly understood that managers react, rather than facing the harder challenge of developing a strategic understanding. Ignorance, coupled with the fact that many executives are frightened about how the Internet will affect their companies, has led to lots of rapid, ill-conceived, and uncoordinated responses to the Internet challenge.

Strategies should be formal and continuous

We suggest that Porter's overall approach is still valid. It simply needs to be extended and given a new sense of dynamics. In Figure 2.3 we illustrate an e-business strategy process that is conceptualized as a continuous cycle. In effect, the strategy team never completes its task; it simply works to develop a temporary understanding, makes commitments, and then evaluates the results as it

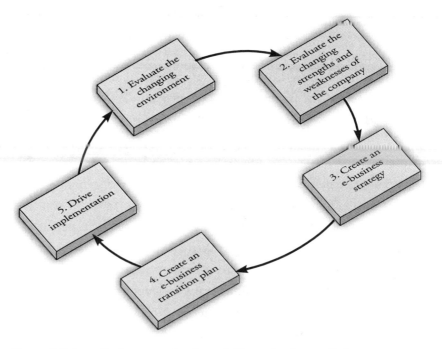

Figure 2.3 A cyclical process for formulating e-business strategy.

cycles through a subsequent cycle in order to arrive at a new understanding.

Obviously a cyclical approach that continues without ever arriving at any final strategy isn't as satisfying as a linear approach that results in a strategy that you can then systematically organize behind. But the linear approach simply isn't viable in today's environment. No one knows how the ongoing shift of customers to the Internet will proceed. Today, most Internet customers are using personal computers. In two years, it's generally assumed that most customers will use phone, personal digital assistants, or TV consoles. But no one is sure which will dominate or exactly how the interfaces will work. Each move by a new e-business company evokes responses by lots of other companies, and innovations occur daily. The best anyone can do is to arrive at a temporary goal and pursue that while watching what others are doing. At any point, a new company may introduce a new approach that will render your temporary solution obsolete, and you'll simply have to revise it in light of the new developments. Hopefully your company can be among the few that introduce innovations that will make others stop and reassess their current strategy.

The best Internet strategy will keep changing

Notice that we've reversed Porter's first two phases in Figure 2.3. The cyclical model assumes that a company has a tentative strategy and that it's less important than the continual changes in the environment. The place to begin is to come to some general conclusions about the changes taking place in the environment. As an example, every company needs to get as close to their customers as possible to assure that they know exactly how their customers currently prefer to use the Internet. And, of course, you also want to be among the first to know when your customers' preferences begin to change. Thus, the cyclical strategy model assumes that everything begins and ends with strategists monitoring changes in the environment.

Developing strategy involves continuous environmental monitoring

The second phase is like Porter's first phase. The company's current strategy assumptions and its strengths and weaknesses are evaluated. In this case, however, they are reevaluated in light of the latest changes in the environment.

Monitoring customers' changing Web practices

The third phase in the cyclical model is similar to Porter's final phase: The company arrives at a strategy that balances the company's strengths and weaknesses with the changing environment. To accomplish this, Porter recommends exploring scenarios. We recommend the same. Instead of starting with the company's products and services and projecting forward to new customers, however, we recommend that the company begin by evaluating groups of potential customers and then working back to how your company could provide value to each group. The Internet may be pushing the current business revolution, but the customers are definitely pulling it, and it's hard to imagine an e-business that's too customer-focused.

Developing and monitoring alternative strategies

Porter assumes that the result of the third phase will be a strategy. We can imagine a single strategy in some cases, but we can just as well imagine that companies will begin to develop portfolios of strategies, each strategy based on a different scenario and each assigned a different probability. In effect, companies will probably move toward focusing on a major strategy, while simultaneously nurturing one or more alternative strategies on the chance that the alternative strategies turn out to be more viable. Allocating resources to alternative strategies will be a challenge, but there are tools available for such tasks, and the risk of pursuing a single strategy in a rapidly changing environment will simply be too risky for lots of companies.

Implementation planning and strategy development

Our cyclical model also introduces two new phases: a phase in which a transition plan is created or updated and a phase that calls for managers to drive the transition. It's easy to argue that neither of these new phases is really a part of the strategy development process, and in the abstract we'd agree. Today, however, it's important that senior strategists be prepared to shift direction very quickly. They can't do that if they don't have a good understanding of the commitments and the constraints entailed by the plan that is guiding the implementation of the current strategy. Hence, we suggest that these phases be added to the strategic process to assure that the information and the feedback necessary to maintain a continuous strategic process be maintained.

The fourth phase calls for the creation of an e-business transition plan. We'll return to this in later chapters, after we have discussed some of the reasons why any transition in a company's e-business strategy also entails a redesign of the company's IT organization. Suffice, at this point, to say that we don't believe any large company can simultaneously reengineer its software architecture and infrastructure and retrain its people to use new, distributed software techniques while also implementing a total reengineering of its business processes as well. Major changes take time. Yet everyone wants a quick response to the e-business challenge. The only realistic way for a company to do this is to imagine a future state in which its IT organization can support any changes the company might make in its business processes. Then the company must design a transition plan that will move it toward that future state in reasonable steps. At the same time that the company is moving toward that future state, however, it must also build e-business applications. The trick is to create a plan that links business applications with the steps you want to take to get to the future state. Depending on the nature and extent of the changes a company proposes to make in its core business processes, it will probably also have to phase in the changes in its business processes. Thus, the e-business transition plan becomes a key document that defines how the company will successively approximate the implementation of its strategy.

An e-business transition takes time and planning

We have already suggested that the company's strategy will need to change rather frequently. When it changes, the transition plan will also have to change. The smart company will keep information flowing back and forth between planners and strategists to minimize the amount of backtracking and waste that results from what will be a necessarily messy process.

The final phase is included to remind managers that the e-business transition involves changes in the company culture and major reallocations of organizational power and responsibility. There will be fear, confusion, and resistance. The only large organizations that survive the e-business transition will be those with senior managers who can make the transition happen. Those managers will need to communicate the vision, define the necessity, and when necessary, demand the cooperation of the managers and employees who report to them. Given the extensive nature of the changes that most companies will be undertaking, feedback from senior managers about the cooperation or the resistance being encountered will be a key element in the strategic process.

Put another way, the senior management of even large companies will need to behave more like an entrepreneurial team managing the creation of a new e-business company. Speed to market, in many cases, will be very important, and coordination will be imperative. At the same time, in large companies, groups will be disintermediated and there will be resistance to change. Only constant oversight and pressure by the CEO and other senior managers will make the transition possible.

The Classic Model of Competition

To provide a summary of the changes that an e-business strategist must consider, let's review the notated version of Porter's model of industrial competition (see Figure 2.4). We could suggest that Porter's model still provides a good summary of the environmental challenges facing any firm. In that sense, the model is still of value. On the other hand, the model has changed from a model that generally comforted the managers of large, established businesses to one that describes most of their worst nightmares.

The protection that size and capital investment formerly provided to large firms is rapidly disappearing. Worse, in some cases, the very assets—the numerous stores and large inventories—that used to secure a company's position are now liabilities that increase its cost of doing business. The minimal costs of creating a Web site and entering a retail market provide a new entrant with an even greater strength as long as the stock market is willing to buy the

Today, challengers can easily raise money

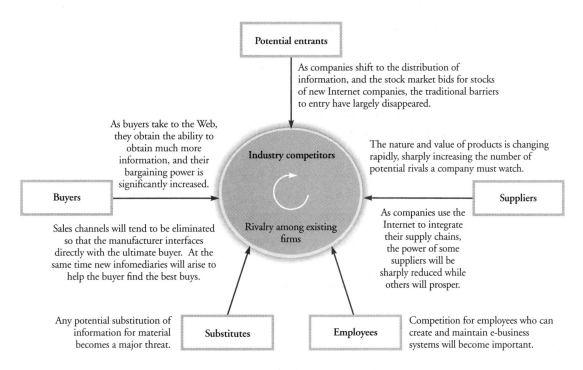

Figure 2.4 A modified version of Porter's model of the forces driving industry competition.

new entrant's stock and provide it with capital. The stock market is going through adjustments as we write, but we suspect that after a short period, venture money will once again be flowing to the more innovative Internet startups. Their IPOs may not provide them with the lavish funding Internet startups enjoyed in 1989–99, but we suspect they will still have more than enough to challenge established companies whenever their founders have a really good business plan.

The importance of the role of information

Obviously not all companies or industries will be under siege in the same way. If customers will buy via the Web, then retailers that depend on expensive stores and warehouses will be vulnerable. Companies that manufacture valued products, like cars and stereos, however, should still be able to benefit from their investment in plant and machinery. The key is the role that information plays in the value of the product or service.

Today's products mix information and materials

The major value of Philip Evans and Thomas S. Wurster's book, *Blown to Bits,* is its emphasis on the changing role of information. Historically, both buyers and sellers have lacked adequate information. In different industries, the information advantage has been on one side or the other, and the buyer or seller with more information has traditionally exploited the situation to increase or decrease a product's price. Over time, companies have tended to mix information and material (bits and atoms as Evans and Wurster would have it) in various value propositions. In extreme cases, the product is virtually given away and the information is charged for, or vice versa.

E-business changes the value of information

The key to understanding what the Internet is doing lies in realizing that it is now possible to separate information and material elements and to distribute them independently. Moreover, as Evans and Wurster illustrate in various ways, the economics of materials and information are very different. If you create a toaster and then sell it, you no longer have the toaster. If you create a software program and sell it, you still have the program to sell again.

Most managers have never thought of their businesses in terms of independent flows of information and material. Hence they don't immediately see where they have weighted their value propositions in favor of one or the other, or what would happen if they were separated. If an industry has evolved to the point where its major costs go into manufacturing a product, but its major revenues result from the use of information, then it is in serious trouble. In effect, it is a target for anyone who wants to move in and sell the information portion of its value proposition, via the Internet, for a fraction of what it currently sells it for. A trivial example is provided by companies that sell music CDs. Although music companies have traditionally paid noteworthy sums to recording artists, overall their real costs are in creating CDs, packaging them, and distributing them via stores. The music on a CD is information. The CD disk is just material. Once someone begins to distribute music via the Internet, downloading the bits to customers who can store it on any of a variety of media, including their PC's hard disks, the CD industry is in serious trouble.

Companies that misprice information face serious problems

We don't want to go too much further into this problem at this point, but we urge you to read *Blown to Bits* and to think about these issues as you begin to reconceptualize your company's strengths and weaknesses. Each company strategist needs to develop a very clear idea of what value proposition their business is really based on, and how their existing products and services combine and price information and materials. Products and services that we thought we understood are rapidly changing.

Where before a company may have faced a half dozen rivals each selling a package more or less like every other, suddenly the company can find itself facing several dozen rivals, most selling only one or another part of the package the company is selling. In the worst case, one of the new companies is selling an element of the package that contributes 40% of the company's income for a fraction of what the original company can sell it for. An example

Startups that sell the information separately are rewarded

would be a newspaper company that earns most of its revenues from advertising, even though advertising is only a small part of the total cost of a newspaper. If an Internet startup can draw a critical advertising audience—say, landlords and renters who are willing to use the Internet to find each other—the newspaper suddenly finds itself with a rival who can sell its services for a fraction of what the newspaper can. At the same time, the Internet service is pushing the newspaper, which is committed to using the sale of information to support the sale of material (newspaper), into bankruptcy. In this case, the barrier to entry has been shattered, while at the same time the company's rivals are multiplying and fragmenting into lots of different specialists.

The Web increases the buyer's power

At the same time, buyers who are willing to use the Web suddenly have access to lots more information. In most cases, this significantly increases the buyer's bargaining power. In a matter of minutes, a buyer shopping for a TV can access sites that compare brands and offer test information. Then the same buyer can quickly use an intermediary to identify dozens of firms that are willing to sell the TV that the buyer wants. Quick checks can determine the price, the service offered, and so forth. Any company that presents the buyer a Web site that is unfriendly is dismissed with a mouse click.

The Web forces sellers to reduce prices

At a minimum, the Web is putting all companies that sell via that channel under terrific pressure to reduce their prices. That, in turn, has forced most manufacturers to reevaluate their sales channels. As a generalization, manufacturers of commodities are moving toward selling directly to buyers over the Web in order to eliminate all of the costs associated with intermediary distribution and inventory. In several industries, salespeople and distributors are rapidly being disintermediated.

At the same time, new "infomediaries" are establishing themselves. An *infomediary* is a company that offers itself to customers to help them quickly identify and evaluate the choices available on the Web. Thus, a customer could use a search engine to find all the companies selling TVs on the Web. Or the buyer could go to an infomediary who would quickly assemble information sources and sellers and order them to minimize the time it takes the buyer to find and purchase the TV.

Continuing to examine Porter's model in Figure 2.4, we can see that the relationships between the company and its suppliers are also changed, although the change can vary sharply from industry to industry. If the company in the middle is a distributor of items manufactured by one of its suppliers, it may find itself disintermediated, as its supplier goes to the Web to establish a direct relationship with the ultimate buyer. On the other hand, if the company can establish a brokerage and force its suppliers to compete in real time, it may succeed in forcing the suppliers' prices down. (In the case of Ford and GM, they hope their parts brokerage will afford significant savings to suppliers, which they will pass back to Ford and GM, thereby reducing the cost of parts without necessarily reducing the profits of the suppliers.)

The relationship between companies and suppliers

In some cases, companies are committing to tight integration with their suppliers. In this case, the company is providing the supplier with direct access to information about its manufacturing activities so that the supplier can time shipments of new parts more accurately. This kind of system has already been developed between some large companies and key suppliers using Electronic Data Interchange (EDI) technologies available a decade ago. Unfortunately EDI systems were expensive to build and maintain. The Internet promises to accelerate the entire process of integration. In effect, in some cases, companies will be forced to reconceptualize their business processes as subsystems within a multicompany business supply chain process.

Company processes and supplier processes are integrated

Finally, it's worth noting that in some cases, the changes being driven by the Internet have supported more conventional responses. For example, most companies using the Internet have

Some conventional companies are thriving

realized that they don't want to try to establish worldwide, next-day delivery services and have outsourced their delivery process to a specialist. Thus, delivery services, like Federal Express and UPS, that combine information, trucks, and warehouses are thriving and buying new trucks and warehouses like mad in an effort to keep up with the growing volume.

Information is being substituted for materials

We've already indirectly discussed substitutions. The economics of the Web places a huge premium on substituting information for material whenever possible. And it places a similar premium on packaging information for distribution over the Web, rather than via media that embed information in material formats.

Finally, as a reminder, we added a new box to Porter's model. In the world that Porter described when his book first appeared in the 1980s, employees were not considered a major competitive factor. That's changed. In the next decade or so, companies that want to succeed on the Internet are going to find themselves competing for employees just as they compete for customers. The skills necessary to compete successfully in the rapidly changing world of e-business are scarce, and it's a zero sum game for the foreseeable future. Expect to read of major companies that fail because their personnel policies aren't adjusted to the new realities and they find that, for lack of key employees, they simply can't create or maintain the systems they need to compete with their rivals.

E-business companies will compete for employees

Summary

Companies must make changes to transition to e-business

Whatever strategic process your company follows, it will eventually arrive at some description of your company competencies and some understanding of the new business environment being created by the Internet and the Web. If you keep in mind the changes we have described above and apply them to your own company, you will probably conclude that your company needs to get very serious about redesigning most of its business processes. Most companies, for example, will find they have unsustainable mixes of information and material product and that they need to sort out the implications of having the two split apart. In some cases the decision will be stark: They should either specialize in producing and selling information, or they should focus on producing and selling material goods. In these cases, the company will need to redesign its business processes, making them slimmer and more focused, and then they will need to figure out how to work with others who will specialize in information or material processes that the company decides not to specialize in.

More commonly, companies will decide, at least initially, that they will need to divide some business processes, but should continue to offer both material goods and information. In this situation, they will still need to divide their existing processes in order to assure that each subprocess is as efficient as possible. If they don't do this, they are simply waiting for some Internet upstart to figure out how to decompose one of their processes and begin to sell a portion of their package much more efficiently than they do. It's better to be proactive and deconstruct your own business processes rather than to wait for someone else to show you how to do it.

Most companies will attempt a dual-track response

In a similar way, most e-business strategy gurus advise companies to focus on creating new value propositions rather than focusing on revising their current products and services. This advice is designed to counteract the tendency of traditional strategists to define their company competencies in terms of the existing products they produce. This is especially acute in cases where companies rely on large-scale production to obtain great efficiencies of scale. The tendency of companies of this type is to think primarily in terms of the product they manufacture. They assume that, because they are

Some companies will create entirely new value propositions

currently the best or the most efficient at manufacturing a product, that is their core competency. In fact, as we have already noted, the current product is probably a mix of material and informational efficiencies, which may become quite inefficient if they are disentangled.

Another way of approaching the same advice is to simply note that customers are about to become much more powerful. Companies are well advised to focus on customer value propositions first, and only consider how to supply the value once they have arrived at it.

At this point, we'll leave strategy considerations and shift our focus to the actual problems a company encounters when it tries to redesign an existing corporate business process.

3

Redesigning Business Processes for E-Business

The e-business challenge facing companies is complex and can't be easily described from any single perspective. It involves major changes in the way companies do business, including changes in marketing, sales, manufacturing, inventory, and service and product delivery. It involves creating new organizations, redesigning business processes, and moving to a different mix of employees with different skills. In many cases, it involves different products. It certainly requires different computing architectures,

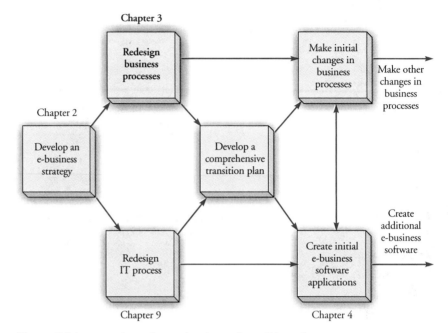

Figure 3.1 An overview of an e-business transition plan.

infrastructures, new development tools, and a whole new approach to developing software applications.

Moving to an e-business requires extensive changes

In Chapter 2 we provided a brief overview of the kind of conceptual changes that company strategists would need to make in order to formulate new goals and policies for their companies. In this chapter we will describe some of the specific changes in business process that companies will need to consider in order to respond to the Internet challenge (see Figure 3.1).

Transitioning to an E-Business

Web site applications are easy

Most companies have probably already begun to experiment with the Internet and the Web. Small-scale exploration and experimentation, however, is very different from a serious commitment to change your company from a traditional business to an Internet

or Web-based business. The commitment to change is a commitment to reengineer the company, to change company business
processes, and to create new systems and new ways of doing
business that will take advantage of the Internet. Some theorists
now distinguish between first-generation Web applications and
second-generation e-business applications. First-generation Web
applications can be constructed without making major changes in
a company's existing enterprise systems. In effect, a Web application is simply a Web site that is more or less independent of the
company's other applications. E-business applications, however,
require much more extensive changes, and they normally need to
be integrated with a company's legacy applications. Thus, the
decision to create a company Web site is easy, but the decision
to undertake major changes in core business processes and to
develop second-generation ebusiness systems is a serious
matter.

A serious effort cannot begin or proceed without the commitment of senior management. Companies that are serious about
making the transition usually begin by creating a committee that
includes the CEO, COO, CIO, and most of the company's division or department heads. If you are talking about changing the
very nature of the company, all of these individuals must be involved in the discussions that lead up to the commitment. Once a
commitment is made, a subcommittee is typically created and em-
powered to draw up more specific plans and, once they are approved, to oversee implementing them. In many cases, the subcommittee is headed by an individual especially hired for the job.
The task of heading a transition committee requires a rare mix of
skills. The individual has to be equally sensitive to the business
problems and the information systems problems involved in the
transition. In addition, if the company decides to acquire new e-
business companies, or to set up a subsidiary, this individual needs
to be able to help plan very high-level corporate strategies.

*E-business systems
require a major
management
commitment*

Once the company has made a commitment and set up a committee to oversee the actual transition process, the committee turns to the actual work of business process reengineering (BPR).

Business Process Reengineering

An overview of BPR   To assure we are all talking the same language, we'll begin with a very high-level overview of the basic terms commonly used, and a generic methodology that defines the phases in a common BPR project.

Basic BPR Terms

Figure 3.2 provides an overview of a hypothetical auto dealer. The shaded columns provide an idea of how the dealership is organized. There are five departments, each with a manager who reports to the owner.

Business processes are sets of activities or tasks that deliver value. External processes are processes that are originated by customers of the dealership and end when the customer is satisfied. Internal processes take place within the firm and are originated by a department or by one of the external processes.

External processes are divided between core processes, which generate most of the money for the firm and employ the real expertise of the firm, and secondary processes, which add some money but aren't critical to the survival of the firm.

Suppliers from outside the firm provide people, capital, materials, and services, which are consumed by the various company processes.

Business processes tend toward horizontal integration. A single process integrates everything that is required to move from the original customer request to the fulfillment of the customer re-

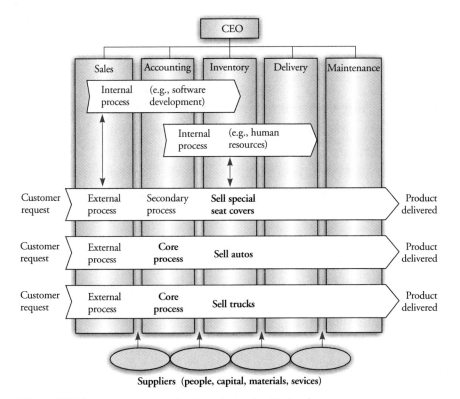

Figure 3.2 A company organizational chart with business processes overlaid.

quest. When possible, companies often try to achieve vertical integration as well. In that case, they seek to link to suppliers to extend the control the company can exert over the performance of the task. Most computer manufacturers, for example, have good horizontal control, moving from order to assembly to delivery in a systematic way. They do not, however, have vertical control, since they depend on others for the chips and other hardware elements that they use to actually assemble the computers they sell. IBM, on the other hand, owns its own chip manufacturing facilities and the research groups that design and create the chips it uses in its computers.

Most companies made an effort to identify business processes in the mid-1990s. The key element in most BPR efforts is the identification and analysis of business processes. Companies seek to reduce the number of steps in their processes while increasing their efficiency. At the same time, they try to focus on customer needs and what makes customers happy. The goal is to be the best at providing a particular product or service by perfecting the business process involved. At the same time, BPR theorists have usually urged companies to focus on processes that embody the company's real expertise and to subcontract secondary processes and even some internal processes to other companies that can specialize in those processes.

Early BPR efforts tended to focus primarily on horizontal integration and not on vertical integration. There were some efforts to link with suppliers to increase the efficiency of order and inventory systems, but nothing like the focus on vertical integration that is being advocated by e-business experts.

The term BPR is often associated with radical reengineering. Some users prefer "business process redesign" or "business process improvement" (BPI) to stress their commitment to evolutionary improvements.

Figure 3.3 provides an overview of a generic approach to reengineering a company and a business process. There's no broad agreement on exactly what phases every BPR effort should include, but we've used five in the model in Figure 3.3.

Phase 1: Create an enterprise model

Phase 1 involves creating a high-level enterprise model, which might look very much like Figure 3.2. The enterprise model specifies all of the company's business processes and defines the major relationships between them. Internal and external processes are identified, and external processes are classified into either core or secondary processes. This phase usually requires inputs from senior company managers and department heads. In the early 1990s, it was common for companies to set up high-level BPR management

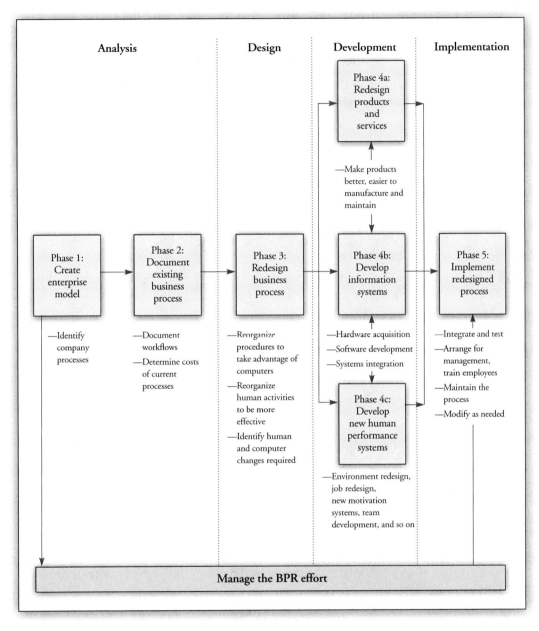

Figure 3.3 An overview of the generic phases in a traditional BPR project.

teams to establish such an overview and then manage the ongoing BPR projects the company undertook. Most large companies have already worked their way through this process. The Web and the Internet offer new challenges, and most companies will want to re-create this committee if it's been allowed to lapse and to reanalyze the company's processes, but it shouldn't take as long this time as it took in the early 1990s.

Phase 2: Document the existing process

Phase 2 focuses on documenting process workflows and determining the costs and efficiencies of the company's existing processes. In the early 1990s, this portion of the effort put a special emphasis on eliminating unnecessary jobs and steps and on comparing the efficiency of a company's processes with those at related companies. Thus, for example, one auto dealer might determine that it cost them $500 to sell a typical car, including advertising, delivery preparation, a sales bonus, and so forth. A comparison of their costs with costs for similar efforts at other auto dealers might have revealed that competitors provided the same value for $350, providing the first company with a goal: to reduce their costs accordingly.

As a result of mid-1990s BPR efforts, most companies have better documented processes and a better idea of the costs of their current processes than they did before their BPR projects. As companies move toward e-business processes, however, the emphasis is on quick change and on responding to the moves of new Internet companies and less on efficiency. Presumably most companies will spend what it takes to develop an adequate Internet presence and then worry, later, about making their e-business processes more efficient.

Phase 3: Redesign the business process

Phase 3 focuses on the actual redesign of business processes. This is usually undertaken by a committee that includes folks from the existing business process, from IT, and from management. The redesign of business processes always involves changes in a variety of different elements that contribute to the business process.

Some BPR gurus suggest that at this point the team forget the existing process and envision a new, ideal process from scratch. Most companies aren't willing to be so radical and focus on simply improving an existing process. They usually start by checking the steps in the existing process to see if a different order or a combination of existing tasks might result in greater speed, greater efficiency, or greater customer satisfaction.

Usually some changes are required in management policies or the rules that govern the performance of a task. We know of one company that made a huge gain in procurement efficiency simply by issuing each manager a credit card and assigning a spending limit. It made it possible for managers to acquire small items they urgently needed without having to go through a time-consuming and frustrating special-order process. It exposed the company to some risks that foolish purchases might be made, but it was better than delaying the majority of special purchases and significantly reduced manager frustration with procurement regulations.

Small changes can yield large gains

At the same time, most redesign efforts require that jobs be modified and that employees learn new skills or new ways of doing things to facilitate the changes in the business process. Most companies insist on having representative employees who will be affected by the change on the committee that redesigns the system. Too many efforts have failed because technologists made changes that the company couldn't get the workers to implement.

Changes in the use of hardware or software systems can also result in great improvements in business processes. In the early 1990s, a lot of attention was focused on automating jobs by providing desktop computers, or handheld devices, and on linking computers via local area networks so that electronic versions of documents could be passed over the network to save time. This, in turn, meant that documents needed to be scanned for electronic distribution. But it also meant that several different employees could receive a document at the same time and that processing could proceed in parallel. This was also the period in which most companies began to convert from mainframe systems to early client-server systems that relied on PCs linked to databases supported on Unix servers.

Workflow systems were closely associated with email systems and with groupwork systems that helped groups of employees work together, online, on a document or a problem.

In the early 1990s, there was a good deal of emphasis placed on companies linking with suppliers to reduce resupply times and to minimize the amount of inventory that a company needed to maintain. Unfortunately, the technology available before 1995–97 didn't make it easy to link large numbers of suppliers in networks. Because of costs and development problems, most companies only focused on linking key suppliers.

Phase 4: Make the necessary changes

During the fourth phase, all the changes specified in the business process redesign document need to be made. In some cases, the products and services themselves need to be changed to accommodate the new processes. At the same time new hardware needs to be acquired and put into place and new software systems need to be created to automate the new processes. Finally, new jobs need to be designed and training needs to be developed to provide the employees with the skills they will need to function in the redesigned environment. During Phase 4 different groups of specialists work on each of these development tasks.

Phase 5: Implement the changed business process

During Phase 5 all of the results of the efforts undertaken in Phase 4 are brought together and implemented. All of the changes need to be tested and fine-tuned. Once the actual changes are implemented, they need to be monitored to assure they work as they should, to provide data to determine if the changes result in the anticipated efficiencies, and to be prepared to improve the processes whenever possible.

In addition to the various phases, the entire BPR change process needs to be continually monitored. That overall management function is indicated by the box at the bottom of Figure 3.3. Obviously this overview doesn't begin to cover all of the tasks involved in a large corporate BPR effort. It is sufficient, however, to suggest that BPR involves a lot more than software development. Indeed, in the mid-1990s, most companies obtained the largest gains simply by reorganizing the order in which tasks were performed, consolidating tasks, and eliminating redundant employees.

The BPR change process must be carefully managed

Computers didn't contribute as much to most early BPR efforts as was hoped, simply because most IT groups were engaged in transitioning to client-server systems and they ran into lots of problems making those systems work efficiently.

BPR had already begun to fade by 1996 when people began to discover the Web and IT managers began to embrace the Internet as a universal distributed communications standard. During 1996–98 most companies were simply experimenting with Web sites and watching with amazement as new startups showed what could be done by selling directly over the Web. During this same period, software vendors began to introduce new tools and technologies, like Java, Enterprise JavaBeans, EJB application servers, and COM+, that would facilitate serious Internet systems development.

The Internet necessitates another round of BPR

By 1998, every business newspaper, magazine, and conference decided that companies would either become e-businesses or perish. The transition to the Internet was in full swing by 1999. And large companies once again found themselves faced with the need for serious business process reengineering.

To sum up: During the first half of the 1990s, when BPR enjoyed its first round of attention, companies used it primarily to improve their back office processes. They streamlined processes, consolidated steps and tasks, and eliminated employees whenever possible. Computer systems were used to improve processes, but didn't play a major part in most BPR efforts. The main computer emphasis was getting PCs for most employees. IT often didn't provide the boost that was expected of it, simply because IT faced too many problems moving to put client-server systems in place. Links between companies proved difficult because distributed techniques weren't ready to support the plans that companies wanted to implement. In the end, most companies wouldn't go as far as BPR gurus recommended because the pain of change was simply too great and the benefits of changing weren't large enough to justify the pain. Radical BPR gradually changed into a more modest improvement strategy that slowly faded.

BPR for E-Business

The advent of the Web and the possibility of selling goods online and linking to suppliers via the Internet has led companies to embrace a new round of process reengineering. This round, driven by fears that companies that don't adapt to the Internet will disappear, seems likely to embrace more radical changes than companies were willing to contemplate in the 1990s. One wag has termed the return of BPR as "BPR on steroids"!

E-business BPR focuses on online customers

BPR for e-business has emphasized reorienting business processes to facilitate marketing and sales over the Web. Product manufacturing is often being redesigned to support tailoring products for customers. At the same time, everything possible is being done to cut costs, since the Web clearly will allow customers to compare prices and features in ways never before possible, bringing many companies under intense pressure to reduce prices.

Equally important, this round of process reengineering is extending the concept of a business process beyond the boundaries of the company in a major way. To support tailoring and rapid response times, companies are integrating their processes with other companies' processes in ways unimaginable just a few years ago. This supply chain integration not only automates the ordering and shipping of parts but also integrates billing and payment systems in many cases.

E-business BPR also focuses on supply chains

In effect, e-business reengineering is finally leading companies to consider the deep and radical redesigns that Hammer and other BPR gurus first advocated in the early 1990s. What was too radical then is simply necessary to survive now.

Many companies have approached the transition in a very haphazard way—simply responding to challenges by startups rather than planning a systematic response. Indeed, some e-business BPR gurus have argued that the e-commerce challenge calls for a new approach to BPR—one that puts a heavy emphasis on responding quickly. Thus, they advocate avoiding companywide planning in favor of task forces that specialize in quick redesigns that can be extended later. As time has passed, however, more thoughtful companies realize that to survive the challenge, they will have to be much more systematic, both in the redesign of their processes and in their approach to software development.

BPR takes time and systematic planning

For many companies, the reengineering of the software group is one of the highest-priority tasks. The good news is that the Internet, IIOP, XML, Java, COM+, ActiveX, and EJB technologies make it possible to build the kind of new Internet-enabled business processes that companies only dreamed of in the early 1990s. The bad news is that to take advantage of these technologies, companies need to adopt new software architectures and learn to use distributed component-based development techniques. In effect, they need to reinvent their IT organizations at the same time that they must also reinvent their core business processes.

Reengineering the IT process is a high priority

Converting to an E-Business

Focus on customers
who will buy online

Before considering any specific processes that might be affected by the Internet or the Web, let's take a broad view of the business environment in which companies now find themselves. Some customers, although by no means all customers, are using the Web to seek information about products, to buy products, and to request service support. Although these Web-oriented customers are still a minority in almost all areas, they are often the wealthiest and the most sophisticated customers. And their numbers are growing rapidly. Similarly, some companies that buy or sell products are relying on the Internet or the Web to facilitate the distribution of information, to handle orders, and even, in some cases, to deliver the products that other companies seek to buy or sell.

To make matters more complex, new companies are being founded to do business with these new Web-oriented customers and suppliers. Moreover, the current financial market is such that these new companies are able to find lots of startup money and, with luck, go public rapidly and have access to even larger amounts of money via the stock market.

Figure 3.4 provides an overview of the situation we are describing. Each company must consider its own business environment

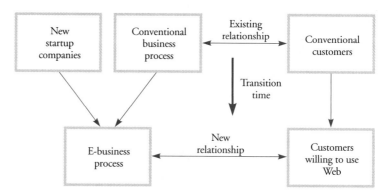

Figure 3.4 The transition of customers and business processes.

very carefully to determine what its customers are doing or are likely to do in the near future. Are your company's customers likely to buy over the Web? You must also consider what your competitors or new e-business startups might do. This is especially hard for large existing companies, since they have been successful, in the past, by knowing their market and responding to it effectively. Suddenly, the company's managers are being told that the company may not understand its market, or that the market is about to undergo a radical change. It's hard for those who have worked in an industry for years to forget all their assumptions and rethink their business in fundamental ways. Nonetheless, that is what survival in the e-commerce era will require. Companies need to consider how quickly their customers might migrate to the Web. The smart company will want to be prepared to sell its products and services on the Web when its customers arrive there.

Figure 3.5 provides another simple overview of the elements that company managers must consider. (This is a variation on the competition model that we considered in the last chapter.) Ignoring for the moment the internal processes that take place at the company, managers must consider who their customers are and

Some questions to consider

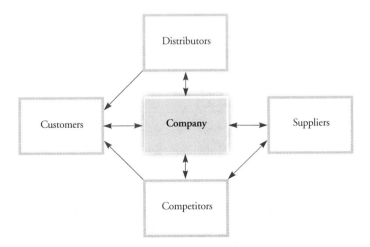

Figure 3.5 Some of the basic relationships to be considered.

how likely it is that they will change. They must also consider who their suppliers are and how likely it is that their relationships with their suppliers could be changed.

The key questions every executive group should be asking itself include the following:

1. How does your company interact with our customers? (Identify all of the different interactions.) What products and services do we provide? Could we provide any of them over the Internet, and if we could, would it please our customers?

2. How does your company interact with its suppliers? (Identify all of the different interactions.) What products and services do we buy? Could we buy any of them over the Internet, and if we could, would it increase the overall productivity of our business or make the products and services we sell more pleasing to our customers?

3. What are your competitors doing? Are they making moves that suggest they will be transitioning to an e-business model? Are there any new startups that are targeting our customers? Exactly what products and services are our competitors offering over the Web, and if they are successful, how will it affect our financial situation?

4. How vulnerable is your business or industry to penetration by new startups? Are there significant barriers to entry, and are they really barriers in the Internet age?

Many retailers might have said that the cost of their stores and their distribution system that supported their stores was a barrier to entry. It turns out, however, that these "assets" aren't really barriers in the Internet age. If customers are willing to shop online, then stores are a liability. On the other hand, if a company manufactures a product, the manufacturing machinery and know-how are probably a barrier to entry. Moreover, if a manufacturer decides to tailor products for customers, they probably have a significant advantage over an Internet startup that must buy its products from manufacturers. Each company needs to determine for itself how vulnerable it is. A company that decides that its core business isn't vulnerable to an attack by an Internet startup can hardly relax, of course, since it still faces its historical competitors and any of those companies may use the Internet to change the competitive situation.

5. If your company is vulnerable to an attack by a startup that can create a new way of business while significantly reducing the costs of doing business, will you modify your own business processes, or set up a new company to conduct business over the Internet?

Initially, the idea of forming a new company to compete with itself can be threatening. It comes down to a very hard-nosed analysis of how difficult it would be to change the existing company. If a company is in a market that is vulnerable to an attack by an Internet startup, then the new company will probably enjoy an advantage since it can create new procedures, hire new people, and build new software systems, all tailored to take advantage of the Internet. The existing company, on the other hand, has to deal with all the inertia of its existing legacy procedures and systems and must retrain people who have spent years learning how to do things in a pre-Internet manner. Change is always hard, and in many cases, provided you have the capital, you can move much faster if you can start from scratch rather than retooling an existing organization.

6. Should your company consider buying other companies to acquire needed technologies?

Speed is very important at the moment, and capital is relatively plentiful. Under the circumstances, if your company can buy another company that knows how to perform some function, it is usually better to make the purchase and obtain the new capabilities quickly than try to reinvent the new functionality internally.

Everything must be reevaluated

These six considerations hardly constitute a comprehensive list, but they provide a good beginning. The changes taking place in business are fundamental and profound. They are at least as great as the changes that took place when companies began to adopt telephones or changed to take advantage of the railroad. They may be as fundamental as the changes that ushered in the Industrial Revolution—the establishment of factories, production lines, and the use of energy sources like steam and electricity to run large machines. The point is that nothing can be taken for granted, and everything must be subjected to a radical reevaluation.

The New Role of the Customer

Online customers behave differently

Most detailed analyses of how e-commerce will change business processes begin with a reevaluation of the role of the customer. If customers are willing to use the Net to shop, then they have the ability to quickly check many different suppliers to find the product that best suits their needs. If by simply clicking on a new Web site name, they can move from one company's site to another, they don't have to put up with poor service, waits, or confusing product descriptions. Moreover, by using new intermediary services, they can actually use software tools to search for the seller offering the best price, or the best delivery dates, or a product tailored to meet their specific needs.

There may be some markets in which customers will be unwilling to use the Web. Some analysts have suggested that customers will use the Web in "low-touch" areas where products come in standard units and they can rely on formal descriptions to make their decisions. On the other hand, if the purchase depends on "touch and feel," customers may be reluctant to rely on the Web. For example, customers have been quick to buy computers on the Web, but have been slower to rely on the Web to buy clothing or food. In spite of this kind of generalization, however, company executives should be very careful in concluding that their business models can remain unchanged just because their products are high-touch products. Lots of new Internet companies are exploring ways to make customers more comfortable buying high-touch items over the Web, and, to repeat, nothing can be taken for granted. For example, some clothing Web stores have created three-dimensional models. A customer can enter their measurements and the model will be adjusted to reflect the customer's body size. Then clothing items can be dragged and dropped on the mannequin to allow customers to see what the clothing might look like if they tried it on. It's too early to know how well approaches like this will work, but it's clear that no area is completely safe from Web-based approaches. After all, enough high-touch items are already sold via mail catalogs to undermine any simple analysis of products that can be sold via the Web.

What can be sold over the Internet?

What is clear is that the Web is going to change customer expectations. As customers become accustomed to visiting sites, like Amazon.com, that offer tens of thousands of options, they are going to become impatient with stores that don't have the items they want when they want them. Similarly, as customers become accustomed to buying from stores that apply heavy volume discounts, they are going to become less tolerant of the higher costs common

Online customers expect to compare offerings

at smaller, local stores. In effect, using the Web, customers can now shop anywhere in the world and buy from the vendor that offers the best prices. Obviously this advantage won't be as valued if the Internet store can't deliver the item quickly. Hence, Web-based companies are clearly going to compete to offer customers quick delivery.

Online customers expect custom tailoring

At the same time, customers will increasingly expect not only a wide selection but custom tailoring. Web-based vendors will compete by offering customers more options. You might imagine that this would be more expensive, but many Web companies have decided that they can actually save money by providing tailoring and eliminating inventory. In the past, a computer vendor would try to anticipate what models customers might want. They would ship several different models to warehouses and to retail stores. Some would sell better and run out while others would move more slowly. Any large company could calculate how long items were in inventory before they were sold. Today, computer vendors like Dell are only manufacturing computers after they receive an order. Since the computers are made from standard parts, the company finds it easier to maintain an inventory of parts and assemble them into specific models requested by customers upon demand. As long as the assembly is done quickly and the product is rushed to the customer, it's actually cheaper than the traditional way of doing things.

So customers will increasingly expect more options and more tailoring, while simultaneously demanding the best prices and rapid delivery. And they will expect excellent support and service, available instantly over the Internet.

Companies buying online expect better prices and service

So far, we've spoken of customers as if they were all individual consumers. The same analysis applies to industrial customers as well. We have already discussed how Ford and General Motors expect to create brokerage systems that will allow them to buy parts via the Web. In the past, Ford or GM would enter into long-term contracts with parts manufacturers and buy parts in quantity. There has been a steady movement to reduce inventory times by coordinating supplies with manufacturing needs, but Ford and GM now expect the Net to make it possible for them to increase this coordination by an order of magnitude. In effect, their brokerage system will be set up to allow them to ask for bids for parts at any time and in any quantity. (Keep in mind they will increasingly be selling tailored cars to their customers and will thus be less able to anticipate long-term needs.) Parts manufacturers selling to such demanding and sophisticated buyers will need to reengineer their own systems to respond quickly and efficiently, or lose out to those who can.

The place to begin thinking about how your company or industry might change is to imagine customers like the ones we have just described. Once you can imagine how your customers might change, you can begin to consider how you will have to change your business processes and your interactions with your suppliers to satisfy such customers. You will also be in a position to reconsider how you distribute your products to your ultimate customers. You may decide, for example, that you can provide the service your customers demand by interfacing directly with your ultimate customers via the Web.

Imagine what your customers will want online

In most cases, of course, a company will not decide to change everything overnight. A company will decide that customers are beginning to change and that it will need to evolve in response to a changing customer body. Deciding how quickly customers will change and therefore how quickly the company must change to remain competitive will be a difficult problem. As we have suggested elsewhere, many companies have decided to establish a separate company to handle Net sales to assure that the existing company can continue to service older customers and existing distribution

Understand how your customers might change

channels at the same time that a new system is put in place to deal with new customers. Once you can describe how your customers might change, you are in a position to consider how you might change your company to provide products and services to those new customers.

Changing Business Processes for the Web

To make our discussion a little more concrete, let's consider the hypothetical order fulfillment process illustrated in Figure 3.6. Let's assume this business process belongs to Stereos-R-Us and that this

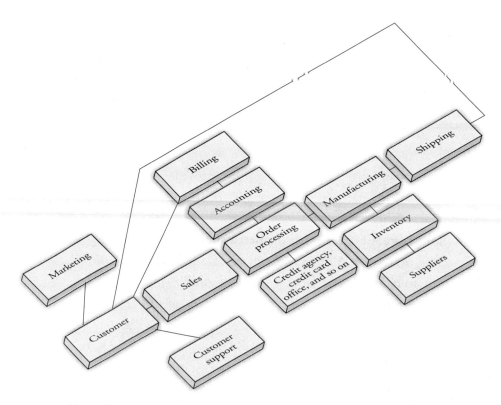

Figure 3.6 An overview of the Stereos-R-Us order fulfillment process.

process sells a variety of different types of stereo sound systems to individuals and wholesalers. While hardly comprehensive, we've illustrated the major steps or groups involved in the stereo order fulfillment process. This process is a conventional business process that was improved somewhat in the early 1990s, but is otherwise much the same as it was in the early 1980s.

The Stereos-R-Us marketing department runs ads in trade magazines and cosponsors occasional ads on television. In addition, it sometimes runs a direct mail campaign to encourage the purchase of stereos. The sales force takes orders. Stereos-R-Us offers tailoring options to its customers. Thus, for example, stereos come in silver, metal, or black. Similarly, they can have regular or heavy-duty parts, and so forth. The salesperson indicates the tailoring options as part of the order. Salespeople visit major wholesale sites and they talk with others by phone. They fill out an order form when they make a sale and submit it to the order processing department. Order processing does three things. First, it determines that the customer is creditworthy. To do this, it requests information from credit card or credit rating agencies. If appropriate, the order is approved.

The Stereos-R-Us marketing and sales functions

Once the order is approved, order processing alerts accounting of the order and instructs manufacturing to produce the order. To produce a stereo unit, manufacturing obtains parts from inventory. Inventory is constantly replacing parts that are used by ordering new parts from various suppliers. When a stereo is manufactured, it is passed to shipping, which arranges to ship the stereo to the customer. At the same time, shipping notifies billing, which sends the customer a bill for the stereo. At any time during the process, or after, a customer can call customer support to determine the status of the order, to obtain help in actually using the stereo, or to seek to resolve some problem.

The Stereos-R-Us manufacturing and delivery functions

As we suggested, this is a very generic process and could easily illustrate, with minor variations, processes at thousands of

Stereos-R-Us has already improved its processes

midsized companies. Over the past dozen years, lots of companies with similar processes have used computers to improve their processes. The emphasis on reengineering in the mid-1990s focused primarily on making processes like these more efficient. In the first place, a major effort was undertaken to link all the processes together and eliminate bottlenecks. Paper sales orders were phased out. New business rules were instituted to assure that credit checks didn't cost more than the order was worth. Thus, for example, very small orders are now shipped with a minimal credit check, since historical data makes it clear that most orders are paid and it isn't worth holding up the smaller orders for elaborate credit checks. Similarly, Stereos-R-Us linked its inventory computer system to a number of key suppliers so that they could send parts in a more timely manner to minimize the actual parts in inventory at any one time.

Reengineering always meets resistance

Depending on the company and the industry, the reengineering that took place in the early 1990s might have introduced major efficiencies—many due to better business rules, but most due to the wider use of computers and to efforts to link computers together more effectively. Cutting-edge companies, which Stereos-R-Us wasn't, started down the path toward the use of new software technologies and distributed-component-based software systems. Most companies didn't, however, because they discovered two things. First, it's very hard to change a large organization. Department managers fight for turf and technologists are quick to explain how difficult and costly it would be to make the desired changes. In many cases the pain proved greater than the benefits that the company hoped it would obtain. Second, given the technology available in the early 1990s, building distributed systems proved very difficult. Linking the company's inventory system to those of its suppliers proved time-consuming and complex. The suppliers all used different hardware and different software protocols, and

the hand-built bridges that Stereos-R-Us developers had to construct were very costly to create and maintain, since everyone
seemed to be constantly changing some aspect of their overall software system.

In 1996, however, everything began to change. The Internet
and the Web have changed how managers, customers, suppliers,
and developers look at the process. The Internet provides a common, basic communication protocol that everyone has adopted.
Because the Internet protocols use telephone lines, whether public
or dedicated lines, it's much easier to establish links between various sites. The Web, with its graphic interface and easy-to-use formatting protocols, makes it much easier for customers, suppliers,
and internal company employees to pass information to each other
or to access information online. In effect, the whole world of computing has made a quantum leap. Now, instead of thinking of
computers as processors of some kind, people are beginning to
think of them as nodes in a communication network. As Sun
Microsystems keeps saying, "The Network is the computer."

*Computing made a
quantum leap*

Initially, potential customers used email and the Web for personal communications and amusement, but by 1998 most potential customers were also considering how to use the Web to locate
products and services they wanted to buy, and many were actually
acquiring them over the Net. Every study of this phenomenon pre-
dicts that this trend will grow rapidly, both in the United States,
where it is already having a major impact, and abroad, where it is
still just picking up momentum.

*More customers buy
more on the Web*

The frenzy to adapt to the Web gripped Stereos-R-Us just as it
did lots of other retailers. To date no new e-business company has
been established to sell stereos. This makes sense when you consider the considerable cost of manufacturing quality stereos. Anyone who wanted to enter this business would need to duplicate
Stereos-R-Us's manufacturing investment, which is considerable.

*Stereos-R-Us tries to
decide about the
Internet*

Thus, in this particular market, the main competition will probably come from other stereo manufacturers. The CEO of Stereos-R-Us has decided that she wants her company to be the first to offer quality stereo systems online. With the CEO applying pressure, everyone at Stereos-R-Us has begun to think about how to manage the transition. Obviously there is a broad continuum of options. Stereos-R-Us can make some minimal changes, to explore the e-business process, or it can take more risks. For example, Stereos-R-Us can begin by creating a Web site that provides customers with a catalog of the stereos the company sells, but doesn't allow customers to order online.

Some Stereos-R-Us managers suggest major changes

Let's assume that the CEO of Stereos-R-Us is a hands-on CEO and that she is determined that the company needs to make major changes. She takes her senior management team away, locks them in a hotel room, puts the process shown in Figure 3.6 on the board, and asks how they can use the Internet and the Web to totally transform the way Stereos-R-Us does business. Some of the executives, who have been reading and thinking about the implications of customer online sales, have suggestions for major changes.

Others think major changes will be disruptive

Others are extremely nervous about the possibility of making major changes while continuing to maintain the profits that their stockholders expect. They argue that the changes that are being proposed will change all the company's business processes at once, eliminate many jobs, and require major new investments in software technologies. Worse, during the transition, the new e-commerce systems will be competing directly with the existing Stereos-R-Us process. Each e-commerce sale, bought at a high price, will be made at the expense of sales that would otherwise be made by the conventional system, at a much lower price. No matter what the ideal outcome in two or three years, in the meantime managing the transition will be very, very hard. Many of the issues being discussed, these executives point out, came up when Stereos-R-Us reengineered itself in 1992 and were rejected as too disruptive.

The CEO of Stereos-R-Us listens to all the reasons not to change, not to change too quickly, or not to change too extensively, and rejects them. She is convinced that the worldwide transition to e-commerce is akin to the transition to the use of the railroad or electricity that occurred late in the last century. "We either change quickly and succeed in this new business environment, or we will bleed to death over the course of the next few years and disappear," she asserts. "This is a time for boldness and risk." Once the management team accepts this position, they begin to look again at their business processes and see what they might do.

Stereos-R-Us opts for major changes

Changes in Marketing and Sales

The Stereos-R-Us managers began by assuming that their customers would increasingly shop by means of the Web. Individual customers would come to their Web site to look and then, perhaps, to buy. Corporate customers (wholesalers) would probably begin to use intermediary marketing systems that would let them compare the prices and features of the major stereo system manufacturers and buy from the manufacturer offering the best terms. This led the management team to focus on two separate goals. One was to determine how to sell stereos via their Web site. The other was to determine how they would need to change their product to compete in the brutal competition they would face if their major wholesale customers used an intermediary and then chose stereos primarily based on price.

Implications of an online orientation

Marketing was unsure how much effort it would need to put into conventional advertising campaigns and how much should be allocated to online marketing efforts. They elected to explore a mixed strategy, while monitoring the results very carefully. What marketing was very sure of was that the Web site would play a

Marketing targeted both online and conventional sales

major role in the image the company projected in the future. Thus, they wanted to take the development of the Web site out of the hands of "IT techies" and use professional advertising companies that had helped them develop magazine ads in the past.

At the same time, both marketing and sales wanted guarantees from the IT people that they could keep the Web site running 24 hours a day, seven days a week without any failures. They pointed to the major PR problems that other companies had experienced when their Web sites crashed for a few hours and argued that the image of the company would gradually shift from current image campaigns to the Web site, making the management of that site very important.

Salespeople would be phased out

Sales reluctantly accepted the fact that it would be gradually phased out. If customers gradually shifted their habits and preferred to buy stereo systems online, then the company wouldn't need either the field salespeople or the phone order people. Obviously this transition would only happen if customers found it easy to buy on the Stereos-R-Us Web site, and they wanted guarantees that Web site would be designed by people who focused on ease of use and customer feedback. As the sales manager said: "It's one thing for our salespeople to use the order entry system that IT developed in '92, and it's another thing to expect customers to enter orders using those interfaces. It takes a long time to train our salespeople to use that system. Don't expect customers to put up with the frustration involved, they'll simply go elsewhere." Everyone agreed that the actual ordering screens and the steps in the order process would need to be considerably simplified. Meanwhile, the sales manager would have to project how quickly the transition would occur and figure out how to maintain a gradually declining sales operation.

Customer support would go online

In a similar way, everyone agreed that most customer support should be provided via the Web site. Different techniques were considered, ranging from (1) having a list of commonly asked questions, to (2) allowing customers to check manufacturing and shipping schedules, to (3) letting customers send emails to customer service agents who would answer them by return mail. The customer support team drew up a whole range of issues to be investigated. They wanted to know if manufacturing information could be made available to customers online and in what form it could be provided. They also decided that they would need to acquire new "call answering" software that could handle both phone and email contacts. And, of course, they decided they would need to retrain the existing customer support people to use computers and email.

It was decided that the order processing operation could be largely automated. Most orders would now be originated by customers online. Customers would provide information and expect approval and shipping information in a matter of seconds. Credit checks would need to be automated as would scheduling information. Links between credit systems and manufacturing systems would have to be developed well beyond what they were at the moment, and an interface would need to be developed that would make it easy for customers to determine the status of their order.

Customers would order online

A completely new software application would be required to interface with wholesalers who used intermediaries to buy stereo systems. This application would need to be able to evaluate requests from wholesalers and then generate bids in something close to real time. A team was set up to figure out what kinds of rules would need to be applied to requests of this kind.

Changes in the Manufacturing Process

Discussions about the kinds of purchase requests that Stereos-R-Us might be asked to respond to led to discussions of how the stereo systems they currently sold were configured. To remain competitive, the manufacturing, marketing, and sales managers argued that Stereos-R-Us would need to begin to sell systems that were much

Stereos-R-Us lets customers tailor their systems

more tailored to specific customers. "The customers want more
choices, and if we don't provide them, we'll lose sales to those who
do," the sales manager argued. Manufacturing initially talked
about how expensive offering more options would be. Whole new
manufacturing systems would need to be put in place. Accounting,
however, argued that it might be cheaper to tailor each stereo system and ship it as soon as it was manufactured, rather than manufacture batches, as they did now, and store them until they were
ordered.

IT committed to an
integration effort

Questions about tailoring and offering customers more options
led to discussions about how the management of inventory could
be improved. In the past, Stereos-R-Us had made various efforts to
link their manufacturing processes to specific suppliers. The process has often proved painful, since the systems of the companies
were so different. Now, however, between the Internet and new
middleware systems like Java and CORBA, IT felt that it could integrate most of the suppliers into a complete supply chain application that would largely automate the acquisition of parts and components required for manufacturing stereo systems. At first they
talked about simply sending orders to suppliers via email, but as
the conversation evolved, the Stereos-R-Us team began to consider
a stereo components brokerage system of their own. If they could
get their suppliers to participate in an online brokerage system,
Stereos-R-Us could post requests for parts and have their suppliers
bid to provide them. In either case, accounting urged that they not
only build a system to buy parts when needed, but that they automate billing and payments to eliminate all the paperwork normally
involved in parts purchases. No one was confident how quickly
they could set up the acquisition system or how efficiently it would
operate, so it was agreed that the inventory management people
would need to run a dual operation for awhile, automating what
they could while simultaneously maintaining a regular inventory to
assure that the company could fulfill orders in a timely manner.

Changes in Product Delivery

The CEO next asked the team to consider how they would manage the delivery of stereo systems to individual customers. The company was accustomed to delivering stereo systems to stores in bulk, but it didn't have a system in place to deliver individual units to individuals in a matter of two or three days. Everyone agreed that the Web would generate more orders from more locations worldwide. To support this very distributed group of customers while providing accurate information on when deliveries would be made, the management team suggested phasing out the shipping department and subcontracting the entire delivery operation to Federal Express. According to the IT manager, Federal Express already offered software components that could be integrated into the Stereos-R-Us Web site to allow customers to track their orders. It would be far simpler, the IT manager argued, to use what Federal Express offered rather than to try to develop their own software to do the job.

Shipping is phased out and delivery subcontracted

In the long run, everyone agreed that Stereos-R-Us should consider how it might regain control of the delivery process to assure it was run efficiently, but in the meantime subcontracting seemed best.

Managing the Transition

In summary, the Stereos-R-Us CEO noted that several departments would be largely phased out and their work would either be automated by software or subcontracted to outside companies. "This is going to be a delicate process that will extend over a year or two," she remarked. "If it isn't well planned and managed very carefully, we'll lose critical employees before we are ready." A team was assigned to develop a personnel management plan and to see what incentives the company could offer to make it worthwhile for the employees to help make the transition as smooth as possible.

Stereos-R-Us planned on a two-year transition

Changing the Software Development Process

Reengineering IT was a priority

Equally important, the entire transition process would depend on the ability of the IT group to create the new applications that would be needed to support all the changes that were being discussed. This comment led the head of IT to explain to everyone present that IT, as it was currently organized, couldn't provide the needed software. "Before IT can provide the software we need," the CIO explained, "the IT group itself will need to be reengineered." The software development methods and the company infrastructure currently in place wouldn't support the distributed and much more integrated applications that the company managers were asking for. "Just integrating the applications that we currently use inside the company will take a whole new approach," he explained. The order processing and customer service applications were done at different times, using different hardware and software techniques, and so forth. Integrating the existing manufacturing application with inventory modules and over one hundred parts supplier applications would be even more challenging.

Some IT reengineering goals

"We'll need to reengineer how we develop software," the IT manager explained. "We'll need to create a new software development approach, a new infrastructure, based on the Internet, and a new way of handling integration. We'll need to retrain most of our developers to create new types of software and hire some new people to create and maintain the user-friendly Web site that everyone wants. We'll also need new people to negotiate the supply chain integration with our suppliers and to create a brokerage application that we can all use to acquire new parts. The transition from where IT is now to where it will need to be to do all the things everyone wants will take time. It will need to be done quickly, of course, but it can't be done too quickly or we'll create more problems than we solve. For example, maintaining a Web site that can scale from handling a few hundred customers to thousands of customers per hour, while assuring that it will continue to operate every hour of every day without fail, is hard. It will take planning, a new software architecture, a new infrastructure, and lots of new technologies. It will have to be phased in over a period of time and carefully tested to assure that it does what it needs to do."

Considering what Stereos-R-Us had spent on its Y2K project, the CEO was pretty upset to hear what the CIO had to say, but she respected him and decided that he was probably offering good advice. She asked him to draw up a plan to reorganize the IT group that they could review at their next meeting.

The First Draft of the Revised E-Business Process

Figure 3.7 illustrates the initial revised business process that the Stereos-R-Us management team came up with. When the meeting broke up, each manager was assigned to teams to work up a plan to revise what was necessary and a schedule for the revision. When the entire team met the next month, the CEO suggested they create a corporate plan and schedule that would combine all the independent plans.

As the various Stereos-R-Us managers reviewed what they had agreed to do over drinks after the meeting, most were amazed that they had committed to the changes. They were making radical changes in almost every aspect of the existing company. The changes, coupled with transition planning and personnel dislocations, would guarantee that the company operated in a state of flux for the next several years. Most of the company's long-established business practices and rules would need to be radically revised. The information technology group was about to assume a much more important role in the operation of the company, while other managers would become increasingly dependent on IT to achieve their own goals.

E-business would make IT much more important

Some thought the new integrated Web site would be the most difficult development. Others thought that a more flexible manufacturing system that linked a highly tailored manufacturing pro-

Stereos-R-Us agreed to massive BPR changes

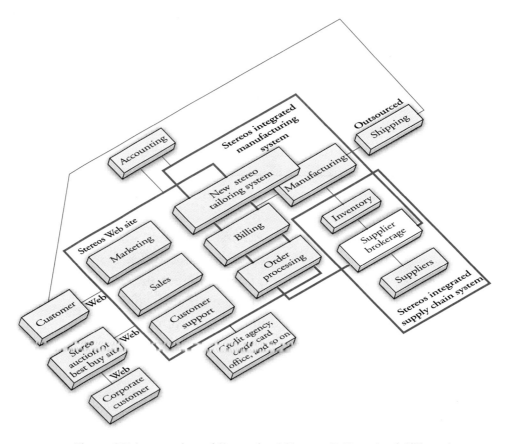

Figure 3.7 An overview of the revised Stereos-R-Us order fulfillment process.

cess to a supply chain that made the company dependent on the prompt and consistent responses of suppliers would be the key. Still others worried about how effectively Stereos-R-Us could control the delivery of its products to a worldwide audience that would expect more tailoring and would probably also expect lower prices. The potential for lower prices was certainly suggested by the new business process that the group had outlined, but the cost of creating the systems that would deliver the productivity gains while slowly phasing out the existing systems would be costly and very difficult to manage. Indeed, as one manager remarked, "We never would have agreed to do anything like this if we hadn't absolutely been convinced that the company would disappear if we didn't do it."

And lastly, everyone worried about the IT group's ability to deliver everything that would be necessary in the time allowed. Everyone had memories of other times in which IT failed to deliver. The good news, according to the IT manager, is that new technologies would make it easier to do what had to be done. In the past, just as the others had never forced themselves to make major changes, so IT had resisted major changes. Now, however, to survive and meet its obligations, the IT group would need to transform itself into a completely different software development group. The bad news, of course, was that such a transition would take time, cost money, and require lots of work to assure that it happened as planned. "The whole transition," one of the managers remarked, "will be like redesigning and rebuilding a ship while it is at sea in a storm."

The reengineering of IT was radical

"This reengineering effort will certainly go far beyond anything we tried in the early 1990s," the head of manufacturing remarked. "We'd have rejected this plan out of hand, then. And today, we accepted it and agreed to come up with a schedule in a month. I hope the sales we get over the Web will justify all this."

Summary

This chapter hardly begins to describe all of the different problems and possibilities that companies reengineering for e-business will face. It does, however, provide managers with a general approach and suggest some of the arguments they will encounter.

More importantly, it lays the groundwork for the focus of the remainder of this book. Companies may undertake first-generation Web applications without worrying about reengineering their IT operations because Web applications can be undertaken by a special group that simply focuses on creating a Web site. Second-generation e-business systems are different. To develop companywide enterprise systems that can integrate existing legacy applications and provide complex services to hundreds or thousands of users, IT groups must significantly alter the way they develop software. They must learn new techniques and methodologies and retrain their developers. The remainder of this book focuses on the nature of the changes IT must make and on effective ways to make those changes.

4

E-Business
Applications

In this chapter we want to provide readers with an introduction to

the problems of developing software applications for Internet envi-

ronments. We'll begin by discussing the new e-business climate

and describing the new requirements imposed by it. One special

requirement, that of highly scalable applications, will be examined

in more detail to determine the requirements it places on the com-

pany and its applications. Another is component-based develop-

ment, which we'll consider briefly in this chapter and in more

E-business brings new challenges

detail in the next chapter. Finally, we'll wrap up with an overview of some of the generic types of e-business applications being developed today.

The Challenges of the E-Business Environment

A new generation of applications is required

In order to compete in the global marketplace, businesses today must build a new generation of applications. Many of the requirements for e-business systems were not part of past application design. Enhanced user expectations and increased competitive pressures must be accommodated, along with changes in technology and a new business climate.

The Web is responsible for the biggest changes in business systems since the introduction of the computer itself, including new usage patterns, new user expectations, increased competition, and shortened product life cycles. The previous chapters provided several examples of these forces at work.

The Web has dramatically changed business systems

In this chapter's discussion of these factors, we sometimes use Web-based customers as an example to help clarify the points being made, even though some studies predict that interactive Web users will account for only about 30% of e-business activity. The larger portion of e-business may come from electronic commerce applications such as supply chain management. However, the requirements we discuss pertain to all e-business applications, including internal (intranet) systems and business-to-business e-commerce as well as external (Internet) end user applications.

New Usage Patterns

One dramatic change caused by the Internet is the new usage patterns of customers. The days of 9-to-5 customer interaction are over. With the Web, customers can, and will, access online systems 24 hours a day, 7 days a week, 365 days a year. This fact has two important implications. First, because customers want to use the systems at all times, the systems must be available at all times. So applications must have a way to perform maintenance and up-grades without taking the application offline (at least not for long or very often). Second, applications can no longer depend on off-hour batch-based processing for most tasks, especially if such batch processing interferes with the availability of the application.

E-business customers operate 24 hours a day

Although the Web brings customers at all sorts of crazy hours, it has the potential to bring lots of them. With the Web, your application has access to potentially millions of customers and vice versa. Thus, the application must have the ability to scale up to millions of customers a day, perhaps thousands simultaneously.

Word spreads quickly on the Web, and an application that expected to grow to a few thousand customers per day may suddenly experience several orders of magnitude more usage. Stories of initially successful applications that couldn't handle the load are not hard to find. Some enterprises, like AOL, managed to survive and prosper in spite of such problems. Others found themselves in the out-of-business category, as fickle Web users quickly lost patience with nonperforming applications.

Millions of potential customers can visit your business

This last point is important and bears elaboration. Web customers in general do not have any particular loyalty to your site, and thus are much more mobile than traditional customers. If they cannot get the products and service they want from you, chances are that there are dozens of other sites they can find that will provide what they want. And once customers leave, it is very hard to get them back.

But they can just as easily go elsewhere

The Web is just one example of a new type of customer access (see Figure 4.1). Other types of access devices are ATM machines,

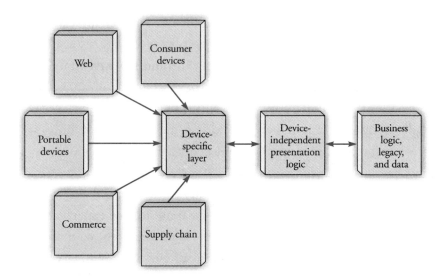

Figure 4.1 Applications must support many types of customer access.

handheld devices, cell phones, and so on. A new e-business application needs to go beyond simple Web browsers for user interaction models. The application may need to support several of the
devices we've already discussed, plus some that haven't been invented yet. Some estimates suggest that there will be more
nonpersonal computers on the Web by 2002 than there will be
personal computers. As we mentioned earlier, Charles Schwab is already preparing to have people trade by phone and from personal
digital assistants of various types. An effective e-business architecture must be able to accommodate this variety of current and future interaction models without requiring significant changes.

New Customer Expectations

Not only do electronic customers have new usage patterns, they
have new expectations of the system—expectations different than
those of your internal users or existing customers. Taking an existing application and just putting a Web front end on it—without

rethinking the user interaction requirements—is a recipe for failure.

Web customers are typically less skilled and less well-trained than your own employees, so the applications must be easier to use. While an employee will struggle with a bad application because they are paid to do so, a customer won't. The application for the new Web user must be more intuitive, easy to use, and foolproof.

New Systems must meet new expectations

Remember, however, that foolproof doesn't mean expert-proof. The application has to be equally easy to use for the experienced user as it is for the beginning user. Because these users cannot be expected to know the policies and constraints of your application (the way your employees are expected to), the rules that enforce these will have to be implemented as part of the new application.

Customers expect easy and powerful interfaces

Perhaps it's obvious, but your applications must have an acceptable level of performance. Studies have shown that customers will happily wait 1–2 seconds for a response, but will almost never wait more than 30 seconds. The rule of thumb is that 5 seconds is the maximum response time that an application can exhibit before customers go elsewhere.

Applications must also perform well

Easy-to-use and responsive applications are still not enough to attract and keep customers. Companies must become more customer-focused than ever before and must compete for customers by providing them with a personalized experience. Several different styles of personalization are possible. Customers may be categorized (e.g., as standard, preferred, and premier) and different levels of service may be provided based on those categories. This is the model used most commonly by airline frequent traveler programs.

Customers want a personalized service

An individual profile may be maintained for every customer, thus keeping track of their preferences and history. This information can be used to offer specific products and programs as well as to provide customers with a user interface tailored to their prefer-

Personalization has business advantages

ences. Companies such as Amazon.com have shown the incredible potential of this type of customization. No matter what level or combination of customization desired, the application must accommodate some form of customer profile storage and retrieval and some form of personalization based on that profile.

Increased Competition and Shortened Product Life Cycle

E-business means increased competition

The Web has greatly increased competition between suppliers. Customers now have unprecedented access to you and also to all of your competitors. Comparison shopping (with respect to both prices and services) is easy, and the overall Web shopping experience can be better than that offered by brick-and-mortar suppliers (e.g., ease of use, personalization, and time savings).

Competitive pressures require constant innovation and change

When your competitors introduce new products or services, your customers will expect the same from you almost immediately. Thus companies are under enormous time pressures to introduce new products and services, either to establish a competitive advantage or to play catch-up. And that means that your processes and infrastructure must support rapid application development.

This situation implies that new applications will need to operate in an environment of constant change, precipitated by external pressures to compete and gain competitive advantage and by internal pressures to increase efficiency and accountability and to cut costs.

Constant change requires new infrastructures and techniques

The traditional methods of application development cannot satisfy the requirements for constant change and rapid development. A new application cannot be built each time new products are to be offered.

Component-Based Development

Instead, flexible applications will be constructed by assembling a variety of functional software modules (components) to create new products and services. Once constructed, applications can easily be enhanced by adding new components or modified by replacing existing components.

Components are required for e-business

Some components will need to be built from scratch for a new application. Other components may already exist from other applications. Over time, applications will be assembled more and more from existing components, requiring fewer new components to be constructed. So rapid development and competitive pressure require an organization to achieve maximum reuse of their components and applications.

Consider two existing applications that are constructed of components. Each application consists of a user interface, some process controllers, and a legacy access and data component. These components represent processes and entities that are fundamental building blocks of the overall business. In Figure 4.2, a new application has been quickly developed simply by creating a new user interface. The business parts of the application have been con-

Component-based applications can react quickly

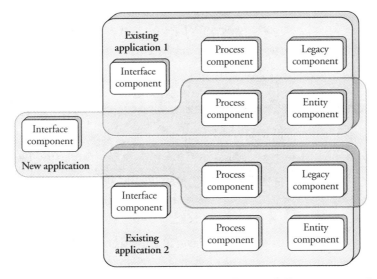

Figure 4.2 New applications are constructed from existing components.

structed of business building block components that were already available as part of the existing applications.

*Enterprise
component
architecture
harnesses component
technology*

To accomplish this, software needs to be designed as component-based applications and an infrastructure needs to exist to support this new style of development. An *enterprise component architecture* defines the enterprise's infrastructure for components. It also defines what all components in the enterprise must be able to do, how applications should build compliant components, how applications make use of the infrastructure, and how existing components are found and cataloged such that they can be reused.

An enterprise component architecture does not define what the application components should be or should do—that is the responsibility of each application. But it does provide a common environment for all components in any application. This leads to more reuse of components and to a common set of tools for administration and management of component-based applications.

*Traditional
application
development is too
complex*

One more key element is required to support rapid development—a simplified programming model. Currently, application software is too complicated to build as designed. Most companies have already experienced the shortage of available software expertise for building new distributed applications. In many cases, it is the single largest impediment to creating new applications.

*Component
technology simplifies
programming tasks*

This shortage will continue to exist and will probably get worse. This fact argues that these scarce but highly skilled software engineers should be utilized to solve only the most complex and critical problems. Most of the application should be assembled by less specialized staff and by those whose expertise lies with the application itself, rather than with the technology used to implement it.

The proliferation of Visual Basic applications and the armies of VB programmers are the best examples of how a simplified, but

powerful, programming environment has increased the speed of
application development. Up to now, however, the increased productivity has been limited to client-based applications. The same
model (and many of the same programmers—retrained, of course)
must be extended to server applications in order to meet the flexibility demands of today's e-business climate.

*High productivity is
necessary for server
development*

Integration and Interoperability

Most organizations today have a huge existing investment in applications and information systems. Much of a company's processes
and policies are contained in the code of these applications. In
many cases, the applications work just fine, and there is little appe-
tite for replacing them. As they say in New Hampshire, "If it ain't
broke, don't fix it." However, regardless of how good these applications may be, they are nonetheless large, monolithic systems that
are difficult to upgrade or extend. How can we support the constant change and rapid development required to be competitive
and still use our legacy systems and applications?

*Legacy systems
represent enormous
corporate assets*

The answer is to integrate these legacy systems into the new
component-based application infrastructure. As we described in
the examples in the previous chapters, redoing the process did not
mean reimplementing everything, but rather making better use of
existing capabilities. The new infrastructure uses the legacy systems to perform the tasks they already do well today, and extends
them by making their functions available in new usage environments. Frequently, capabilities in the new systems will be needed by
many different applications (including legacy applications) at the same
time. These new capabilities can be added outside of the existing applications, avoiding both the need to modify existing code and duplication of effort. This style of approach is referred to as *legacy integration,* or the more fashionable term *enterprise application integration.*

*Legacy functions
must be made
available as
components*

"Legacy components" bridge the old and new

Package applications, sometimes called commercial off-the-shelf (COTS) software, also needs to be integrated. Figure 4.3 shows the integration of legacy and packaged applications into the new infrastructure. On the left of the figure are the new components and on the right are the existing systems. The legacy and application components bridge these two worlds by making the capabilities of the existing applications available as components in the new infrastructure.

Other systems and applications must also be integrated

Integration does not only apply to the legacy systems. A company's assets and resources reside in many different areas and applications, which must interoperate together. Interoperation means

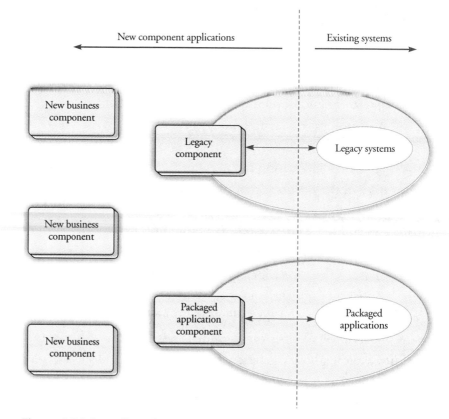

Figure 4.3 Integration of legacy systems and other applications.

that different applications can share the things that they have in common. This may be common data, such as customer information, or it may be common functions, like "send a bill to the customer." The current business climate of mergers and acquisitions makes this requirement even more important, since each merger or acquisition typically creates numerous cases of replicated data and functionality that need to be integrated.

Of course, an organization may have its own historical integration problems, without having been part of a merger. In the past, ad hoc development of departmental applications was not concerned with interoperation. As a result, there is duplication of data and functionality and a corresponding difficulty in getting these applications to work together. However, one of the new customer expectations is for consolidated account interaction. A customer should not receive more than one bill or more than one statement from the same company (unless, of course, they want to). This competitive pressure alone makes it imperative to integrate applications, and the enterprise architecture must provide a solution for this requirement. It does this by defining standard ways for applications to be built (ways that make interoperation easy) and by describing a generic interoperation model that can be applied to all existing and future applications.

Integration means combining things together into a unified application. Interoperation is the cooperation of different things working together. The distinction may seem minor, but it is important. Different applications interoperate together, but are managed and operated separately. These different applications may be owned by different units within the same company, or by completely separate companies, as is the case for business-to-business (B2B) e-commerce. For these applications to interoperate, they must support some mutually agreed upon protocols both for network transmission and for application-specific semantics. And this

E-business demands an integrated environment

Interoperation between businesses requires industry standards

means that support of and conformance to standards becomes very important for effective e-commerce.

Enterprise Application Requirements

Enterprises have additional requirements

Business applications run as part of a company's IT assets. Requirements for IT come from several sources: the specific application, the e-business environment, and the enterprise's operational requirements. We discussed the need to develop applications that can be scaled up to the new e-business requirements, but scalability is just one of several "enterprise requirements" that these applications must meet. These enterprise requirements fall roughly into three categories:

- Scalability
- Deployment
- Management

Challenges of Large-Scale Applications

Resource utilization is key to scalability

The difference (at least at a high level) between just any application and an application that can become very large scale can be summed up in two words: *resource utilization.* The keys to building a large-scale application are (1) understanding what the critical resources in a system are, and (2) having a mechanism that not only allows you to use those resources efficiently but also lets you selectively add more resources as required.

Before we examine the critical system resources, let's look at what we mean by a large-scale application. Any application is made up of three main constituents: *clients* (users), *servers* (performing business operations), and *data*. In a component-based system, data is frequently represented as components within the system.

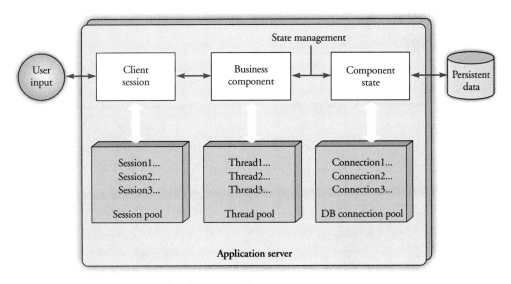

Figure 4.4 Resource utilization in application servers.

A large-scale system is one that is capable of supporting tens of thousands of clients simultaneously, dozens or hundreds of servers, and millions of components. Each of these constituents has an associated set of resources that must be managed intelligently in order to reach larger scales. In Chapter 6, we go into more detail about how component technologies help manage critical system resources. Figure 4.4 illustrates the various resources involved in implementing components. The components run in a server, which utilizes several different resource pools to manage the critical resources.

What is large scale?

Client Resources

For every client, there is some kind of *client connection* to the system. This may be a customer session on a Web site or a customer service representative using a dedicated workstation. The connection links the client to the application via a server. For each client connection, there is an associated connection on the server,

Every client consumes some system resources

and some information about that client and connection is also maintained by the server.

Client resources must be managed

These connections represent processing overhead, which must be handled by the server in addition to the processing required by the business functions. If the application is to support tens or hundreds of thousands of clients, these connections must be managed by specially designed processes that concentrate the sessions into a smaller number of connections that can be more easily managed by the business servers, as shown by the session pool in Figure 4.4.

Servers are also clients to the database

The server has several other resources that must be managed in addition to client connections, most importantly, data connections and components. Data, by definition, is stored somewhere. It is typically stored in a database or some other persistent data source. In this situation the server is acting as a client to the database.

We have the same connection problems between servers and databases as we have between clients and servers—each server has one or more connections to the database. The primary reason that traditional (two-tiered) client-server applications do not scale very well is due to the number of connections and associated contention at the database.

Server connections to the database must be managed

For applications to scale well, the connections to the database must be carefully managed. For example, a server should use a database connection pool to share database connections among all of the components being used by all clients, rather than have one connection for each component or client.

State Management

The next important resource on the server is components. A component is composed of two important things: behavior (the business functionality) and state (the business entity that the function is being performed on). When a component is executing its behavior, it is using processing resources on the server, typically in the form of process threads. The server will maintain a pool of threads to be shared among the many components that need to execute. Each component may actually use several additional resources such as memory, database connections, locks, and so on. In a large-scale system, it is not uncommon to have 1 million or even 10 million components. How can a server support this many components concurrently? The answer is simple: It can't. However, it can provide the *appearance* of supporting this many components concurrently.

Every application component consumes server resources

This means that when a component is needed, the server can create an instance of the component (by getting, or restoring, its state). The component is then available to be used by whatever application needs it. When the component is no longer needed, the server can save the component's state, flush the component from the server, and reuse those resources for another component. Figure 4.5 illustrates how state management allows a small number of active components to be in memory, while supporting a much larger number of inactive components that can be made active when needed.

The action of saving and restoring a component's state is known as *state management* and is critical to a server's ability to handle large-scale applications. State management is completely transparent to the applications using the component, as long as the server satisfies these important guarantees: (1) A component will be available (usually re-created) when it is needed, and (2) the component's state will always be consistent.

State management allows servers to support many components

In other words, the server must guarantee never to lose state in the process of saving and restoring a component. Chapter 7 goes into more detail about state management and how to use it when building an application.

The server not only uses resources, it is itself a valuable resource within the system configuration. Just as a server manages a pool of

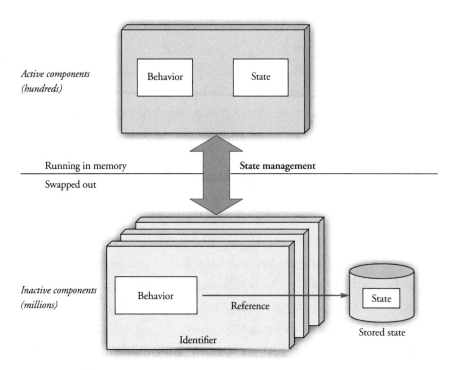

Figure 4.5 State management.

Servers are an important system resource

components, the "system" must manage a pool of servers, which are most likely running on several different machines. The "system" is an infrastructure that supports many servers, mediates the coordination between them, and balances the workload among them. The modularity of our enterprise component architecture allows us to increase the throughput of our system (that is, to scale up) by adding more server resources to the system configuration.

Application Management

Application management includes setup and ongoing operations

The ability to have many servers in a configuration, and to add new servers to that configuration, highlights the enterprise requirement for management. Management can be thought of as the tasks necessary to set up the application and to keep the application running successfully. Building the application is only a part of the problem. It is equally important to be able to keep the application running once it has been developed and deployed. Management tasks include system configuration (and reconfiguration), activity monitoring, and application management.

Configuration is the ability to set up the system and assign resources. For example, this includes the assignment of components to servers and of servers to machines. It also includes specifying how many of each server will be present, how many clients will be supported simultaneously, and so on. More sophisticated systems allow the configuration to be changed dynamically, while the system is operating. This capability is important for high availability.

Servers and other resources must be configurable

Monitoring is the ability to get statistics about the system's configuration and operation. This includes information such as how many clients are connected, the status and resource utilization of the servers, throughput and response times, and so on. More sophisticated systems automatically monitor certain information, such as server status, and respond to errors or other specified conditions. For example, if a server fails, the system monitors this event and automatically starts a new server. These capabilities are important for high availability and for tracing and trouble-shooting.

Monitoring helps predict and avoid problems

Application management is the ability to control (rather than just monitor) the application. This includes the ability to start or stop servers or components, modify parameters, and so on. Application management is the mechanism that performs the changes to a system configuration. Management (including configuration and monitoring) requires that all of the parts of the system (components, servers, etc.) are capable of participating in monitor and control activities. That is, an application should provide management-related information when queried by the monitor and control mechanisms. It also requires tools that perform the

The entire system must cooperate in management

monitoring and control tasks. Tools must provide an easy-to-use GUI interface as well as a script capability that allows these tasks to be automated.

Application Deployment

Thin clients avoid deployment hassles

Finally, we need to understand the requirements for application deployment in an e-business environment. In looking at this, we must consider the issues of deploying the application initially, securing the application, and evolving or upgrading the application (redeployment). In an application with 10,000 or more clients, there are significant drawbacks to a design that requires deploying the application to each client. It is much easier to simply avoid this problem rather than trying to solve it. The best deployment scenario involves no special software on the client at all, as is the case with browser-based "thin" clients.

Deployment tools help with "rich" clients

In many applications it is impractical to eliminate application-specific software on the client's machine. These applications tend to have significant processing of input data and/or the need to exchange large amounts of data with the server. Such "rich" client applications may be appropriate in corporate intranet environments, but should not be considered for external clients. For external clients, an automatic distribution mechanism must exist for publishing the software to the client systems.

Even the best applications will need to be updated or enhanced. This is simply a fact of the new e-business environment and must be part of the requirements of an enterprise architecture. A good application will also have many different users, and in most cases, not all users will immediately be able to use a new version of the application. This implies that the architecture must support application versions and the ability for multiple versions of the same application to operate simultaneously. The system must transparently connect clients to the right versions of servers and application components.

The use of a thin-client architecture can avoid client version problems because no application-specific software ever resides on the client. In contrast, a rich-client architecture aggravates the problem. But in either case, internal server-to-server interactions will still require support for multiple versions.

Multiple versions must be supported

Security is a critical requirement for the deployment of an application, especially in the e-business environment. External clients are coming into your system as end user Web customers and as B2B business partners. Because the e-business environment requires these types of access, security can no longer be based on restricting users by limiting access points (as most systems do today).

A hacker's attack can range from simply being an embarrassment (e.g., a graffiti attack or a denial-of-service attack that shuts down a Web site) to the theft or destruction of valuable corporate resources. A new mechanism must be used that restricts clients from using certain resources or doing certain types of operations based on how they accessed the system. This new mechanism should be used in addition to the traditional user identification (login-based) security.

Security is critical

Types of E-Business Applications

Perhaps the best way to think about the changes that will occur in the near future is to look at some of the types of software applications that current e-business companies are using today. Different companies in different industries will adopt these generic types of applications in different ways. In Figure 4.6, we've identified five

E-business applications can be simple or complex

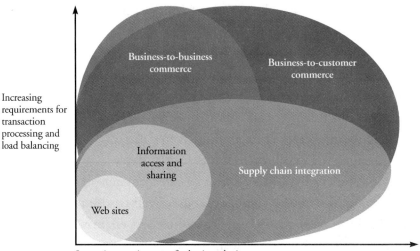

Increasing
requirements for
transaction
processing and
load balancing

Business-to-business
commerce

Business-to-customer
commerce

Information
access and
sharing

Supply chain integration

Web sites

Increasing requirements for business logic

Figure 4.6 Types of e-business applications.

of the most common types of e-business applications that you see today.

Simple Web Site Applications

Web sites are the simplest e-business application

At the bottom left of Figure 4.6 we show Web sites. Most large companies now have Web sites. Some refer to their Web sites as "brochureware." Earlier, we referred to these applications as first-generation Web applications. Early Web sites were largely static—simply a set of HTML pages that browsers could load and read. Most of today's Web sites are linked to company databases so that the site can be more easily maintained. Similarly, most of today's Web sites incorporate applets, ActiveX, or CGI elements so that they can save information that users provide. That, in turn, allows companies to incorporate forms and questionnaires, to tailor the sites for individual users, or simply to make them more stimulating and entertaining.

Information Access and Information-Sharing Applications

The next, larger circle at the bottom left of Figure 4.6 is labeled "Information access and sharing." This refers to a wide variety of intranet applications that companies have developed to allow employees access to corporate applications and databases. In some cases employees can check the status of their company benefits. In other cases salespeople can browse the latest parts catalogs or check their sales and bonus figures to date.

Most would probably exclude Web sites, in themselves, from the e-business category. On the other hand, most people would include a company's Web-based information access applications in the e-business category. Both provide good ways to begin to explore the use of the Internet, but neither is really vital to the survival of a company.

Web sites can share company information

Increasingly, however, when people talk about e-businesses, they refer to companies that are conducting business-to-business commerce, integrating their supply chains with other companies, or selling products and services to customers over the Web. These types of applications tend to make the company's survival dependent on the Internet. We have indicated each of these types of applications in Figure 4.6. We have used circles to suggest that these applications require increasing effort because they increase the demands for high-speed transaction processing and the need for more sophisticated business logic.

But there is more to e-business

Business-to-Business (B2B) Applications

For most companies, business-to-business commerce makes the most sense. Company A simply uses the Internet to contact a computer company and order new desktop machines. Both organizations have people who understand the use of the Internet, and the product lends itself to an efficient transaction. In fact, however,

B2B commerce is another application

business-to-business commerce is rapidly expanding in a variety of different ways. There are already steel and plastics intermediaries that sell future production runs by auction. Thus, the small steel mills announce their upcoming production plans on a Web site where companies that want to buy steel come to bid for the output. Similar auctions go on among the producers and consumers of specialized plastic products.

New interaction styles are exploiting B2B

In the near future, this kind of market-based allocation should significantly increase the efficiency of producers and reduce the cost of goods to consumers. There are a wide variety of other on-line trading schemes being investigated. In many cases, businesses are developing sophisticated computer applications simply to take part in auctions and to track prices of commodities they wish to acquire. Many of these new trading systems incorporate very sophisticated business decision-making capabilities. In most cases, the Web sites that support business-to-business commerce are heavily used and need both transaction processing capabilities and the ability to scale rapidly when trading is especially intense.

Supply Chain Integration Applications

Supply chains use B2B to increase efficiency

Similarly, once companies begin to explore supply chain automation, the process can rapidly evolve into very sophisticated systems. Initially, companies may simply pass plans, schedules, or orders to allow suppliers to anticipate their needs. In many cases, however, the suppliers find themselves integrating their systems with the final producer. In sophisticated cases, the suppliers learn what new materials are needed by being tied directly into the producers' manufacturing and inventory systems. As the suppliers respond, accounting entries are created and paid automatically. This entire process requires trust, serious quality control on behalf of the supplier, and entirely new ways of thinking about who is responsible for what. The higher the speed of the manufacturing process, the more business logic needs to be incorporated directly into the supply chain systems. In the most sophisticated integrated supply chain systems, companies are changing their requisitions daily to support the production of highly tailored products, assembled to meet the orders of individual customers.

Any software developer who has ever been involved in trying to link one company's computer systems with the systems at another company will be aware of the huge challenges that large-scale supply chain integration will create. We'll return to some of the issues raised by multicompany application integration a little later. Suffice it to say that some of these applications are more complex than anything being attempted on the sales side.

A variation on supply chain integration is e-marketplaces or auction systems designed to allow the buyer to announce that it needs some specific item in a particular quantity, as, for example, 100 units of a specific auto part. In this case, suppliers check the site and when new requests are announced, the suppliers offer bids, specifying what they can provide at what price. We discussed how the large automakers are moving to this approach in Chapter 1. This approach doesn't tie one buyer with one supplier, but instead builds in a market mechanism so that a bidding process occurs. Of course, suppliers may take part in many different e-marketplaces, and it's possible that no one will have exactly what the buyer wants when it asks for bids.

Many industries are turning to e-marketplaces

Business-to-Customer (B2C) Applications

Business-to-customer sales over the Web have received most of the news media attention to date, even though it is probably the smallest of the three major types of e-business. In many cases new companies have entered the field, like Amazon.com and eToys,

B2C applications can cut sales costs

and promptly begun to take market share away from established giants who, until a couple of years ago, felt completely secure in their markets. In most cases, in fact, the new ventures haven't taken too much market share away from the established companies. What they have done, however, is to demonstrate that they can sell products at a fraction of the cost of the established firms.

The difference between developing a Web site or an information accessing and sharing application and a B2B, supply chain, or B2C application is quite large. The former can be done with relatively simple tools and techniques, while the latter tends to require very sophisticated techniques. The high-end e-business applications must integrate existing enterprise applications with new Web applications and make decisions and process information in complex ways that go beyond the skills of traditional departmental developers.

E-marketplaces, Intermediaries, and Portal Applications

So far, we've been talking about e-business applications as if they were constructed by a single company for its own use. Some of the more interesting Internet developments involve Web-based systems that link companies together. We have already hinted at this when we discussed how steel companies were using an e-marketplace or auction system to sell steel. Similarly, we have briefly discussed the fact that the major automakers would soon be buying parts from suppliers via an e-marketplace system. In these cases the companies involved have to tailor their e-business systems to fit with those of other companies involved in the brokerage or auctioning system.

Intermediaries offer customers ease and value

A different example, but one that impacts companies in a similar way, is the various intermediaries that offer to compare prices and suggest to customers which site offers the best deal. Company A, which sells cameras, may develop a site and hope to use a number of value-added features to sell its product. Consumers, however, may prefer to use an intermediary that "shops" a large number of sites offering cameras and reports the prices to the consumer. In such a situation, Company A's site may never be visited by a consumer that decides that Company A isn't competitive. Increasingly, retail sites will have to study the criteria the intermediaries use when they conduct surveys, decide if it's worth competing in such a market, and, if it is, adjust their prices to be competitive. Airlines have built systems to help them do something similar when it comes to seat pricing. Airlines regularly "shop" other airlines to see what they are pricing seats on specific flights and use the information acquired to assist them in adjusting their own seat prices.

Another example of an extra-business Internet linkage is provided by portals. At its simplest, a portal can simply refer to a Web site that provides access to a number of other Web sites. Any large company could build this type of portal to provide an overview of the products and services sold by its various divisions or subsidiaries. A narrower use of the term "portal," however, refers to a site that functions as a shopping mall. There is quite a bit of competition currently among vendors who provide browsers, to establish their sites as the place that the customer goes they sign on to the Web. Thus, for example, Netscape, Microsoft, AOL, and Yahoo! all offer portals that provide the consumer with popular services. Many companies will probably want to advertise on these sites. Others will want to place content on portals. A company may maintain a minisite on a portal in hopes of hooking customers who will subsequently visit the company's main Web site.

Portals are a special kind of intermediary

By the same token, companies may want to join up to offer focused portals. Thus, for example, auto insurance vendors may want to have space on auto sales Web sites, and flight insurance vendors may want to have space on air travel Web sites.

Summary

In this chapter we have discussed the new requirements for applications that will operate in an e-business environment, which include

- 24 × 7 availability
- scalability
- variety of devices/interaction models
- intuitiveness
- customer profiles, personalization
- constant change
- rapid development
- simplified programming model
- legacy integration
- application interoperation
- management/configuration/monitoring

We have explored some of the implications of those requirements for future IT infrastructures and discussed a variety of different e-business applications ranging from simple Web sites, to B2B and B2C applications, to e-marketplaces and portals.

The scope and variety of e-business applications is currently beyond anyone's imagination. Over the next few years new ways of organizing and selling over the Web will proliferate. The best any company can do is maintain as much flexibility as possible and build a component-based infrastructure so they are ready to take advantage of interesting opportunities as they arise.

chapter 5

Components

Internet applications are necessarily distributed applications. Customers from anywhere in the world can access a Web application using a Web browser. The application's developers can't be sure what types of hardware or software the customers will be using. If an Internet-based supply chain application is designed to allow one company to interact with another, it can even be more complex, since the variety of different hardware, software, and legacy applications that will need to be integrated will be even more diverse.

IT groups need new techniques

To remain competitive, companies will want their new e-business applications developed quickly, and they will need to change them rapidly as business practices and Web technologies evolve. At the same time, software developers will have to learn and use new technologies to meet the new e-business requirements described in the last chapter. This suggests that IT groups will need all the help they can get. IT groups that try to stick with older ways of developing applications will flounder and fail. IT groups that succeed will use off-the-shelf products and open standards whenever they can to minimize their development effort. In other words, successful IT developers will focus on strategic business software development tasks and buy infrastructure and software components whenever they can, to minimize their involvement in tactical development.

Component infrastructures will be required

The key open standard for the new era is obviously the Internet itself and other protocols like HTML and XML that are supported by W3C, the Internet standards consortium. The basic Internet standards, by themselves, however, are insufficient. They don't provide security, transactions, or support for persistence, for example. Thus, companies will need to supplement Internet standards with standard distributed component infrastructures that will allow them to link diverse applications together quickly.

Business components provide application building blocks

Distributed components offer two advantages. To begin with, they offer a way of providing common interfaces for the diverse legacy applications that need to be linked to build Web applications. Longer-term components offer a way to significantly reduce the cost and time involved in developing new applications by shifting from writing code to the assembly of prebuilt components. Most companies already rely on the use of small components for the rapid development of user interface screens and for tasks like linking applications to databases. The new emphasis, however, is on larger business components that can provide functionality similar to what is currently found in off-the-shelf applications.

Companies that opt to use distributed component middleware will need to consider which of the popular distributed component standards or architectures they will employ. The most popular models, at the moment, are Microsoft's COM+/DNA, Sun's JavaBeans/J2EE, and the Object Management Group's CORBA/OMA architecture. If companies decide to use more than one of these models, then they will need to consider how to link multiple component systems together.

Three main standards for components

In each case, the development task can be considerably simplified if a company opts to not only use a distributed component system but to also use a component-based application server. COM or EJB application servers not only provide basic support for a distributed component model but also provide a wide range of integrated services and utilities that the developers would otherwise have to create and link into the application. In this chapter, we will consider components and servers in more detail.

Application servers bring additional value

What Is a Business Component?

A *business component* is a self-contained unit of software that consists of its own data (or state) and logic (code). One reason for building software as components is that it provides a convenient way to separate concerns about component function (either business logic or utility functions) from development and deployment details. To do this, the component must conform to several conventions.

A component separates out business logic

A component has well-defined connection points for integration with a component framework and well-defined business interfaces that other software can use to access its capabilities and functions. A component is designed to be reused in the development of multiple applications, either with or without further customization.

Components support well-defined interfaces

Components provide interfaces that expose business functions

Because components are designed to be reused, a component's primary job is to make its functions available to other software. It accomplishes this by way of its interfaces. In essence, an interface is the collection of related functions (called methods) that can be invoked on a component.

The "connection points" mentioned above are simply specialized interfaces that allow two-way communication between components and their containers. Containers provide services to the components via these interfaces, and components use them to describe themselves and their needs to the container. For example, a Web browser is a container of client components, and it may provide screen management services via such interfaces. Or a server component might use such connection points to alert its container that it has special needs with respect to transactionality or persistent storage.

Stable interfaces localize changes within a component

The implementation of a component   that is, the *way* in which it performs its function—can and will be changed over time. But as long as the interface does not change, other components can continue to use it without needing to be changed themselves. Thus interfaces provide the mechanism by which applications can be built as a stable set of cooperating components, and changes to a component are localized to that component. Pieces of the application can be modified or replaced without disturbing the rest of the application as a whole. In this way, standard interfaces make it easier for components to provide functions to other components, to consume the functions provided by other components, and to be assembled into applications.

Components can publish and receive events

The ability of a component to handle events, that is, to notify other components—or to be notified—when something of interest has happened, is an important and very powerful feature of components. This mechanism is usually referred to as a "publish and subscribe" function, in which components can ask to be notified (subscribe) when a given event or class of events happens. Conversely, a component can announce (publish) an event to those components that have expressed interest in that event or class of events.

Types of Components

One way to categorize components is to examine how they are used in software applications. The earliest popular components were graphical user interface (GUI) components, modules of code designed to allow developers to quickly develop graphical user interface screens by dragging and dropping graphical images on a screen. Thus, using Microsoft's OCX components, a developer could quickly assemble buttons, input boxes, windows, and slider bars to form a Windows interface for a new application.

The type of component depends on its use

Some GUI components are very simple and handle something like a single button. Others are more complex and incorporate other simpler components. A form component, which reproduces a paper application form on the screen, for example, would be made up of lots of smaller components.

GUI components support user interfaces

Following quickly on the heels of GUI components, vendors introduced a wide variety of utility components—components that packaged a specific bit of functionality that was useful in speeding the development of an application. Thus, utility components were introduced to handle access to specific databases, generate SQL, generate reports, or pass HTML code back and forth. As with GUI components, utility components can be very simple, or they can be made up of several other components. Initially, GUI components and utility components were sold by independent vendors, and while many still are, most are now packaged with operating systems, like Windows, or development packages, like Sun's Java Development Kit.

Utility components provide common capabilities

In the past few years, most component development efforts have focused on larger components that combine GUI and utility components with business logic to create business components. An

Business components
represent business
concepts

ideal business component performs some recognized business function or represents a common business entity. Thus, for example, there are business components that function as accounts, as an account reconciliation process, as machines, or as a credit checking process. Major business components are large modules that contain lots of smaller components—some are smaller business components and others are utility components.

Recently, it has become popular to speak of even larger components that function as small applications. These large-scale components are often referred to as domain or system components. In effect, a domain component is made up of several business components.

Figure 5.1 provides a component continuum that illustrates how these components relate to each other.

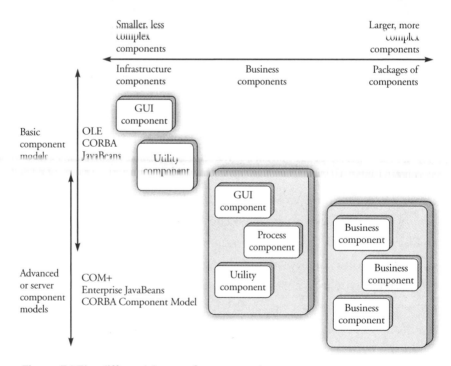

Figure 5.1 The different types of components.

The vertical axis in Figure 5.1 is divided between basic component models and more complex component models. Basic models have been around since the early 1990s. A basic model simply packages a module of code or an object inside an interface. Good examples of basic models are OLE, OCXs, ActiveX, and COM, before MTS was incorporated into it. Any object wrapped in an OMG IDL interface for use with CORBA is a basic component. Similarly, JavaBeans is a basic component model.

Basic components support simple tests

Starting about 1997, second-generation, advanced, or server-side component models began to appear. Examples of advanced component models include MTS or COM+, Enterprise JavaBeans, and the OMG's new CORBA Component Model (CCM). Advanced or server components are designed to reside on a server platform. Moreover, the advanced component is a collection of components, some designed to provide services needed by server applications and some provided to function as business components.

Complex components support business tasks

When you construct a system using components, you "wire" components together by specifying the messages that will be sent between the interfaces of the components you will use. Since the late 1980s, developers have dreamed of rapidly constructing applications by simply reusing existing components, much as computers are assembled by wiring together prebuilt hardware components.

Applications are constructed by connecting components

Although it might seem as though any individual component can be reused, this is typically true only within the same organization—because every development organization has certain barriers to use of code owned by another organization. These barriers range from simple communications difficulties, to the "Not Invented Here" (NIH) syndrome, to company politics. Thus, for a component to have reuse potential, it must provide enough value to overcome these barriers to reuse.

*Components need
enough functions to
be worth connecting*

As developers have gained experience with component development, they have realized that if component development is really going to save significant time and money, the components that are used need to be relatively large. Studies of application development explain why this is the case. Only about 30% of the time involved in most application development projects is spent actually writing code. The rest of the time is spent in analysis, design, and testing. If developers use GUI or utility components, they reduce the coding time involved in development, but the most they can save is something less than 30% of the entire development effort. On the other hand, if a component can incorporate not only code but analysis and design logic, then component development can begin to reduce the entire development process.

*Business components
have enough
functionality*

Business components represent entities that developers normally consider when they are first analyzing an application. Early analysis diagrams typically show entities like customers, order processing, accounts, machines, and shipping. If a developer can buy a prebuilt component that actually incorporates all the functionality and data representation needed to handle an account or store information on a customer, then a developer can really begin to think of creating a high-level analysis and then moving directly to the assembly of components that will provide the needed functions. The move to domain components represents a further step in that same direction.

*E-business
components support
Web applications*

To date, the differences between businesses, coupled with the fact that early business components were not robust enough to support large-scale application development, has limited the market for business and domain components. The rapid development of e-business applications, with new business processes, like taking an order at a Web site or shipping an item by means of an outside delivery service, has stimulated the interest in reusable Internet-ready business components.

Component Containers

While components are logically self-contained units of software, they are not stand-alone programs that can be individually executed or launched. Components must run within the context of some other program, which is called the *component container.* Containers provide services to components, and this capability is another step on the road to relieving application programmers from the burden of worrying about things other than application logic.

Components run inside a component container

The first component containers were Web browsers, and the components they contained were portions of the graphical user interface itself. But there are several other types of component containers as well. Some of these other types—for example, Enterprise JavaBeans and the CORBA Component Model—are on the cutting edge of component technology. All these container types are described in more detail below.

Components and their containers have a symbiotic relationship that is made possible by their respective understanding of the other's capabilities. Components typically know what functions a container can provide, and containers can determine—dynamically, at run time—the interfaces and functions of a component. Dynamically determining the functions of a component is made possible by interfaces that allow the component to describe itself to the container.

Components can describe themselves to their container

Another way of dividing components is to distinguish between components that are designed for and used on client computing platforms and those used on server platforms. Since these platforms and functions are substantially different, the containers that support these types of components will also be different.

Two kinds of components and containers

Client platforms include desktop personal computers, computer workstations of various kinds, and laptops. It could also include telephones designed to allow access to the Internet or any of a number of different kinds of personal digital assistants, as, for ex-

Client components support user interfaces

ample, a Palm PDA. As a general rule, distributed applications place interface and utility components on client platforms.

Server components support business functions

Server platforms range from computers running Windows NT, Windows 2000, and various types of Unix to midsized and mainframe computers of all sizes. As a generalization, distributed applications place business components and application frameworks on server platforms. Some utility components are also placed on server platforms, and of course, databases are associated with server machines.

Client Components

Client component containers manage user interface tasks

As mentioned earlier, a component is self-describing by virtue of the interfaces it provides. Thus, the component container can dynamically determine how to use the component by invoking these interfaces. Similarly, the container (i.e., a browser) provides interfaces that allow the component to signal events such as a change in data or the need for a screen refresh. These capabilities work together to allow the application developer to focus on the business problem and to leave the mundane tasks of managing processes and windows to the component container.

A client component typically has one or more of the following characteristics or capabilities, as illustrated in Figure 5.2:

- Visual presentation: A visual depiction of the business object, such as text, fields on a form, or a chart, graph, or picture
- User input and output: Some mechanism to get input from and present data to the user, such as a form, text fields, drop-down lists, buttons, and so on
- Local processing: Some limited amount of processing of data

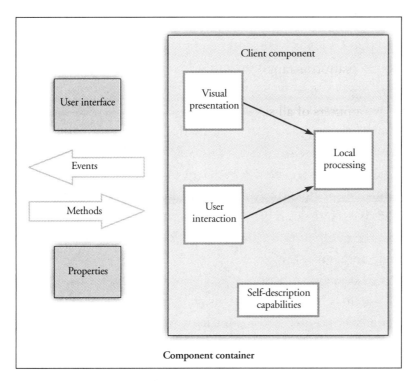

Figure 5.2 Client components.

within the component, such as validating fields in a form before
sending it to the business object

● Properties: A set of information that describes the visual and
processing aspects of the component, such as the background
color or text font

The component uses these capabilities to provide a specific service to the client application. If the service has been defined carefully, it can be reused in multiple different applications. Client
applications can then be constructed from a set of cooperating
components and only a small amount of additional programming
to tie the components together.

Client Component Technologies

Recall that COM is Microsoft's component model for the Windows (Windows NT, Windows 95/98, and Windows 2000) platforms, which is clearly the predominant client (desktop) platform in enterprises today.

COM provides powerful user interface tools

Part of the popularity of these platforms is the availability of powerful tools, such as Visual Basic or Delphi, for building user interface applications, and the excellent integration between custom and off-the-shelf desktop applications such as Microsoft Office. These characteristics reflect COM's heritage as a technology for managing compound documents and its emphasis on document linking and embedding.

ActiveX control components for COM are widely available

Another major function of COM was support for user interaction—such as management of visual display real estate among applications—and mechanisms for user input such as drag-and-drop, cut and paste, and so on. Subsequent generations of COM technology evolved to support packaged software components (VBXs, OCXs, or OLE controls, and now ActiveX controls) that have made a major impact on visual programming. (ActiveX controls originated as OLE controls, or OCXs, that were modified for more efficient use on the Web.) Today there are literally thousands of third-party, off-the-shelf ActiveX control components that can be used to construct user interface applications.

Java is perfect for multiplatform Web-based applications

Java and the Web are practically synonymous. Java (which was originally designed for programming "set-top" television controllers) has come to be known for its multiplatform applications for Web-based user interfaces. As part of its target environment (the Java Virtual Machine or JVM, within which Java components run), Java provides an inherent security model to prohibit downloaded applications from maliciously accessing system resources.

Because of its enticing programming model, Java has emerged as a major new object-oriented language for both client and server applications. JavaBeans is a technology for building reusable client components in Java. (Note that JavaBeans and Enterprise Java-Beans or EJB, which we will discuss later, are not the same thing). Several easy-to-use and powerful development tools have hit the market to support the development of Java and JavaBean applications.

Java is also popular for server development

The trend in client development is clearly toward "thin clients," meaning that the client contains an absolute minimum of client-side programming logic. The thin-client approach tries to avoid downloading any component or applet if at all possible. There are third-party tools for all styles of client component development. In fact, the line between "Web publishing" tools and application development tools for browsers/thin clients is a blurry one. But here again, there is room in the enterprise for all these styles of client components.

Most applications are going to a thin client architecture

Both JavaBeans and ActiveX provide technologies for building reusable user interface components. In addition to the obvious benefits of reuse and increased productivity, there are several characteristics of client components that make them ideal for large-scale enterprise applications.

Enterprise Considerations for Client Components

A major advantage for an enterprise is that client components are downloadable. In other words, they can be pulled down to a client desktop as part of normal usage of the application, rather than having to be installed or otherwise deployed to each client machine. When there are thousands or tens of thousands of desktops in an enterprise, the deployment and upgrade of the client machines becomes a major consideration in terms of maintenance, usability (training), and cost.

Components are ideal for an enterprise

*Client components
help meet
deployment
requirements*

Components can be upgraded without a major redeployment effort. When an application is used, it can automatically download the latest version of its components. The business object represented by a given component can evolve over time, and such changes affect only one component, thus minimizing the impact on the overall client application.

*Client components
can be downloaded
as required*

Like all things in life, these features are not without cost. Being downloadable is a major advantage, but it also raises a big question. What should the system do with the component when it's finished with it? There are two different approaches to answering this question: *sticky* and *nonsticky* components.

*Sticky components
for an intranet*

Sticky components are copied to disk when downloaded, and there they remain. They may be automatically updated with newer versions, but unless they are manually removed by an administrative action, they continue to take up disk space. Sticky components work well in an intranet/enterprise environment where a client is typically using the same components over and over again. With a sticky component, the application does not constantly download the same things again and again. But this model does not work well in an environment where there are many different, infrequently used components.

*Nonsticky
components for the
Internet*

Nonsticky components remain on the client system only for the duration of the process that downloads them; when the browser is stopped, the nonsticky components go away. This is a good model for an Internet environment where a client is frequently encountering components that are used once or twice. However, in an environment where the same components are used many times, a nonsticky component will have to be downloaded over again each time.

*Most enterprises will
want both types*

An enterprise may require both types of components. For internal, intranet applications, where a small number of components are frequently used, the sticky model will be appropriate. For external, Internet applications such as a customer-accessible Web page, the nonsticky model may be more appropriate. The trade-off is between bandwidth usage and disk space usage. While bandwidth and disk storage are becoming less expensive, components are increasing in size. So this trade-off still bears watching.

ActiveX controls are sticky components, while JavaBeans are nonsticky. In addition, JavaBeans have recognized the value of being able to control this aspect of behavior in a component, so they have added the ability to make a component sticky or nonsticky, depending upon a user-determined setting within the browser.

Client Component Security

Another difference between the JavaBeans approach and the ActiveX approach results in their having two different models for component security. JavaBeans execute within a special environment called the Java Virtual Machine, while ActiveX controls execute in the same environment as any other PC program.

Security is another difference

Thus the Java approach is to provide a secure JVM, where "secure" means that JavaBeans executing within the JVM have no direct access to system resources (e.g., communication links, memory, or disk space) outside the JVM. This approach prevents any malicious access to system resources, but some might argue that it also prevents a component from doing many very useful things.

The secure JVM prevents malicious access

In contrast, the ActiveX approach is to provide a means for authenticating (by way of an encrypted digital signature) the author/source of a component and giving the user the choice of downloading the component or not. The component can also be unsigned, in which case the user is asked if it is okay to download an unsigned component, and the component will either be downloaded or discarded depending on the user's answer. This model works well when there is a relatively controlled environment and a fixed set of acceptable, identifiable sources for components, such as

ActiveX depends on user-controlled authentication

may be encountered within an enterprise intranet. However, it is far too easy to allow unacceptable components to be downloaded for this security model to be adequate for general Internet usage.

As was the case with stickiness, many enterprises will find that both types of security are required to satisfy different needs and scenarios within the enterprise.

Client Component Model Comparison

ActiveX controls run on Windows platforms only

The biggest difference in client component models is where the component can run. ActiveX controls are distributed in binary format, which means that they need a specific hardware and software configuration on which to run. Since a large majority of client systems are Windows-based and run on an Intel platform, this restriction may not be a problem. However, in a mixed-platform environment, this restriction can be a showstopper because specific hardware is required. While ActiveX has the capability to allow a client to ask for a control that runs on alternate hardware (such as a Compaq Alpha system or a PowerPC), most controls are only available for the Intel platform.

The trade-off here is that, on one hand, ActiveX controls are able to take direct advantage of operating system features that may provide better performance and functionality, but these same capabilities make it possible for malicious components to do severe damage to a system.

JavaBeans run in any browser

JavaBeans are designed to be platform independent, as illustrated by their catchphrase, "write once, run anywhere." They are downloaded in byte code format so they will run on any platform that supports the JVM. However, because the Java Virtual Machine can run in any browser, it provides a "least common denominator" set of features to the application. While the Java Development Kit (JDK) 1.2 has many features to support development, not all browsers or platforms support it yet.

Another aspect of where a component runs is the container applications that support it. ActiveX controls run in a wide variety of Microsoft containers, including Visual Basic and Visual C++ programs, any of the tools in the Microsoft Office suite, and Internet Explorer. There are also plug-ins for Netscape browsers to support ActiveX controls. JavaBeans run in Java applications and Java Applets inside of a browser. Some vendors have introduced Java-based office tool suites that will allow integration with JavaBeans.

Standard office applications are also component containers

Server Components

Starting about 1997, second-generation, advanced, or server-side component models began to appear. Examples of advanced component models include MTS or COM+, Enterprise JavaBeans, and the OMG's new CORBA Component Model (CCM). Advanced or server components are designed to reside on a server platform. While client components are mainly focused on the GUI, server components exist primarily to provide business functionality. Client components brought a huge productivity increase to GUI programming. Server components (and their containers) attempt to provide similar productivity increases for server applications and may be even more successful at achieving this goal. As illustrated in Figure 5.3, there are three ways to view what makes up a server component:

- Container viewpoint: Defines interfaces and interactions between the server component and its container
- Business viewpoint: Describes the type of component, its interfaces, properties, state and events, and the factory that creates the component
- Packaging viewpoint: Describes the information the compo-

Three different views of a component

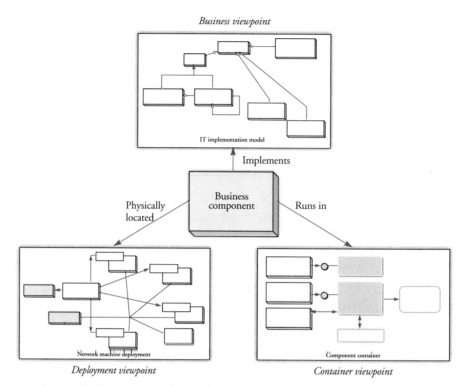

Figure 5.3 Three views of a business component.

nent presents to the container to aid in installation/deployment
and design time construction of component instances and
packages

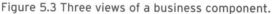

*Container view is
determined by
technology*

The container viewpoint is defined by the particular component
technology it uses (such as EJB, CORBA, or COM+) and is not
really visible to the application programmer, except to the extent
that the container model provides functions that the application
programmer would otherwise have to code.

*Business view is
determined by
analysis and design*

The application developer is most concerned with the business
viewpoint of the component. Standard design and programming
tools, such as UML, and various integrated development environments (IDEs) are used to capture the business model and may be
able to generate some amount of code from it.

IDEs have built-in support for one or more containers, and they typically automate the tasks of creating the particular container artifacts needed to connect the business components to the framework. Similarly, IDEs have support for component packaging and also provide GUI tools and automation of tasks for packaging of components.

Packaging view is determined by operations

To provide clarity, these three views are described in three different architectural descriptions that are explained in Chapter 6. The container viewpoint is described in the implementation architecture, which isolates the container specifics from the business model so that the same business functionality can be implemented in different containers. The business viewpoint of the component is derived from the overall business model and described in more detail in the component and implementation models. The deployment of the component is described in the operational architecture so that the same component can be deployed in a variety of different scenarios.

Component architecture describes the different views

Container Viewpoint

The container provides a set of fundamental support services for the application, services that would otherwise have to be implemented as part of the application development effort (see Figure 5.4). These services include support for

Containers provide fundamental services to components

- distribution
- integration with system services (component creation, security, transactional semantics)
- persistence
- state management

A distributed system of cooperating components requires a variety of services and artifacts. These include the creation and regis-

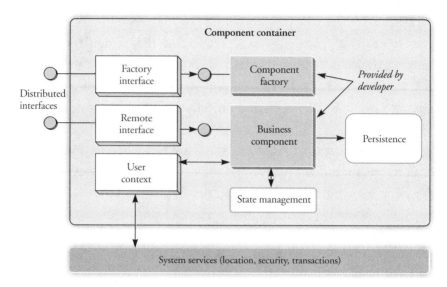

Figure 5.4 Server container environment.

*Containers take care
of distribution for
the components*
tration of component instances, as well as the creation of stubs and
skeletons to connect client-side and server-side components to the
mechanism that actually transports information across the network. In addition, because the distributed system may be composed of different platforms, information must be *marshaled* into a
common format for transmission, then unmarshaled into the particular machine format used by the recipient. The component container can take care of all these needs, making these details transparent to the developer.

*Containers provide
security and
transaction services*
     The ability to automatically integrate an application with sys-
tem services, such as security and transactions, meets a critical enterprise requirement, especially when these requirements are met
by services that are based on industry standards. For example, if
the transaction services provided by the container are XA-
compliant, the chances of being able to participate in transactions
with other systems are greatly increased, since almost all databases
support the XA protocol.

Components that represent business processes or entities may also have state. The state needs to be updated and saved (persisted) as part of the normal business processing. This interaction (typically with a database) can be a major part of the complexity of application development. In addition, state needs to be managed more intelligently when systems are scaled up in size. Both of these functions can be provided by the component container.

Containers manage persistent state for the component

Application Servers as Containers

Chapter 4 described some of the challenges faced by large-scale application systems, including the need for scalability, deployment support, and resource management. Application servers are relative newcomers to the scene, but hold out the promise of addressing these challenges in a way that is very cost-effective as compared with developing these services from scratch. This section describes some of the similarities and differences between application servers.

Application servers provide server component containers

The current crop of application servers has its roots in one or more of these three product types:

- "Traditional" Web servers, that is, products using CGI-BIN, HTTP, HTML, servlets, and so on. For as long as such products have existed, they have emphasized how information is presented to the user, in terms of both data transfer and GUI issues.
- Object storage, that is, products whose roots are either in object/relational mapping tools or object-oriented databases.
- Enterprise run-time infrastructure, that is, object request brokers (ORBs) and transaction monitors.

But not all application servers are created equal

It is fairly easy to discern which of these three categories applies to a given application server product. But while its roots can indicate a product's strong suit, you should not pick a product based

Application servers reflect their heritage

solely on that pedigree, because all three categories are extremely important.

Another important aspect when considering these products is their respective tool sets and integrated development environments. Usually, the tool sets and IDEs that best support a particular application server are those that the product "grew up" with, and this means that the choice of an application server product may result in an implicit choice about tools.

An enterprise class infrastructure is especially important

While all three of these categories are important, enterprise runtime infrastructure is a much bigger category than the others. A reliable middleware infrastructure will provide features that support the large-scale applications requirements that were discussed in Chapter 4 (i.e., state management, configuration control, logging, recovery, security, and transactions). Other enterprise requirements, which may or may not be addressed by a particular application server product, include

- openness
- interoperability
- security (CORBA Security Service, Secure Socket Layer, firewalls, security configurability, and appropriate granularity)
- transactions (XA compliance, multiphase commit)
- scalability (load balancing, instance management, state management)
- configuration control
- management (administration, configuration, operational management, client deployment)
- availability

Application integration is also important

Since one of the strongest drivers for component-based development is the "Web enablement" of existing business functions, and since such Web enablement usually involves the integration of legacy business systems, the legacy integration features of an application server may be an overriding concern. For example, IBM's

WebSphere products can make integrating MQSeries and TXSeries applications much easier than it might otherwise be.

A wise enterprise will carefully evaluate its requirements in all these areas before choosing an application server product. The bottom line is that an application server can be an extraordinarily useful tool. It provides so many of the capabilities needed by today's enterprise that you should have a good reason *not* to use one. If you do not use an application server product, you may find yourself building a lot of infrastructure that can be purchased as a commodity today.

Figure 5.5 illustrates the relationship between a business component and its server platform container. The container runs within the application server, which is responsible for providing the resource pooling and resource management that we discussed in the previous chapter. The object services, such as naming, cre-

Application servers solve critical enterprise requirements

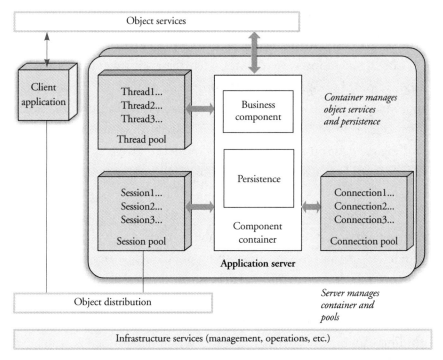

Figure 5.5 Server platform environment.

ation, transactions, and security, are implemented by the container rather than the business component, thus simplifying the task of component development. The persistence of the component can also be managed by the container. Finally, the server itself runs as part of the enterprise infrastructure.

Business Viewpoint

The business viewpoint represents a component's primary purpose

The business viewpoint for a server component is the component's reason for being. The most important aspect of the business viewpoint is the business/application logic, as accessed through the business interface(s). In addition, a business component must deal with the issues of

- creation
- persistence
- events

The business interface describes what a component does

The business interface defines what the component does and is a reflection of the processes and entities identified during the business analysis phase of the project. The component's business interface adds additional concepts such as distribution, relationships, and logical grouping to the analysis model to arrive at the business interfaces. These design considerations will be discussed in detail in Chapter 7.

A component's factory interface is used to create instances of components. As described in Chapter 7, the factory pattern allows intelligent object creation in support of characteristics such as concurrency, location, and partitioning.

Components have a choice for managing persistence

As mentioned earlier, components (and objects) usually have state, and containers can provide support for managing state, including caching and persisting state. When persistence is managed by the container, the result is called container-managed persistence (CMP). Using container-managed persistence can significantly reduce development effort.

These two container persistence options are illustrated in Figure 5.6. In the bottom of the figure, the component is relying on container-managed persistence. In order to implement CMP, the container maps between the properties of the component (entity mapping) and the actual storage of those properties in the database (data access logic). In the top of the figure, the business component is implementing the persistence itself. In order to do this, it is using another component, called a *persistence adapter* (recall that we can construct components with other components). The adapter does a similar mapping of the component to the actual storage (object/relational mapping) and uses a variety of mechanisms including stored procedures to access the actual logic.

Persistence involves data mapping and access

The main difference is whether the component container automatically handles the mapping and data access, or whether it needs to be explicitly written. As beneficial as CMP is, there are occasions when persistence must be managed by the component itself, rather than by its container. For example, if the container-managed persistence supports only a limited set of capabilities, only very simple objects can be stored this way. With better capabilities, fairly complex objects can be stored. Some CMP mechanisms will have object caching, which can significantly increase performance. Typically, containers that evolved from an O/R mapping or database environment have stronger CMP capabilities.

Container-managed persistence is dependent on the container

Thus component-managed persistence (also called bean-managed persistence in EJB) is required when CMP isn't sufficient. Some of the reasons for choosing component-managed persistence over CMP include unsophisticated CMP implementation, very complex object/component mappings, extreme performance requirements, or mapping to legacy data.

Component-managed persistence is required for complex data

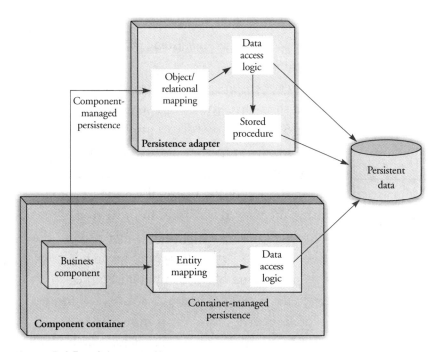

Figure 5.6 Persistence options.

Most applications will use both CMP and component-managed persistence—CMP wherever possible (perhaps 60–80% of the time) and component-managed persistence the rest of the time.

Packaging Viewpoint

Components are a unit of deployment

A component is both a unit of business functionality and a unit of deployment (though a set of cooperating components can also be specified as the "unit of deployment"). The explicit designation of deployment units is one of the biggest distinctions between components and objects. The fact that an object or set of objects was typically *not* built as a self-contained unit of deployment was often a key reason for a given object-based implementation's failure to achieve reuse goals.

For a component to be more generally reusable, certain of its characteristics should be easily modifiable or customizable. This includes system characteristics like security and transaction support and custom properties that a particular component may have created. Because these items are specified in the deployment descriptor, the application source code need not be modified.

Deployment descriptors allow for runtime customization

Transactional policy, as specified in the deployment descriptor, determines how the component behaves under different transaction scenarios. For example, the component might always require transactional semantics, or it might optionally use such transaction support based on the context, or it might never need transactional semantics.

In Chapter 7, we discuss how a well-designed component can execute in more than one of these scenarios. For such components, the transactional approach it should take can be specified at run time in the deployment descriptor. Although there are significant similarities, different component models have different options for specifying these basic behaviors.

Components can be used in different transactional scenarios

In a deployment descriptor, the security information simply describes which users or roles are permitted to perform what methods on the component. The descriptor lists the allowable roles for each method. The container automatically implements the specified security authorizations in a way that is completely transparent to the component.

Components provide role-based security

Thus deployment is managed through the use of deployment descriptors, which specify the following types of information:

- Run-time configuration
- Deployment
- Packaging

The deployment characteristics also describe dependencies on other components (such as required interfaces or events) and information on specific platform requirements. If a component uses container-managed persistence, then the mapping of the component's state to a particular database is described in the deployment descriptor.

Figure 5.7 shows an assembly of components. Each component has its own descriptor that conveys its needs with respect to transactional policy, security, and persistence. The assembly itself has a descriptor that lists the components in the assembly.

Component
assemblies are a set
of components

Although a single component can be designated as a unit of deployment (as described above), in many cases (such as the higher-level business component) a set of cooperating components must be deployed together, and such an assembly can thus become the deployment unit. For example, in such an assembly of cooperating components, not all of the interfaces of the components are necessarily exposed outside of the assembly, yet the assembly may rely on some of those interfaces to operate. Today, the tool support for packaging and deployment of components is rudimentary, but this will improve over time.

Descriptors can be
XML files

A deployment descriptor is typically implemented as a file (i.e., a descriptor file), and XML is becoming a standard format for such descriptors. Many development tools provide a mechanism for the automatic generation of such descriptor files.

Server Component Models

At the moment there are three popular server component models: Microsoft's COM, Sun's Enterprise JavaBeans (EJB), and the OMG's CORBA Component Model.

COM+ is Windows
only

COM only works on Windows platforms. You can write COM components in VB, Java, or C++. COM is tightly integrated with the Windows operating system, and Microsoft is about to make a significant change in the model. Thus, you are faced with lots of

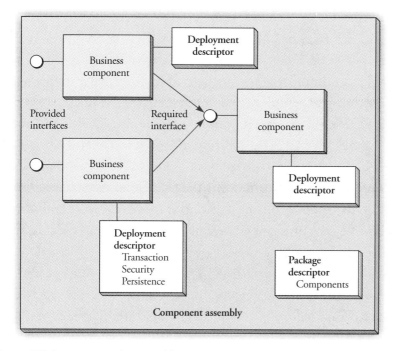

Figure 5.7 A component assembly.

constraints, and some are nearly impossible to work around. For this reason, COM has been most popular with GUI developers and with utility component developers, but not nearly so popular with business component developers. When COM+ ships with Windows 2000, developers who have ActiveX and MTS components are going to find they need to do recoding to port their applications to the new operating system.

Sun's Enterprise JavaBeans model runs on almost any platform, but it requires that you write your application in Java. Enterprise JavaBeans offers a more flexible model, and that flexibility requires that a new developer work harder to master the options available. In COM+, for example, transaction processing is built into Windows 2000. It's relatively simple to link your COM components to the TP engine, but you can only use the Microsoft TP engine and

EJB supports only Java

you are limited by its constraints. Using EJB you can either use a default TP service or link to any popular TP engine. You have more options on how you handle transactions and you can do a better job of optimizing performance, but you have to know what you are doing to assure that you choose the right options.

CORBA components are late to market

The Object Management Group specifies the CORBA Component Model. The CCM specification defines a standard container for CORBA objects and simplifies the process of developing business components. Unfortunately, the OMG has taken a long time to finish its component specification. It may be a while before any vendor offers an implementation of the specification. Meantime, the EJB model has become very popular among enterprise developers, and Sun has extended the EJB specification to support OMG's IDL and IIOP. Thus, EJB components can access legacy applications or components written in other languages by means of CORBA.

CCM is the more advanced and more complex

The advantages are obvious: Using CCM you can create a component in any language and then place CCM components written in different languages together in the same CCM container. The CCM approach will be easier than working in straight CORBA, but it will still be more complex than EJB or COM, simply because it will support more options and thus require more knowledge to use skillfully. CCM was specifically designed to make it possible to place EJB components in the CCM container and run them without any changes. Thus, the real key will be to see how Sun evolves the EJB container. In a sense, the CCM container is where the EJB container will probably be in five years. If Sun chooses, it can evolve its EJB container into a CCM container, just as Sun has, in effect, evolved RMI into IIOP.

Abstract and Implementation Component Models

Companies that embrace a distributed component approach are, in effect, adopting a component software architecture. In this sense, a software architecture simply describes the high-level elements and relationships supported by a software development organization. Thus, whether you speak of a component specification or a component model, the more generic way of speaking of the entire assembly of components and a middleware or supporting infrastructure is to speak of one of the standard component architectures.

Component architectures are both abstract and specific

Any discussion of component architectures must begin by making a distinction between abstract component architectures and component implementation architectures. Component models can describe abstract component systems or they can be designed for implementation. Thus, when an architect is first laying out a high-level business model, they rely on an abstract component model. (For example, an architect can create an abstract component model using the OMG's Unified Modeling Language (UML), a notation convention that need not assume any specific implementation decisions.) The abstract model allows the same component to be implemented on more than one component model, and provides protection from changes in technology, vendors, and so on.

An abstract model is technology independent

As the development process shifts from focusing on a high-level design and toward implementation, a specific implementation model is required. The specific implementation model describes how the components are built using a specific technology, like COM+ or EJB. The model is derived by mapping the technology-independent design to the specific component technology. This mapping is described in a specific implementation architecture.

An implementation model is technology specific

Summary

In this chapter we have discussed the technology used to implement component systems, the specific component technologies available on the market now, and the use of application servers as a host for components. These application servers provide a solution to many of the enterprise and e-business requirements that companies are facing.

We also made two important distinctions about the types of components, those used for client systems and those used for server systems. We also differentiated the size or complexity of components, ranging from simple components to business components. Business components offer the best opportunities for reuse because they represent useful business concepts and because they overcome barriers to reuse.

Finally, we made an important distinction between abstract and implementation-specific component models. We will explore these in more detail in the next chapter.

chapter

An Enterprise Component Architecture

In several chapters, but especially in Chapter 4, we stressed that

any company transitioning to e-business development must first

develop a comprehensive software architecture that will support all

its subsequent application development efforts. In Chapter 5 we

stressed that an enterprise e-business architecture was necessarily a

distributed, component-based architecture. In this chapter we want

to define such an architecture in more detail.

What Is an Architecture?

Definition of "architecture"

The term "architecture" is currently used in computing circles in so many different ways that it is meaningless without a specific definition. Broadly, most organizations have corporate hardware and software architectures. In general, these architectures are statements of the various types of hardware or software the corporation has decided to employ. The goal of architectures at this high level is simply to minimize the number of hardware platforms or software techniques used in the hope that standardization will make integration easier and reduce staff training and maintenance and support requirements.

There are many different software architectures

Throughout this book, we ignore hardware architectures and focus only on software architectures. In Figure 6.1 we've listed four popular corporate software architectures. Most companies currently endorse, by a variety of different names, one of the software architectures listed in the left-hand box within the overall corporate software architecture space. Thus, for example, a company with a major commitment to off-the-shelf, back office applications

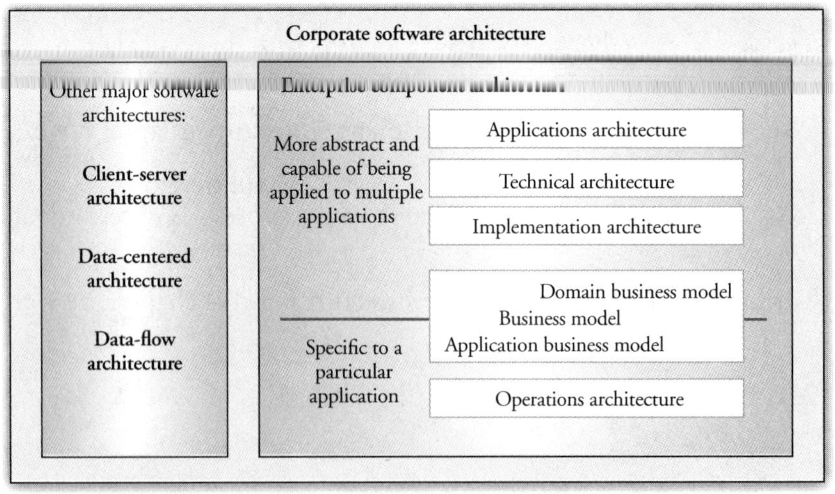

Figure 6.1 A hierarchical classification of some types of architectures.

from SAP or PeopleSoft is committed to a client-server architecture, while a company that primarily relies on older mainframe applications is probably relying on some kind of data-flow architecture.

There are lots of ways of talking about e-business architectures. In essence, however, most companies that have developed e-business applications have relied on some kind of distributed component architecture—what we refer to in Figure 6.1 as an "enterprise component architecture."

E-business architectures are usually component-based

The enterprise component architecture, in turn, can be broken down into a number of subarchitectures, as shown on the right of Figure 6.1. The applications architecture refers to the set of applications that a company supports and how they relate to each other. The technical architecture describes the overall design of company applications. Specifically, it describes the functional layers and the tiers into which an application can be divided. It also describes the frameworks, services, and patterns that the company intends to rely on as it develops component-based applications.

Component architectures are made up of subarchitectures

The implementation architecture derives from the requirements imposed by the specific standards and products used in a specific application. Thus, if you use an Enterprise JavaBeans application server, you will necessarily implement components in a specific way.

The implementation architecture depends on the component technology

These architectures are generic in the sense that they apply to all of the component applications the company will develop. Obviously the application and technical architecture will evolve as new applications are undertaken, and the implementation architecture may expand to support additional products, but they are relatively stable. They need to be determined, at least in general terms, before any specific applications are undertaken.

The business model describes the components that are used in a specific business process. Many architects divide the business model into two parts: a domain business model, which is generic

The business model describes business processes

and could apply to a set of applications, and an application business model, which is specific and is, in effect, a component design for a single application.

The operational architecture depends on performance and other requirements

The operational architecture derives from the specific operational requirements of the application. Thus, for example, if the application will be supporting a bank's electronic banking system, it will need to provide redundant servers and failover databases and to support a large number of simultaneous users, while performing very quickly. These requirements will also have implications for the implementation architecture chosen and for the design of the actual components, and so on.

A Component Architecture

All applications have an architecture

Now that we have a general overview of the various types of architectures, let's bore down into some specifics. A component architecture is a high-level description of the major components of a system and the relationships between them. Most companies have architectures that define how classes of applications will be designed. At the same time, any component-based applications will have an architecture specific to that application—whether it is one we carefully and explicitly create or one that just happened in an ad hoc fashion when we built an application. Not all architectures are equally useful, however.

Architecture describes how a system works and how it is built

An enterprise-class software architecture defines how certain things must be done to be in conformance with the architecture. Before we present our enterprise architecture, let's discuss some of the things that characterize a good architecture. We start with a description of what an architecture is supposed to accomplish, how it attempts to solve certain problems, and the environment in which it must solve them. An architecture must address two major problems:

- How to construct a software system that meets the requirements of the enterprise
- How to construct an environment and infrastructure that simplifies the task of building systems that conform to the architecture

In order to address these problems successfully, the architecture must be communicated to the intended audience. Successful communication of architecture requires

- using abstraction to simplify the problem so that it can be understood and communicated
- keeping a consistent level of detail within an abstraction
- being rigorous and precise
- being well documented

The architectural prewcepts to be communicated are

- separation of concerns
- accommodation of change
- independence from technology
- phased approach to implementation

Development of software systems is a complex endeavor. It involves many different tasks, ranging from the collection and specification of business requirements, to the actual software development process, to deploying and maintaining the systems in an operational environment. Each of these activities involves a different set of concerns, people, and solutions, and all of them are aspects of a true enterprise-class architectural solution (see Figure 6.2).

Software systems involve a wide range of concerns

A common approach to software architecture is to attempt to create a solution that addresses all of these aspects simultaneously. Experience teaches us that this approach is not workable. And if it is pursued to the bitter end, the artifacts it produces arc incompre-

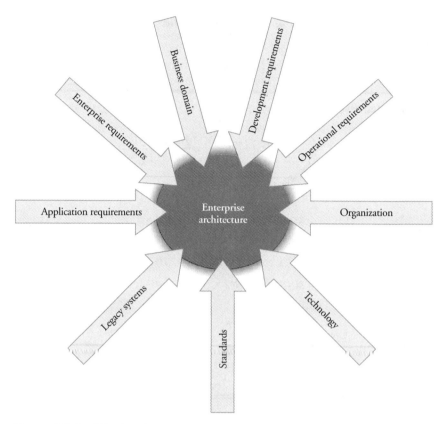

Figure 6.2 Architectural concerns.

First principle: An
architecture
separates different
concerns

hensible to all but a very few. Thus we come to apply the first architectural principle—separation of concerns. Separating concerns
means that the architecture problem space is divided into a set of
related subarchitectures, each of which addresses one or a few related concerns.

This separation has two main benefits. First, artifacts created by
this process are simpler. And second, the information can be communicated in a format and style that is meaningful to the intended
audience.

We call such a separation of architectural concerns a *viewpoint*
because it addresses the architecture from a particular point of

view. For example, a detailed UML model might be appropriate to express how to construct software components, but is probably not the best way to describe hardware and software platforms and other deployment concerns to an operations person. And it is certainly not a useful way to describe the structure of the system to businesspeople.

Different concerns are represented by viewpoints

Given the fast pace of the computer industry, as well as all of the things that must be accounted for in an enterprise software architecture, the only thing that we can really be sure of is that things will change. And this is another area where the role of architecture becomes critically important.

A fundamental characteristic of a good architecture is the ability to accommodate change. The analysis done in support of the architecture identifies what is likely to change in the system, so that any developed solution insulates the rest of the system from changes in those areas.

Second principle: Architecture accommodates changes

For example, rather than having applications writing directly to a specific database, an architecture defines a database *abstraction layer.* This layer presents an unchanging interface to the system components that use the database, and it takes care of communicating with a specific database or databases.

If the need arises, the existing database can be changed simply by implementing another version of the database abstraction layer—one that supports the new database. This kind of architectural approach also supports the use of two or more different databases simultaneously, and all of this is transparent to the rest of the application.

An abstraction layer isolates areas that may change

The same principle can be applied to the choice of middleware technology. We can develop an *implementation-independent architecture* that accommodates the different technology choices that exist today as well as the new technologies likely to appear in the future. We do this by using the same concept of an abstraction layer

Third principle: Architecture should be implementation independent

to present an unchanging model to the rest of the system, and then mapping that model to a specific technology.

Architecture must also simplify building applications

We must never forget that an architecture exists to support business and enterprise requirements, not as an end in itself. Thus it must address the process of developing successful applications as well as the characteristics of those applications. This goal is aided by the key architectural principle of simplification through abstraction. In other words, the architecture must define a simplified model—but not an imprecise one!—which hides the complexity of the system behind a set of frameworks and services that are easy to understand and use.

Just as we apply the concepts of viewpoints (or separation of concerns) to the different aspects of architecture, we can think of the total architecture as supporting two basic and different viewpoints: applications and the infrastructure that supports the applications. We discuss these viewpoints in more detail below.

Fourth principle: Architecture must be phased in

We cannot make the business stop and wait while the architecture and infrastructure are being completed. For many reasons, we find that we must continually release new applications. This fact of life requires that we have a phased implementation process, where pieces of the infrastructure are implemented as part of specific projects and subsequent projects continue to both build on and enhance the architecture over time. We discuss this in more detail in Chapter 7.

The Architecture Development Process

Architectures are general, models are specific

Figure 6.3 provides a more developmental way of visualizing these relationships. It shows how different types of requirements drive the development of the different subarchitectures that make up the

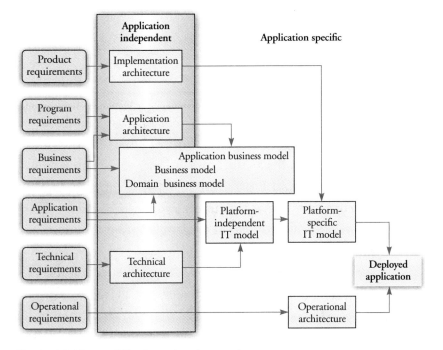

Figure 6.3 The architecture development process.

overall enterprise component architecture. Figure 6.3 shows a mix of architectures and models. As a generalization, any architecture is a more abstract description, while a model is a more concrete description—similar to the distinction between classes and instances in object-oriented development. Another way to think of it is that an architecture applies to several different models. Typically, each application or implementation has a model.

Some theorists discriminate between architecture and infrastructure, but we find that this separation does not address the requirement of simplifying application development. In the approach described here, the infrastructure is part of the subarchitectures to be defined as you build a component-based application.

Infrastructure is defined by the architecture

*Business
requirements drive
the business model*

Starting on the left of Figure 6.3, we see that the program, business, and application requirements feed into the development of a business model (sometimes called an analysis model). This model represents the processes and entities used in the business domain.

*The technical
architecture
describes
component-based
systems*

At the same time, the technical requirements (such as those that determine Web clients, the need for component-based development, legacy integration, etc.) drive the definition of the technical architecture. Although this architecture assumes that component technology will be used, it is completely independent of any specific component technology. Of course this architecture does reflect the common concepts of component technology and how it is used to build systems.

*The IT model
reflects component
distribution
concerns*

When we take the business model and apply the technical architecture to it, we develop a platform-independent IT model (or component model or abstract design). This model represents the components that will be built in the system for this specific application. The IT model addresses concerns such as distribution, relationships, and locality of data when designing the packaging and interfaces of the specific components. As the name implies, the model is still independent of any specific technology choice.

*The implementation
architecture is
specific to technology
and products*

In the upper left of the figure we see the implementation architecture, which is developed by accounting for the requirements and capabilities of specific products and technologies. This architecture describes how to build the components that were specified in the technical architecture, using specific technologies and products. For example, the implementation architecture might describe how to build components using Java/EJB running in an IONA iPortal Application Server and using IBM MQSeries for integration with legacy systems.

*The platform-
specific IT model is
for coding*

When we apply the implementation architecture to the platform-independent IT model, we end up with a platform-specific IT model (or implementation model). This is the model that developers use to write code. It reflects how to build the application components using the specific technologies and products for this application.

The application can have more than one implementation architecture at a time (or put another way, the implementation architecture can describe more than one technology)—it can have one for each technology that needs to be supported. Thus, a second implementation architecture could specify how to build the system with CORBA. The platform-specific IT model separates the business logic from the product-specific code, which means that the same business logic can be used in multiple implementations. Perhaps more importantly, since most of the product-specific code is predictable and has well-defined boundaries, a framework can be implemented to automate much of the task of connecting business logic to a different implementation.

Applications can have more than one implementation architecture

In the lower right of the figure is the operational architecture, which describes the specifics of the application deployment environment. It includes such things as hardware platforms, databases, software, and networks. This operational architecture also describes how the application is actually deployed (e.g., which servers run on what machines) and how it is kept operational (e.g., failover and replication mechanisms).

The operations architecture addresses deployment

By following an implementation-independent architecture process, the application, business logic, and component design decisions are all made independent of both implementation details and technology. Thus the technology can be selected, changed, or evolved without affecting the core business logic, and multiple technologies can be supported with the same business objects.

Implementation-independent architecture isolates business from technology

The implementation-independent architecture also protects against other changes—for example, those that are driven by factors such as mergers and acquisitions, product cancellations, and changes in third-party products. As technology changes over time,

*Implementation-
independent
architecture future-
proofs your
application*

the technical and implementation architectures can be evolved to take advantage of new technologies, while still insulating the existing applications from change.

Although all of these architectures are important, in the remainder of this chapter we focus on the technical architecture. This architecture has the most impact on the structure of e-business applications. This is also closest to what we normally think about when we discuss architecture.

The Technical Architecture

*The technical
architecture contains
the conceptual
model and
development
infrastructure*

The technical architecture describes the structure of e-business software systems. The architecture consists of a conceptual model and a development infrastructure.

The conceptual model provides a conceptual foundation of the software system and describes the details of two basic concepts:

● Functional layers, which describe the responsibilities of related types of components and places them in their respective architectural layers

● Distribution tiers, which describe how different types of components are mapped to a distributed computing system

The development infrastructure provides the tools to support software development, including the following:

● Frameworks, which are customizable generic solutions to specific application problems and may include tools for generating code

● Services, which provide an infrastructure that allows applications to use common functions throughout the system

● Patterns, which are solution templates for commonly encountered problems

The Conceptual Model

The conceptual model shown in Figure 6.4 describes the software architecture in an informal way that conveys the major concepts of the architecture. In this case, these concepts are the functional layering and distribution tiers. Because one of the jobs of architecture is to communicate, the architecture can and must be presentable in a nontechnical, informal manner as shown here.

Conceptual models communicate nontechnically

However, architecture should also be rigorous and detailed, and a conceptual model is not sufficient for those purposes. To address these needs, the architecture should be described in a formal model, in an industry-standard notation such as UML. But be-

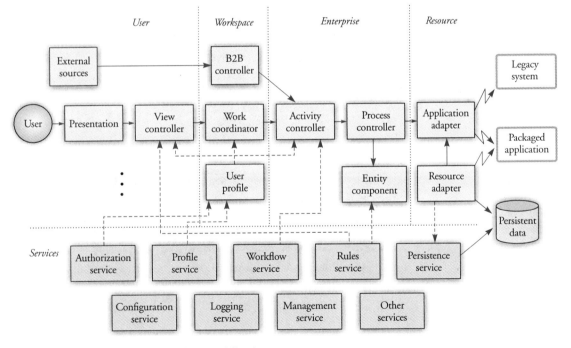

Figure 6.4 An e-business technical architecture.

cause the focus of this book is at the conceptual level, we do not include any formal models.

*Technical
architecture
identifies
application and
infrastructure layers*

Figure 6.4 shows two main functional layers; each light box represents a defined functional construct (or architectural element) in the application layer of the architecture. Together these constructs define application-level responsibilities. The application layer addresses specific application concerns with specific solutions. The darker boxes represent the various services provided to application developers. They form a second "infrastructure" layer and are common for all applications. The service layer addresses a more general set of requirements. Conceptually, beneath the service layer (but not shown in the figure) are middleware, operating systems, and hardware.

Each architectural element can be mapped to a different type of implementation (such as a Java servlet or EJB component), depending on the desired target technology. Some layers—but not all—map to distributed components, and not all applications will have all layers.

The functional layers of the technical architecture address the following:

*Functional layers
address scalability,
distribution, and
technology
independence*

- Distribution: Different functional layers typically reside in different tiers.

- Scalability: Resources can be applied to each functional layer independently as required. Also, distribution tiers can be mapped to different physical processors, and in this way each tier in an application can be replicated. These possibilities, along with techniques such as load balancing between tiers, allow an application to scale up.

- Separation of application development from infrastructure development: All software that is not directly related to the business logic of an application is placed in specific functional layers. Moreover, some services (e.g., authorization and logging) are needed in all application domains, and so are embodied in components that are part of the overall infrastructure.

- Technology independence: Architectural concepts and design guidelines should not be constrained by a particular technology or product. Each functional layer can be mapped to a different type of implementation depending on the desired target technology.

- Device independence: Components use resource adapters to isolate business logic from the specific characteristic of devices. While the presentation of information (i.e., the graphical user interface) may be specific to a particular device, and therefore supported by a view controller designed for that device, work coordinators are device independent.

- Application integration: Components such as application adapters are introduced for integrating legacy and packaged applications.

- Future enhancements and migrations: Functional layers may be replaced or split into finer-grained layers in an enhancement of the architecture. The specific choice of functional layers in the architecture is aimed at accommodating areas likely to change in the future. Separation of concerns allows a designer to replace or enhance parts of the architecture with little impact to the rest of it.

The second fundamental concept illustrated in Figure 6.4 is that of distribution tiers. The dotted vertical lines represent "logical" (as opposed to physical) distribution tiers in the model. The picture shows four tiers labeled user, workspace, enterprise, and resource. These four tiers, or four logical areas of distributed system concern, are defined from the point of view of the application designer, and they provide a general-purpose pattern for distributed systems.

Distribution tiers are concerned with scalable distributed applications

Functional layers are assigned to distribution tiers

These logical tiers are similar to the concept of architectural layering, in that the components in a given tier communicate only with components in the same or adjacent tiers. For example, a component in the user tier does not communicate directly with the resource tier.

Figure 6.4 also shows services, which may span tiers. This means that any component in any logical tier may have the need to use one of the common services, and the architecture supports this.

Distribution tiers can be deployed over physical nodes

A logical distribution tier can be deployed over one or more physical systems or nodes. Conversely, several different tiers can be deployed into a single system, if desired. That is, while separation into logical distribution tiers is necessary to scale up, the concept also scales down nicely. Thus separating functions into logical distribution tiers does not imply the need to deploy the application over multiple physical servers. For example, a three-tier architecture describes a software system that can be deployed over three separate physical host machines and can also be deployed on a single machine.

This is illustrated in Figures 6.5 and 6.6. Figure 6.5 shows how the functional layers might be configured for a small-scale or workgroup-size application. In this example, a Web server and an application server are used.

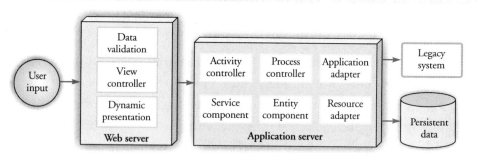

Figure 6.5 Workgroup application configuration.

In Figure 6.6, the same application has been configured for a large-scale enterprise. Now we can see how different resources can be applied for different requirements within the application. For example, we have configured more Web servers to handle the web access, a moderate number of application servers for the business processing, and fewer application servers to handle the services and legacy access. With this architecture, we can apply resources selectively, as required by the application. Comparing the figures, we can also see that without modifying the application code, the same application can be scaled to different requirements.

Figure 6.7 looks at this same application from a layered or multitiered perspective. Let's consider each tier in more detail. The user tier is responsible for managing user interface details, such as

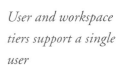
The same application can be scaled differently

User and workspace tiers support a single user

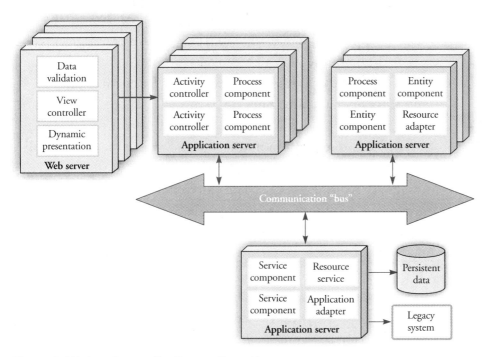

Figure 6.6 Enterprise application configuration.

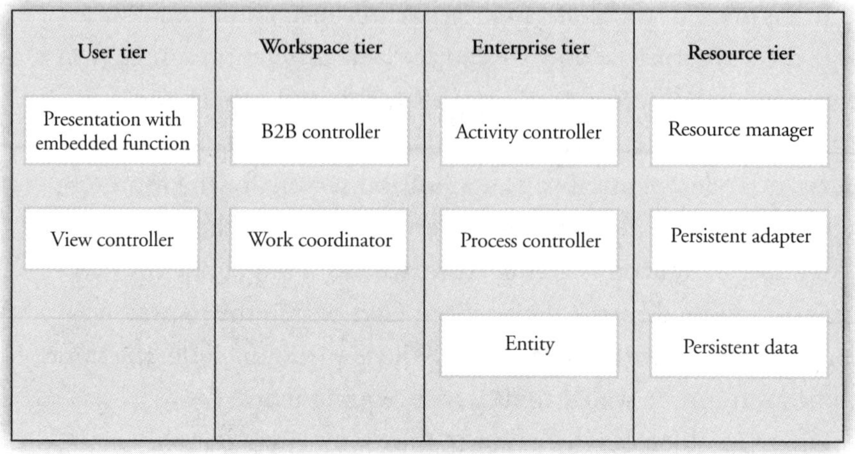

User tier	Workspace tier	Enterprise tier	Resource tier
Presentation with embedded function	B2B controller	Activity controller	Resource manager
View controller	Work coordinator	Process controller	Persistent adapter
		Entity	Persistent data

Figure 6.7 Functional layers and distribution tiers.

presentation of information, data input and output, and navigation within the application. The workspace tier is responsible for coordinating multiple activities for a particular user, executing processes that do not require access to enterprise resources, and getting data from, or putting it to, the enterprise tier. Together, the workspace and user tiers make up what we traditionally thought of as the presentation tier in a typical three-tier system.

The enterprise tier enforces business rules

The enterprise tier is responsible for managing the integrity of enterprise resources, enforcing system-level business rules, and providing services to requestors. The enterprise tier is what implements the business objects—that is, the business entities and business processes that have been identified by the business analysis and modeling activities. The enterprise tier is what we traditionally called the business tier.

The resource tier provides shared access

The resource tier is responsible for providing shared access to the resources and services of the system, particularly the enterprise databases, as well as access to legacy and packaged applications. The resource tier is what we traditionally called the data tier.

Thus far, we have looked at the technical architecture in terms of functional layers and distribution tiers. In addition, the separation of the application developer's concerns from those of the technical infrastructure is critical to productivity, consistency, quality, and cost. The architecture defines an environment for the application developers to work in and provides solutions to common problems encountered during application development. The architecture can also be looked at as having an application developer's viewpoint, which concentrates on using the infrastructure, and an infrastructure viewpoint, as shown in Figure 6.8.

The Infrastructure Viewpoint

The infrastructure view of the technical architecture is aimed at providing the programming environment rather than using that environment to create applications (and by "programming environment," we mean the set of resources available to programs, as opposed to any particular IDE such as Visual C++). So the infrastructure view is focused on making the application programmer

The infrastructure viewpoint provides the programming environment

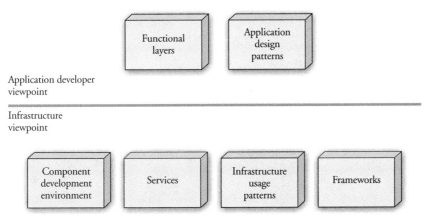

Figure 6.8 Application and infrastructure viewpoints.

more productive. This infrastructure environment provides the
following:

- Design guidelines and framework specifications
- Services to support application requirements, to be used in all
  or most application domains
- Patterns for typical application-specific problems
- Reusable software artifacts—components that can be exploited
  by developers

Guidelines make
developers more
productive

One way to make application developers more productive is to
provide design guidelines and framework specifications for common programming scenarios, for example, providing a harmonious
look and feel by way of a common user interface framework. The
software architecture defines the frameworks that can be used to
help standardize and automate such tasks. Again, some frameworks
may be able to automatically generate application code.

Services provide
common enterprise
functionality across
applications

Part of the infrastructure is the common services that it provides. The software architecture should define these services, their
interfaces, and how the different functional layers within the application use the services. Services should be designed for use by multiple applications in accordance with a common service architecture that provides for consistency between service implementations
as well as integrated service administration and management. Some
typical application services are

- security
- configuration
- logging
- profile
- workflow
- rules
- legacy access

- resource externalization
- management

In recent years, patterns have been used extensively in software design efforts as a way to decrease design and development time and increase robustness and quality. Much has been written describing different patterns for the solution of generic application problems. While these general patterns are appropriate for use within most applications, they alone are not sufficient. There are also specific patterns that apply to the particular business domain or application (or that support the policies of a particular enterprise), and that are not covered in available literature. The technical architecture defines the patterns for these situations.

Patterns provide standard solutions to application-specific problems

For example, in many industries, it is common to build systems by buying packaged applications for certain capabilities (such as customer care or billing) and then tying these systems into the enterprise. This can provide a fast way to obtain the functions provided by these packaged applications, but it comes at a cost since each packaged application has its own set of data. Thus in many cases, applications have different data to describe the same business entity. How does the application deal with this duplication and overlap of data in a coordinated, synchronized manner while providing a consistent view of the business entity? Rather than each integration project developing a different solution for each application or entity, the architecture solves the problem once, in the form of a pattern for packaged application integration that specifically deals with the problem of overlapping entity data.

Example: Packaged application integration pattern

Functional Layer Details

Now we will examine each of the functional layers of the technical architecture. We can think of the user interfaces as having both a form (or a look and feel) and a function (or the processing that goes with the form). The presentation layer is the form or layout part of the user interface. It is responsible for formatting the input and output of information provided by and for the end user.

Presentation provides output for a specific device

One of the requirements for e-business is to accommodate a variety of different presentation devices. And the type of presentation layer to be built is dependent on the physical device and technology used for presentation. For example, an HTML page could be the presentation for a Web browser interface. A form would be the presentation for a Visual Basic interface. And yet another type of presentation would be used for a handheld device.

Embedded functions provide faster feedback

Embedded functions are used to handle some aspects of the presentation function and some aspects of the user input function. This reduces some of the processing necessary in the enterprise tier, reduces communication overhead, and provides faster feedback to the user. For example, a first level of data input validation could be done via embedded functions. Examples of embedded logic include JavaScripts within an HTML page and procedures in Visual Basic.

The view controller manages presentation I/O

The view controller is the function part of the user interface. It is responsible for presentation of specific input and output—in other words, actually sending data to or receiving data from the presentation layer. The type of view controller is dependent on the physical device and technology used for the presentation and must of course match the presentation technology.

Thus, for each type of input device, we have a presentation and view controller (in some cases the same controller could be shared by several devices). For example, if the presentation uses HTML, the view controller would probably be implemented as a Java servlet. In Visual Basic, the view controller is implemented automatically as part of the Visual Basic run time. If the user interface is a telephone, then the view controller might consist of speech simulation, voice recognition, and keypad input technologies.

Providing a unique customer experience is important in a successful e-business application, and that implies the ability to customize the experience for a user. For example, a particular user may be able to perform different functions or be presented a different interface depending on their "customer level" (e.g., normal, gold, platinum, etc.). A customer may also have some set of preferences. And a customer may be restricted from certain things based on security policies. These different factors make up a user's profile. The view controller and work coordinator can use the profile service to get the information necessary to customize the user's presentation.

User profiles provide user customization

An application business process frequently requires more data to be input than can be accomplished in a single screen or presentation. Also, what data is required may depend on specific information entered in another field. The work coordinator is responsible for the collection and temporary storage of information across multiple presentations, for navigation from one presentation to the next, and for sorting out dependencies between information fields. Using the Web-based example again, the work coordinator would typically be implemented as an EJB session bean, linked to the HTTP session object.

The work coordinator manages multiple related screens

Not all data comes into the system via a user interface. This is true for a particularly important class of e-business applications, business-to-business (B2B) e-commerce. Typically, B2B data comes into the system as a whole unit and is most likely to be expressed in XML. The B2B controller is responsible for parsing the message, verifying its correctness, and then requesting functions from the enterprise tier. A different B2B controller might be implemented for each different e-commerce activity that needs to be supported, or a controller might support several activities. It is important to notice that the B2B controller uses the same set of functions in the enterprise tier as the other access methods, such as a GUI. In other words, B2B represents a different entry point into

E-commerce applications are managed by B2B controllers

the system using the same business functionality, not a separate application.

An important technique used during the business analysis phase of a project is to identify business activities to be performed by the application via *use cases,* which are simple narratives of business scenarios that describe interactions between a user and the system or application. These use cases can frequently be decomposed into smaller units of business functionality that can be reused in other use cases.

The activity controller implements business analysis cases

To address performance and scalability concerns, it is desirable to present business functionality to the user interface in "use-case-sized" units of activity. Thus the activity controller is responsible for presenting the higher-level use case functionality to the user interface and then controlling and executing the sequence of business functions required to perform the use case.

Once a "unit of work" worth of data has been collected by the work coordinator (as part of the user interface subsystem), it is ready to be passed to the activity controller. Therefore, the two layers are closely related. Figure 6.9 shows a view of this interaction, which expresses the following relationship cardinalities:

- Many-to-one relationship between view controller and work coordinator
- One-to-one relationship between work coordinator and activity controller
- One-to-many relationship between activity controller and business processes

Work coordinator and activity controller interact

The work coordinator cycles through collecting input and navigating to the next page until all of the input screens for a particular activity have been processed. The activity controller is then called to initiate processing of the data in the enterprise tier. The activity controller starts a transaction (if required) and then executes all

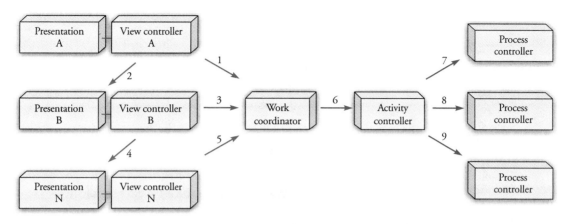

Figure 6.9 Work coordinator-activity controller interaction.

of the steps of the given activity. When that is finished, the transaction is completed and the response is returned to the work coordinator.

Conceptually, the activity controller is a process that is built to order for a given activity, in general maps to a single use case, and is not normally designed to be reused by higher-level artifacts. An activity controller often represents a workflow of business processes. A useful mechanism for implementing the activity is to have a generic workflow system or service as part of the infrastructure.

In this approach, the activity controller essentially retrieves a script that describes the sequence of process steps to be performed and passes it to the workflow service. The script can be made external to the code, allowing it to be modified or updated without having to redeploy any of the application components.

Activities can be implemented as workflows

Business processes represent units of work that are needed to perform the business functions supported by the application. The granularity of the business processes is such that they can be used by several different activity controllers. The business processes are executed by process controller components. The business processes

Business processes are reusable pieces of business functionality

may be new functions that did not exist before or existing application functions to be presented as components in the new system.

Many business processes may be driven by rules. Rules can be as simple as specifying the valid range for the value in a data field, or as complicated as providing control over complex relationships between many different business entities. Sometimes the rules are dictated by legal regulations, which may change frequently. In other cases, they represent the core policies of the business. Rules processing systems (rules engines) can be a valuable technique for executing rules that are associated with business processes. This is an especially useful approach when the rules are likely to change.

Entities have their own identity and represent units of information (data) that are needed to perform business functions. The entities may hold new information or existing information, but they should represent information that is needed by several different business activities. Rules processing can be useful for validating the correctness and consistency of data in an entity.

A goal of the software architecture is to isolate business functionality from the specifics of how those business processes (or data) are implemented or stored. This is achieved through the use of adapters, which act as special insulating layers. In the case of an existing legacy or packaged application, an application adapter is used. In the case of data, a resource adapter is used.

The application adapter provides a new, component-based interface to some existing application function. The adapter must somehow invoke the existing application to perform the work, and this may not be a simple one-to-one mapping. Thus, in order to do this, the adapter must typically communicate with the existing application using some protocol understood by that application. The adapter implements any protocol and/or communications translation that is necessary.

The resource adapter provides access to information resources that exist in one or more parts of the system, such as a database or as part of an existing application. The resource adapter is responsible for mapping the existing data to the format used by business entities. This mapping may not be straightforward and can involve data that is stored in several different applications simultaneously. In this case, the resource adapter is also responsible for managing the dependencies between the data.

Resource adapters map to storage

Summary

In this chapter we discussed software architecture—what it is, why it is necessary, and what it does. We then delved into the details of architectural layers and tiers, in order to understand how architectural structure is applied to meet the needs of the business enterprise.

The architecture example illustrated in Figure 6.4 let's us describe the following attributes and approaches to the requirements of e-business enterprise applications:

- Device independence
- Local rules processing
- User profiles and customization
- Workflow
- Application integration
- Component-based support for accommodating change, for rapid development, and for simplified programming

In the next chapter, we will see how to implement this architecture using component technology. In doing so, we will discuss the design alternatives that need to be considered for each component in the system.

chapter

Implementing a Component Architecture

In Chapter 6 we discussed a technical architecture for e-business

systems. In previous chapters, we described the technology used to

implement component systems and the specific component tech-

nologies available in the market today. This chapter goes into more

depth about how to implement an e-business technical architecture

using components. While this information is presented in a

technology-independent manner that can be applied to any of the component technologies, we present some examples using specific component technologies.

The Component Factory

Architecture should simplify implementation

The enterprise component architecture that we presented has several major goals: to define a high-level system model, to provide standard solutions to common problems wherever possible, and to simplify implementation of applications.

To be effective in e-business, the development cycle must be accelerated. The requirement that the development cycle move "at Internet speed" implies the need for standard solutions to common problems. This need is met in part by implementation platforms that provide common services, frameworks, and infrastructure for applications.

The component factory provides a standard platform for developers

This high-speed, simplified platform for implementation is an important part of what has come to be known as *the component factory*. The component factory, combined with the project management concepts discussed in later chapters, provides the technical and organizational foundation for implementing applications at Internet speed.

The job of the component factory is to relieve application developers of all concerns about infrastructure—so that the only thing they need to deal with is implementation of application logic in business components.

Application developers are freed of infrastructure concerns

As discussed in Chapter 6, the technical architecture describes how to build the entire system. Figure 7.1 is a familiar view of the technical architecture, with the addition of a line that separates application concerns from infrastructure concerns. We can think about these different architectural aspects as being above (application) or below (infrastructure) this line.

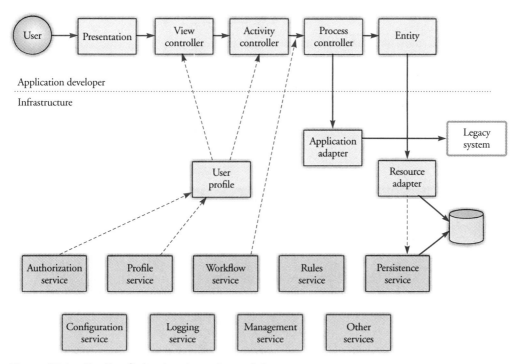

Figure 7.1 Application/infrastructure viewpoints.

No business can wait for the architecture to be fully implemented before seeing the first useful application and tangible business benefits. For this reason, the infrastructure must be built in chunks, with each chunk being a part of a different project.

The first project typically includes building the most important chunk, that is, the basic infrastructure components that any and all applications need. Then each subsequent project adds infrastructure pieces (typically those that are required by that particular project), until after two or three projects, most of the component factory is complete. The component factory continues to evolve with subsequent projects as technology and requirements change (see Figure 7.2).

If you think that this approach requires careful consideration in determining which projects should be done first and in what order, you are absolutely right!

The component factory is built iteratively over several projects

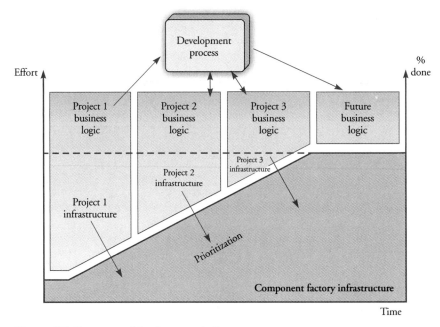

Figure 7.2 Component factory evolution.

Applications follow the component factory's patterns

Thus the component factory consists of architecture, infrastructure, services, frameworks, patterns, project management, and component reuse programs. In this chapter we focus on component development from the application developer viewpoint—their concerns and the patterns they use and reuse to implement applications, rather than the component factory itself. In subsequent chapters, we will address the project management and program aspects of the component factory.

The Component Model

The business model identifies business processes and entities

As we noted in Chapter 6 (see Figure 6.3), the component model (platform-independent IT model) is derived from both the technical architecture and the business model. We will avoid going into detail about the business model except to say that the business model identifies the processes and entities in the enterprise that are meaningful from a business perspective. These business processes and entities have to be implemented in a computer system. We could map them directly to components but that would not make for a well-designed implementation, nor one that would perform adequately. The component model, which maps these business processes and entities to components, needs to factor in several other considerations as well.

The component model must also take into account concerns about the distributed nature of the system (i.e., the network), interface design (e.g., the information that passes among components), relationships and dependencies among components, locality of data, and many other performance considerations. The specifics of these considerations are discussed in the following sections.

Component design must account for many factors

Interface Design Considerations

Let's begin by looking at some of the lessons we have learned about building distributed systems. Fifteen years ago, it was said that 80% of an application's performance depended on the implementation algorithm. Today, we can say that 80% of an application's performance depends on the interface design of its components. And we can certainly say that some of the most important considerations in interface design involve the characteristics of distributed computer systems. Some of the things we have learned about designing interfaces in a distributed system include these "rules of thumb":

Application performance depends on interface design

- Increase request granularity.
- Not everything needs to be a distributed object.

- Understand and manage component relationships.
- Enable collections.
- Do not distribute at the attribute level.
- Isolate distribution decisions from business design decisions.

Distributed design may conflict with OO design

You will not find these precepts in any list of the principles of object-oriented design. It is just a fact of life that the principles of distributed system design are different from—and sometimes in conflict with—the traditional concepts of OO design.

Remote invocations are more costly than local invocations

Traditional OO stressed simple objects with small, fine-grained properties and methods. Theoretically, there is nothing wrong with that. The problem arises because distributed computer systems operate over a real network rather than a theoretical one—the performance cost of a call to a remote object in a distributed system is 1000 times that of a local function call. Thus, in a distributed system, it is imperative to minimize the number of remote invocations and/or to increase request granularity. Below we discuss a variety of methods for doing so.

Interfaces should maximize business function per remote invocation

By "increase request granularity" we mean getting more business function per remote request. This is accomplished by having a single method that performs several actions, for example, returning a collection of data—rather than a single data item—for a single method invocation. While increased request granularity is fundamental to reasonable performance, a thoughtful interface design will likely provide choices. For example, the interface may expose two methods for returning data, one that emphasizes ease of use (by returning a single data item) and another that emphasizes efficiency (by returning a list of data items).

In the context of the design concerns for application distribution, we should first note that there are three types of objects: a distributed component, a value (or data) object, and a local object.

A distributed component has a well-defined interface and is *network addressable,* meaning that other components can find and access it over the network. A value object is essentially a data holder. It may be passed in its entirety as a parameter and then acted on locally, but it is accessible only through its manager object and is not itself directly addressable via the network. The local object is neither passed nor is it network addressable.

Not all objects should be distributed objects

The important point here is that not everything in the system should be a distributed object. In a typical distributed system, many things are implemented as local objects and never distributed.

Objects can reference other objects, which means that any given object can have a fairly complex relationship tree. If all of these related objects are distributed and made remote, then traversing the relationship tree becomes very expensive. For this reason, related objects should be grouped together within the same component whenever possible, and the implementation of that component should not be distributed across multiple systems.

Related objects should be grouped together

For example, a business component may actually be designed as five objects. The designer might decide to do it this way because these five objects are always used together, but in different combinations depending on the business function invoked. So the business component that encompasses these five objects might expose one coarse-grained interface that is quite different from any of the interfaces on the five objects. And the interfaces of those five objects might not be publicly exposed at all. Thus the business component acts as a mediator that presents a single interface but calls multiple interfaces behind it to actually accomplish the work.

Groups of objects can present a single interface

Another way to maximize request granularity, and therefore to improve performance, is to support interfaces that act on groups (or collections) of things. For example, rather than retrieving a single item at a time, a request could retrieve a set or list of items for about the same performance cost.

Distributed interfaces should support collections

Don't distribute single attributes

A special case of a collection is the set of attributes or properties of an object. The object should support a method that provides a get/set method for all of the attributes at once. Only occasionally is there a valid reason to provide distributed methods that get or set a single attribute on the object.

Separate business logic from distribution decisions

We will not go into detail about the reasons for separating business logic design decisions from distribution design decisions. Suffice it to say that it would be embarrassing to have to change business logic because of a change in network topology, or to have to change the network configuration because of a change in business process!

Other Component Design Considerations

Components are concerned with scalability and concurrency

The component model must also provide the critical characteristics of scalability, concurrency, and redundancy in an enterprise-class system. While interface design is fundamentally affected by scalability concerns, those concerns also drive component design decisions that have nothing to do with the interface. Thus, while the design of components must take all three characteristics into account, the resulting design decisions are seen solely in the component's implementation.

Components need to be location independent

To achieve scalability and concurrency, an object implementation needs to consider location independence and object identity. Location independence means that a given component must be able to run on any of a set of servers. By increasing the number of servers on which a given component instance can run, both scalability and availability are increased.

There are two important aspects to location independence: component location and resource location. Component location transparency is provided by the infrastructure through the use of a distributed naming service. When a client needs to get an object, it asks for it by name from the naming service. The naming service then selects among the servers that have registered that object with it.

Resource location transparency is more important in component design. If the component is able to run in any of a set of services, it cannot assume anything about the location of resources. For example, it cannot assume specific disk drive identifiers or file paths, or that the resource will be located on the same machine as the server. As with a naming service, the location of the resource should be looked up rather than being hardcoded in the component.

A component's resources must also be location independent

Component identity is the ability to identify and track a specific instance of a component. In this way, the component's state can be managed, and components achieve greater "mobility"—because a component can be saved on one server and restored on a different server. The component's identity is usually related directly to the (persistent) state of the component. Component identity also controls parallelism (which is the ability for simultaneous access to the same data by multiple clients). Typically, a component system will only allow one component of a given identity to exist in the system at the same time. So, if scalability requirements dictate the need for multiple components to act on the same data, a more sophisticated identity policy needs to be used.

Identity policies are part of component design

Concurrency control is the management of the consistency of data, in the context of the need to have multiple instances of components act on the same data. Concurrency allows similar components to be active on many servers (machines) simultaneously. As you might guess, concurrency is simplest when most of the data is read-only.

Concurrency control must be addressed

Component design must account for concurrent access to data, and that may impose additional responsibilities on applications. The application may provide concurrency control using a variety of standard mechanisms, such as optimistic locking or locking provided by the database or through the use of a distributed locking service such as the CORBA Concurrency Service.

Scalability requirements differ widely

Scalability design requirements vary, since applications range from the use of singleton components to having thousands of simultaneous instances of a component type. In fact, most applications will have different requirements for different components in the same application. Because not all components have the same requirements, we cannot use a one-size-fits-all design strategy. Instead, we use different strategies based on the needs of a particular component.

Components can be stateful or stateless

State-related design considerations depend on whether the object maintains state or not. It is common to build systems using components that represent either business processes or business entities. The difference is that entity components maintain the state of a particular entity (or set of business data). We call this component *stateful*. In contrast, process components do not maintain any state, but instead act on business entities that do. We call this component *stateless*.

For example, "John's account" is an entity component that maintains the information about John's account balance. An "account manager" component acts on John's account, but John's account state is stored somewhere else, not in the account manager object. And, of course, the account manager object can just as easily act on some other account at another time.

Stateless components are much more scalable

Thus, we can perform account activity with far fewer distributed components using the account manager model than would be required if each account were its own component. This translates directly to a more scalable application and is useful in scenarios where we have very large numbers of entities (1 million accounts). However, not all business entities fit this model. For example, since we only have one bank, it would be more cumbersome and less efficient to interact with the bank through a bank manager object.

State Management

We discussed state management briefly in Chapter 4. To recap, state management concerns the saving and restoring of objects in a way that makes it appear (to applications) that the objects are always available for use and that guarantees the object's state is always consistent.

Before digging into this subject more deeply, a word on terminology. Components are referred to as being stateless or stateful. These terms are overloaded, which may cause some confusion. A component may be called "stateless" simply because it has no data (and therefore no state) associated with it. But stateless also means that the component can be deactivated when it is not being used.

Stateless components don't remain in memory

Similarly, "stateful" is used to refer to a component that does have data associated with it and may therefore need to be stored persistently. But stateful also refers to components that must remain in memory (for whatever reason) between invocations. In this discussion, we use stateful and stateless to describe the memory management requirements, rather than the presence or absence of data within the components.

Stateful components consume memory even when not active

State management is determined by the component design and controls a component's activation life, or the duration that an object remains active in memory. This means that the designer specifies the conditions under which the object can or cannot be swapped in and out of memory.[1]

State management controls the use of memory resources

The state management trade-off is between the cost of keeping an object in memory and the cost of saving/restoring the object. The cost of an active (in-memory) object is measured in terms of the resources that are tied up. These include the memory itself,

---

[1] In the context of component-based systems, this memory management is under control of the application system (e.g., the appserver) rather than the host operating system. The OS may indeed manage memory by swapping programs in and out, but this is transparent to the application system.

database connections, and locks on a variety of system and database resources. These costs must be understood in the context of the number of concurrent objects required by the application(s).

State management design: A balancing act

The cost of activating/deactivating an object is usually measured in terms of the resources consumed in writing the object's state to persistent storage and reading it back into memory. However, there are some other interesting cases. For example, an object's state may have to be re-created rather than restored, and the time required for re-creation may have to be considered in the design decisions for a component.

Four models for state management

There are four main models for state management (or, to put it another way, for component/object activation):

- Per method, in which the component is activated each time one of its methods is called and deactivated when the operation is complete
- Per transaction, in which the component is activated as needed after the start of a transaction and deactivated when the transaction is complete
- Per process, in which the component is activated at server startup and deactivated at server shutdown
- Application controlled, in which the component is activated on demand and deactivated whenever the application deems that appropriate

Transaction Models

Transactions are another design decision for components

Another important concept and design decision we must make with components is the transaction model. In general, transactions are used where modifications to a persistent resource (e.g., information in a database) must remain consistent under all circumstances—even if the transaction fails for some unforeseen reason. Two-phase transactions are required if modifications to multiple persistent resources must be performed in a consistent, all-or-nothing manner. And distributed transactions are required if the multiple resources are managed by different resource manager systems.

Transactions, and especially distributed transactions, introduce additional processing overhead and greatly increase the potential for resource contention issues (i.e., livelocks and deadlocks). Therefore, they should be used only where warranted by application requirements. And when transactions are used, they should be as short as possible to minimize contention.

Transactions should be as short as possible

In a distributed component-based application (in fact, in any client-server application), we need to consider who is responsible for starting and ending a transaction. Because we want the transaction to be short, this responsibility should not, in general, be delegated to the client, especially if the completion of the transaction depends on user input. A better solution is to have the transaction automatically started by the system at the point where the client (the application component) invokes an operation that requires one.

Clients should not be responsible for transaction control

In the context of transactions, interfaces should be designed to be as flexible as possible to different transaction environments. Thus the interface should provide choices in how the component participates in a transaction; that is, the component should be able to participate in a transaction; but it should not require one, and the interface controls whether it does or not. If the component does participate in a transaction, the component design should be such that automatic system support for transactions (as opposed to custom logic in the component) is sufficient. Of course, this will not always be possible, and there may be some objects that should never participate in a transaction.

Components must support several transaction scenarios

There are six transaction models:

- Never: Such a component can never be in a transaction. If a method is invoked on such a component while a transaction is active, the request is rejected.

- Not supported: Such a component should not be part of a transaction. If a transaction is active, that transaction must be suspended before invoking this type of component, and the transaction should be resumed after the component completes its task. Suspending and resuming the transaction is done by the system, not the application.

- Supports: This component can participate in a transaction, but does not require that it be part of a transaction. If a transaction is active, the component will be invoked within the context of that transaction. If no transaction is active, the component can still be invoked.

- Required: This component must be invoked within a transaction. If no transaction is active, the system will automatically start one before invoking the component.

- Requires new: The system will always start a new transaction for this component.

- Mandatory: A transaction must be active before this component is invoked. If not, the system will not automatically start one, but will instead reject the request.

Wherever possible, application interfaces should be designed for the "Supports" transaction model. If transactional semantics are required, the component should support the "Required" model. The other transaction models should be used selectively with the understanding that they will limit the general use of the component.

Component Usage Models

So far, we looked at the choices facing a component designer for identity, concurrency, and managing a component's state. Now let's look at the same issues from the vantage point of how components are used in the system. To do this, we will introduce four basic component usage models:

Four major usage models for components

- Service: The service usage model provides the most scalability and is completely stateless. The corollary to this is that in order for a service-style component to act on state, the state must always be fetched. This can be cumbersome and expensive. The service model is useful for natural "processes" (e.g., looking up a phone number) and where high concurrent usage and scalability are requirements. The service model is not good for objects that have a large amount of state, nor for those that are part of "conversations," or where there are only a small number of these objects.

The service model is the most scalable

- Session: The session usage model matches a user session, for example, where the user logs on, performs a number of tasks, then logs off. There is "temporary" state associated with the user's transient session, but this state is typically not persisted to a database (the application controls how long the state is maintained). The session usage model provides for moderate scalability since there is one object per user session. The session ID is assigned automatically and is not visible or meaningful to the application (meaning that an application cannot use this ID to restore a dropped connection). Session objects can also be subject to state management in some technologies. In such cases, the session object has a hidden ID that allows the application server to manage its resources by swapping these objects out and restoring them as needed.

The session model mirrors a user session

The process model best maps to business processes

• Process: The process usage model allows the application to assign a meaningful identifier to a "process" object (although the ID may not be exposed to the client). An example is the "account manager" process component, which keeps track of the total activity each account manager did each day. But note that a client may not care which manager object it deals with. The process usage model typically uses a per-method or per-transaction state/memory management model. The process usage model provides for excellent scalability.

Entities should not be exposed directly to clients

• Entity: The entity usage model maps directly to the business entities that are represented by components. The business entity in question is addressed by a meaningful ID such as its key in a database. The entity usage model is useful within the enterprise tier, especially where entities are shared between processes. However, this is the least scalable model, especially when the entities map directly to clients, as in the example of John's account given earlier. These types of entities can consume significant system resources so they should not be exposed directly to clients.

Table 7.1 summarizes the component models.

Table 7.1   The four basic component usage models.

Component model	Scalability	Concurrency	Identity	State	State management
Service	maximum	N/A	none	none	method
Session	moderate	none	system	some	application
Process	high to moderate	best	application	some	method, application, or transaction
Entity	limited	possible	tied to data store	persistent	application, transaction, or process

Fundamental Interface Design Patterns

Earlier, we mentioned the importance of good interface design and some of the issues involved in distributed interfaces. Now let's look at some examples of distributed interface design patterns. In essence, a design pattern is a reusable approach to certain problems that crop up repeatedly in computer systems. There are more interface design patterns than those described below, but this is a sample of the more important ones for enterprise applications.

Facade/Mediator Pattern

The facade/mediator pattern inserts an "interface" object between the client and one or more business objects. The interface object provides coarse-grained methods for use by the client, and then performs a sequence of operations determined by the method call and its parameters. Thus, the facade presents a consistent interface to a set of differing operations. The mediator object manages the relationships between the process and entities involved in the operation. This is a very important pattern for reducing dependency between process components, thus making the components reusable in a variety of different applications. The activity controller (described in the "Enterprise Tier" section of "Application Scenarios" below) is an example of this pattern. (See Figure 7.3.)

Mediators manage object relationships

Controller/Process Pattern

The controller/process pattern also puts an interface object between the client and one or more business objects. In this case, the interface object presents a process-style interface that then acts on business entities. The interface requires the client to pass an ID to the controller, and this ID identifies the entity to be acted on. An example of this pattern is passing an account ID to an account

Process controllers provide the best scalability

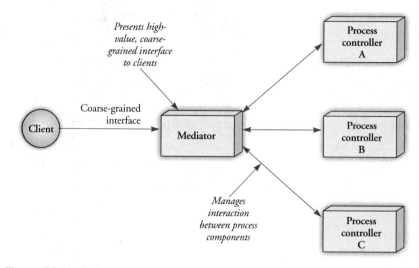

Figure 7.3 Mediator pattern.

manager component so that it can operate on that account. The controller/process pattern is very scalable because it uses stateless, concurrent objects, and few objects are instantiated. In addition, it provides for distribution and management at a higher level of abstraction, it is simpler to use and maintain, and it encapsulates the implementation, thus providing more opportunity for reuse. (See Figure 7.4.)

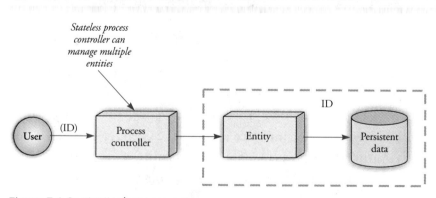

Figure 7.4 Controller/process pattern.

Value Object Pattern

The value object pattern maximizes request granularity and performance by passing the data associated with an object from the
server to the client. The purpose of this pattern is to increase request granularity and concurrency by operating on bulk data. The
client then acts on the data locally. When the client is done with
the data, it is passed back to the server, synchronized, and stored.
Note that when the data is moved, "ownership" of the data is also
explicitly transferred. So this pattern allows client programs to access data without locking it on the server (which is useful in situations where the client needs the data for a relatively long time in
order to complete a business process. Thus, this pattern also handles different concurrency and locking scenarios and is a basic pattern of Java. (See Figure 7.5.)

Value objects
maximize
performance

Component Factory Pattern

The component factory pattern addresses one of the most common (and important) problems in distributed component systems—how does a client find a business object? The component
factory pattern provides a simple and consistent method for doing

Components are
created by factories

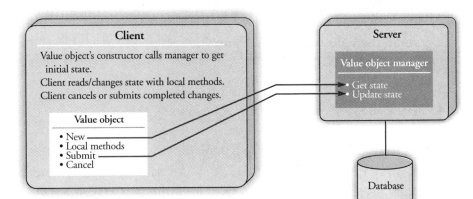

Figure 7.5 Value object pattern.

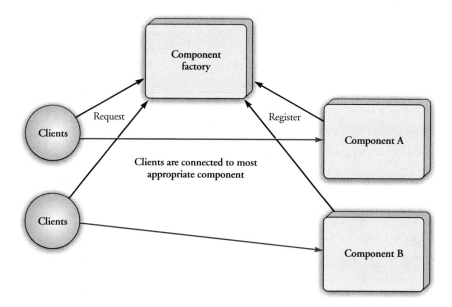

Figure 7.6 Component factory pattern.

this. In addition, the fact that it acts as an intermediary in the component creation process allows the application to make use of external knowledge (e.g., business rules and policies) when creating the reference to the component. Thus things like security, user profile, application partitioning, and so on can be taken into account when the object is created, without involving the client program in these decisions. (See Figure 7.6.)

Application Scenarios

This section shows some sample implementations of the architecture using specific technologies. We show a sample implementation of each tier: the user and workspace tier using Java, the enterprise tier using EJB, and the resource tier using XML and messaging. Remember that these are just examples, and that it is the implementation architecture that provides the details of this mapping for each specific application, including hardware and software products and platforms.

Presentation Tier

The implementation of Web-based clients and Java-based Web servers is shown in Figure 7.7, which illustrates which layers execute within the Web browser and which execute in the Web server. The presentation of information itself—that is, the user interface—is an HTML Web page. Parts of the presentation may also be implemented as a Java applet.

Presentation in HTML executes in the browser

Local input validation is done within the browser environment itself. If the application is using applets, then some of the validation can be done in the applet logic. Validation can also be done in JavaScript, which can be downloaded as part of the HTML.

Local validation is done in the presentation environment

The view controller is implemented as a Java servlet. (A Java servlet is an alternative to a CGI program. A Java servlet is *persistent but stateless,* meaning that once it is started, it stays in memory

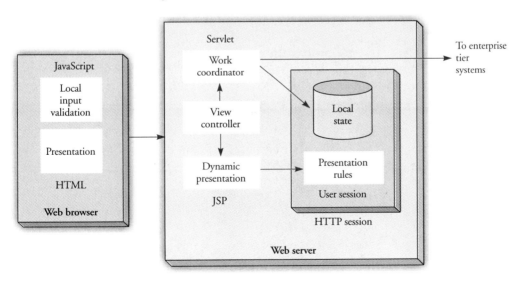

Figure 7.7 Java implementation of the user/workspace tier.

Java servlets process the input/output for the page

and can fulfill multiple requests. The persistent nature of Java servlets means that there is no time wasted in process setup and teardown as is the case for CGI.) The view controller is responsible for

- input of data from the Web page
- interaction with the work coordinator

The work coordinator is also implemented as a Java servlet. In many systems, the view controller and work coordinator will be combined into the same servlet. The work coordinator is responsible for

- interaction with the enterprise tier systems
- preparation of data output for the next Web page
- navigation to the next Web page

Once the next Web page has been determined, the data to be displayed (if any) is passed to the corresponding Java Server Page (JSP) for that page to dynamically create the page's HTML.

JSPs create dynamic presentation content

The specific output (HTML) for each Web page is created dynamically by a JSP. (Java Server Pages are built on top of servlets and provide a way to reduce the amount of literal HTML in servlet code. Thus JSPs provide a programmatic way to generate HTML dynamically.) Each Web page has a corresponding JSP. Part of the processing of the JSP is to apply rules to the HTML presentation (such as whether certain fields are editable or not, which might depend on the rights of a specific user).

Presentation rules can take a variety of different forms and can be applied to both input and output values. Some examples of input rules are

- default values for different fields
- allowable values for different fields

- required versus optional fields
- dependencies between fields

In some complex systems, these presentation rules can be externalized and placed in a "rules engine." However, this is not strictly necessary, and rules can be coded directly in the JSPs. In fact, some rules (e.g., default values and allowable values) can be handled directly by the HTML elements contained in the page. Other rules (e.g., dependencies between fields) can be implemented in JavaScript and appended to the HTML output by the JSP.

Presentation rules control content and allowable actions

In many systems, there is information related to a "session" for a particular user, such as log-in status, permissions, and temporary state storage. Web servers conveniently provide an HTTP session object that is associated with a particular user connection. This object is used to store the temporary session state information required by the view controllers.

Session state is managed by the Web server

Enterprise Tier

A large part of a software architecture is focused on the enterprise tier and the construction of business processes, business entities, and infrastructure services. Figure 7.8 shows how these are implemented as EJB objects.

The upper left of Figure 7.8 shows an activity controller component. An activity controller mediates the flow of control in an application, in support of the business tasks the user wants to accomplish. The granularity of an activity controller maps roughly to the amount of functionality described in a use case and can therefore vary greatly. Note that controlling the flow of an application may also be accomplished by workflow logic, which may be implemented externally in a workflow engine.

The activity controller mediates the flow of control

In Figure 7.8, the activity controller is implemented as an EJB stateless session bean following the service usage model described

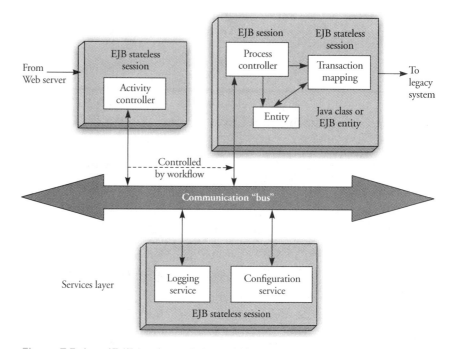

Figure 7.8 Java/EJB implementation of the enterprise tier.

The activity controller provides a service-style interface

earlier. A stateless service provides a request-response–style interface where a client provides input and asks the service to perform some sort of task on that data. The service has no data or identifier associated with any specific request, and so allows for maximum flexibility in scaling, location, and load balancing of the server(s) providing the service.

The activity controller is a stateless service

The activity controller presents a mediator-type interface to the user/workspace domain. Data is collected in that domain and passed to the activity controller. Data is returned from the enterprise tier to the user/workspace domain through the activity controller. However, the activity controller does not itself maintain any user data (although it might maintain some data about the activity itself). Therefore, the activity controller can be thought of as a stateless service.

The scalability requirements of an activity controller will vary according to business activity. There may be some cases where very large scale is required, and other cases where it is desirable to limit the amount of resources allotted to a smaller-scale activity. In either case, the lifetime of a particular activity controller object can be limited to the execution of one of its methods.

Activity controllers can support large-scale applications

One of the responsibilities of the activity controller is to act as a transaction boundary. Here again, the particular requirements will vary depending on the activity—some will require that a transaction span the various services used by it, and others will not require transactions.

Activity controllers manage transactions

At the upper right of Figure 7.8 are the business objects, which include both processes and entities. In order to accomplish a particular task, process controller components may cooperate with entity components. And any component may invoke operations on application adapters and other components.

Processes are called by activity controllers

A entity is implemented as an EJB entity bean and is responsible for presenting an entity interface to the rest of the application. The entity may relate directly to data in a database, in which case container-managed persistence could be used, or it may map to data in a package application, in which case a resource manager would be used for persistence. In either case, the entities are used by the process controllers and not made available directly to the clients.

Entities are used by processes

The infrastructure services are implemented as EJB stateless session beans. Services almost always follow a stateless model.

Resource Tier

The application adapter "wraps" the legacy system and presents a component-style interface to the enterprise tier. The adapter communicates with the legacy system, typically by passing messages through a service like MQSeries. The message passed from

Messages are sent to the legacy systems

the adapter to the legacy system is in XML format, as shown in Figure 7.9.

XML is good for formatting messages

XML allows us to use a standard, self-describing message format that can, at the very least, provide a "least common denominator" foundation for communication. In addition, XML allows messages to be extended *and* it specifies that unknown tags should be ignored.

This is very important because it greatly aids upward compatibility. If a new application adds a new tag, old applications can simply ignore that piece of data while still operating correctly on the data items (within the XML data stream) that they do understand.

XML messages can be extended

XML's popularity is increasing very quickly, and many tool vendors now support it. That is also an important point because for XML to work well in the context of the overall enterprise, tool support—at the very least for repositories of corporate metadata—is a requirement.

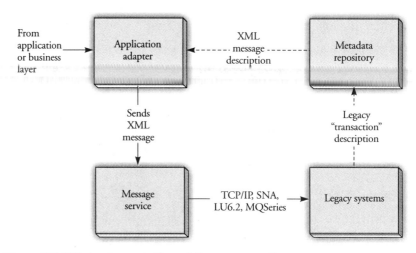

Figure 7.9 XML implementation of the resource tier.

XML tags must be managed such that a given tag has the same meaning, even in different applications. Thus, if a tag for a data item is called *CustomerName,* the format of that data should be the same for every application that uses it—and for every new application that needs a *CustomerName* as well. In order to accomplish this, the XML tags need to be managed in a centralized fashion that allows developers to search for and view tags and their meanings. In addition, the relationships between tags and applications need to be understood so that the impact of changes can be accessed on an enterprise level. These are all features that are supported by a metadata repository.

So to complete the picture, the legacy system interface is described in a corporate metadata repository (typically in UML). Since the system is described in UML metadata (a neutral format), the XML messages and associated software artifacts can be automatically generated from the repository, using tools provided by the repository vendor.

XML tags must be managed

XML schemas can be generated by repository tools

Summary

This chapter began with a description of the component factory and went on to describe various design considerations for components. We then discussed some fundamental design patterns that can be reused to address commonly encountered technical requirements. Finally, we described how components built from these patterns can be assembled into a multitier distributed application.

While it may not be obvious from where we stand today, we are riding a trend that will eventually see the automation of virtually all of the capabilities described in this chapter. Over time, more and more of these capabilities will be standardized in architectural patterns and made part of the component factory.

Over time, much of this will be automated

In this chapter we have expanded on the technical architecture and discussed the important concepts for implementing component systems. However, technology and architecture are only part of what is required to be successful in e-business applications. In the next chapter we will return to a higher-level analysis and consider how a company must organize a transition from conventional software development to the type of development that must be employed to succeed as an e-business.

Managing the Transition to an E-Business

In this chapter we want to pull together a number of different

threads that we have discussed in earlier chapters and provide read-

ers with a generic approach to changing their IT organizations in

order that they can support a corporatewide e-business transition.

CIO magazine recently reported on a survey undertaken by

PricewaterhouseCoopers and the Conference Board. The survey

included 80 large companies. Ninety percent of the 80 companies

had an annual revenue of $1 billion or more. Fifty percent had income in excess of $5 billion. The companies ranged from manufacturing, energy, and transportation to financial services and retail. Seventy-nine percent of the companies said that e-business accounts for less than 5% of their revenues. Sixty percent do not have Internet-based supply chains. Only a quarter of the group has yet to move beyond basic Web "brochureware" applications. Only 28% can process a transaction online. In essence, about 75% of the large companies have yet to begin any kind of serious transfer to e-business. Most may have a Web site, but only a quarter are in a position to build supply chain or e-commerce applications.

Most large companies haven't begun to transition

In other words, in spite of all the articles and commentary about how quickly everyone is moving to the "new economy," in fact most large companies are holding back. In the language of Geoffrey Moore, e-business is still being tried by Innovators and Early Adopters, and has not really crossed the chasm yet, or, if it has, is holding on the Early Majority side of the chasm by its fingertips. This isn't to argue that it won't cross and rapidly move beyond its current 25%, but it is to suggest that many large companies are still thinking about exactly how to go about becoming e-business organizations.

Few companies relish a major reengineering effort

We suggest that this caution is quite reasonable. In earlier chapters, we've surveyed some of the problems companies have developing new strategies for e-business and in redesigning their business processes for the e-business era. We have also considered what's involved in component-based development and defined an architectural approach to developing e-business applications. We repeatedly suggested that any serious move toward an e-business model will necessarily require the company to reengineer its IT organization.

E-business applications are different than conventional applications. Large, serious e-business applications are necessarily distributed component-based applications. They rely on the use of component-based software development techniques and component middleware. This may not seem like a bad thing to those who are comfortable with component technologies, but, in fact, for most companies, for IT to use these technologies would require a major change. It would require different tools and techniques, different methodologies and developer skill sets, and different ways of measuring and testing the new applications. Most large companies have a group that has experimented with large-scale component-based development, but few have more than an elementary knowledge of how to use distributed, component-based techniques on the scale necessary to support a corporate transition to e-business. We imagine that those that have the capability are among the 25% of the large companies that already can process transactions online and are beginning to put supply chain systems in place.

One major transition problem: reengineering the IT organization

In this chapter we want to talk about the experience of a few companies that have already transitioned to distributed component-based development. Our information comes from consulting contracts that were undertaken by Genesis Development Corporation over the past several years. In the process of helping a number of different companies make the transition to distributed component development, Genesis has become expert in helping companies plan transitions. This chapter provides a generic overview of the more detailed transition model that Genesis uses when it helps its clients. We don't propose that this is the exact pattern to follow, but only that it illustrates an overall approach and the major steps that lots of successful transitions have employed.

A proven transition methodology

Types of Transitions

By definition, startups don't need to transition. They simply start from scratch and create an e-business company. Startups don't have legacy systems to worry about, nor do they have programmers left over from another era or experienced in the use of now outdated methodologies. On the other hand, of course, they don't have any

Startups don't need to transition

experience in actually providing products and services to real customers. In 1999 you might have assumed that any e-business startup could quickly raise a large amount of venture capital to facilitate a rapid development effort. Since early 2000, however, venture capitalists have become a little more discriminating, and e-business companies are often asked for reasonable business plans before being funded.

Midsized and large companies must plan carefully

Small established companies probably face the hardest choices. If they want, they could begin a transition and complete it within a year. On the other hand, as a broad generalization, most small companies buy their software from others and are less sophisticated in the development of software systems. Although the techniques in this book can be used in small companies, we are focusing on midsized and larger companies—companies that simply can't transition quickly, or if they do, transition one division or unit at a time. These companies have significant investments in existing hardware and software and trained groups of IT personnel. In other words, they have resistance to any rapid change. A transition at a midsized to large company has to be planned to have any chance of success.

Our assumptions

Some companies find themselves in the awkward position of having outsourced their legacy systems and, therefore, not having control over their software resources just at the time when they will need to be the most flexible. Our assumption here, however, is that we are describing a midsized company that is in full possession of its systems and wants to undertake a systematic transition to e-business as quickly as possible. Assume that the company wants to begin by letting its customers get quotes and buy products online, reducing its field salespeople and store operations, improving its manufacturing operations in order to compete with the newer, lower prices that some competitors are offering online, and, simultaneously, linking with suppliers. The question is, How should the managers think about the transition? More specifically, how should the corporate IT department think about its transition?

An Overview

In Figure 8.1, we've superimposed one diagram over a table. The diagram that fills the top left of Figure 8.1 provides a very generic view of the transition process that a company goes through when it

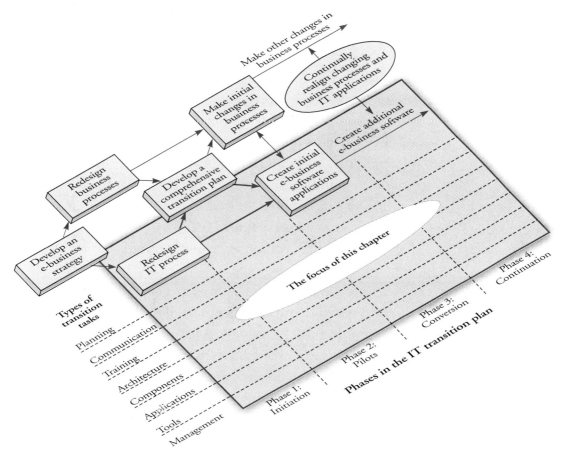

Figure 8.1 An overview of the topics that will be considered in this chapter.

decides to change itself into an e-business. We've used variations of this figure elsewhere in the book to show where we are in the process.

Our discussion of the transition process begins with the leftmost box, labeled "Develop an e-business strategy." In other words, the first step is for senior executives of the company to consider where the company is now and how the environment is changing. Based on this, they can determine if there is a viable e-business strategy the company can adopt.

Reengineering the IT organization

Once the executives identify an appropriate e-business strategy for their company, they are ready to proceed into the detailed planning that will be necessary in order to achieve their strategic objectives. We've suggested, at that point, that they face two more or less independent problems. On the one hand, they need to redesign core business processes that they will need to change in order to change the company into an e-business (Chapter 3). At the same time, however, most companies will also need to redesign their information systems (IT) process in order to support the e-business transition. And that is the focus of this chapter, which will draw together several threads that we have discussed in earlier chapters on components and architectures.

E-business software development requires major IT changes

The redesign of the corporate IT organization involves more than simply developing new applications to support the modified company business processes. That needs to be done, of course, but it can't be done efficiently or effectively unless more fundamental changes are also made. E-business applications require a different approach to software development than most corporations currently employ. The Internet and the Web require a distributed component architecture; a distributed infrastructure that relies on component middleware; the development of business components to support the development of e-business applications; and the use of new software development methodologies, new languages, and new tools. To make matters worse, large Internet applications must be integrated with the large legacy applications that the company currently relies upon. If you want to sell via the Internet, then you need to link your Web application with your accounting applications. If you want to provide information to customers about the status of their orders, you must link the new Web systems with existing manufacturing and inventory systems. And, of course, if you want to develop supply chain applications, the application must be able to link the various different legacy applications of all of the suppliers in the system. Most e-business systems are necessarily enterprise application integration (EAI) systems.

Most large companies have experimented with these new technologies, but they do not have IT organizations that are currently prepared to support these new technologies on a large scale. Software analysts, developers, and programmers will need to learn new techniques and the use of new tools. More importantly, they will need to learn a whole new way of thinking about application development.

E-business development requires a new mind-set

The transition that the IT group will need to make involves major changes and can't be accomplished overnight. Any company that tries to accomplish this transition too quickly is simply preparing itself to fail. The new Internet startups that large companies will often find themselves competing with don't have legacy applications or programmers trained in older techniques. Instead, they have hired new developers trained in the latest distributed component techniques and developed applications that are highly tailored for the Internet environment. Having used the latest techniques, the startup companies are in a position to rapidly change their applications as new developments in e-business take place. This is vital, since all e-business models are so new. Every company must plan on major changes in any e-business process it develops in the next year or two. Approaches that seem valid today will

E-business development methodologies must build in flexibility

undoubtedly be proven less successful than newer approaches that experimental companies will introduce in the near future. Any Internet application that is to succeed must have flexibility built in.

Changes are necessary and take time

Figure 8.1 suggests that any company that wants to redesign its IT process and create new e-business applications will, in fact, have to undertake a major IT transition. The matrix that lies below the "Redesign IT process" and the "Create initial e-business software applications" boxes suggests some of the types of tasks and some of the phases that companies will need to consider. We'll look at the tasks and phases in more detail in a moment. At this point, suffice it to say that an IT transition can't take place too quickly. It takes time to retrain developers and create reusable components.

We've sometimes stated the problem like this: How can a company do quickly what can't be done quickly?

Transition in phases

The answer is that you create a plan that makes the needed changes over time, but that develops some applications before the transition is complete. In effect, you choose pilot applications that require infrastructure and component development that you will need to undertake in any case. Your initial applications may not be as neat and efficient as you might like, but if you undertake the applications fully aware that you are making a transition and aware of where the initial applications are less than perfect, you will also know how to return and improve them when you are prepared to do so.

A Transition Plan

Some organizations set up separate companies to oversee their entry into the e-business arena. Others set up a group within the existing organization or even try to convert the entire existing organization more or less simultaneously. No matter what type of transition the company plans to undertake, it will have major implications for the IT organization.

As you can see by glancing at Figure 8.1, we have divided the transition into four phases:

- Phase 1: Initiation
- Phase 2: Pilot development
- Phase 3: Conversion
- Phase 4: Continuation

In Phase 1 you plan for the transition. In Phase 2 you start the conversion by developing a new architecture and the infrastructure needed to develop a set of pilot projects. You gradually accumulate the infrastructure and the components you need by developing carefully selected pilot projects that solve pressing needs for immediate action while simultaneously laying the groundwork for a more extensive transition. Depending on the size of the company and the pressing needs for e-business applications, there may be a few or many pilots, and the pilots may entail minimal or extensive development efforts. When the pilot phase ends, the company has a core of trained developers and a basic distributed component architecture, an infrastructure, and a core set of components. It also has experience in the use of new methodologies and experience with new software development tools and techniques. During Phase 3 a more extensive transition takes place, and the majority of the company's IT developers are trained and assigned to appropriate projects. Everything that was started in Phase 2 is extended and made more robust in Phase 3. Phase 3 ends when the IT organization is fully up to speed on e-business development and ready to support any new development efforts the company may choose to undertake. Phase 4 is simply the ongoing management of an e-business IT organization.

The transition takes place in four phases

Figure 8.2 provides an overview that shows the phases, the generic tasks, and some of the specific activities that must occur during the transition. We'll consider each of these phases in more detail below. Specifically, we will consider each of the major transition tasks that keep recurring during each phase of the effort and the unique activities that occur in each phase. These tasks are illustrated on the vertical axis of the table shown in Figures 8.1 and 8.2. They include planning, communication, training, architecture, components, applications, tools, and management issues. As we consider these tasks we will arrive at a list of the goals of each

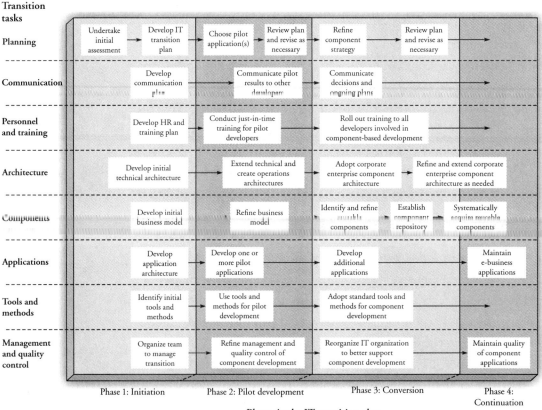

Figure 8.2 An overview of the tasks and activities to be accomplished during an IT transition.

phase, the people involved, the key deliverables, some milestones, and a rough schedule.

Phase 1: Initiation

The overall goal of the initiation phase is to commit the organization to a systematic transition. To do this senior management must become involved and committed, and plans must be laid to assure that the subsequent phases occur in a systematic manner.

The goal

Organization of Phase I

The initiation phase aims at nothing less than planning for the transformation of the entire corporate IT organization. Thus, from the beginning, the top IT management must be heavily involved. Outside consultants are usually hired to provide expertise in what will need to occur, but only internal managers will know how the transition will need to be managed, because only internal managers know the company culture, the historical constraints the specific IT organization operates under, and the strengths and weaknesses of existing staff and resources.

Outside help is usually needed

Most organizations set up a transition team. It is usually chaired by the CIO or the head of the IT group. This team is responsible for developing the plan that results from the initial phase of the transition effort.

The transition team

If the company has a higher-level e-business or BPR team, the individual who leads the IT transition team should also be a member of the higher-level committee, since IT will need to coordinate its efforts with the overall business process redesign efforts.

Planning

The key to the success of the transition effort is to develop a set of pilot projects that provide some immediate value to the company,

Pilot projects

while simultaneously using those projects to incrementally train employees and lay the foundations for a more extensive transition in subsequent phases. Thus, planning should focus initially on what the company is committed to do quickly, and then on how to structure projects to achieve both business and infrastructure development objectives.

As a generalization, most companies will want to hire outside consultants that have experience in developing distributed component systems to help them determine how to maximize the side effects of their initial pilot efforts.

Begin by assessing where the organization stands

Before any planning is undertaken, however, the IT organization should undertake an assessment of where the organization currently stands. Most large organizations already have some experience with distributed component-based development, and it's important that the team begin with an objective assessment of the organization's current strengths and weaknesses. Most organizations hire an outside organization to conduct the assessment to assure objectivity. In some cases the outside organization will simply sum up the strengths and weaknesses. In other cases, they will make recommendations that can form the basis for the company transition plan.

Any good transition plan must take a number of things into account. The pilot projects must provide opportunities for many different things to occur. We have listed the key tasks and activities that will need to be covered in the plan in Figure 8.2 and will consider each below.

Communication

Tell everyone in IT about the transition

The decision by senior management to convert a business into an e-business needs to be communicated. Employees are bound to wonder what roles will exist for them in the new IT organization. Since the job market is very tight and many IT developers have specialized knowledge of their company's legacy applications, it's important that these individuals be assured that the company is committed to training in order to prepare its existing IT people to function in the new e-business IT organization.

Most companies we know of that have undertaken a systematic transition have reported that their IT people were excited to be part of a transition. They were especially happy to be involved in a systematic transition. Nobody likes to be asked to accomplish impossible tasks with unrealistic deadlines. IT organizations that simply launch into e-business application efforts, without considering the broader changes needed in architecture and infrastructure, quickly run into trouble. IT employees know this, and they also know they can find another job rather easily. So it's in the company's interest to plan not only a systematic transition but a systematic communication program that will inform employees of the company's goals, how specific pilot projects fit into the broader picture, and how training will be managed to assure that existing employees become valued members of the new e-business IT organization that the company will develop.

IT people like systematic transitions

Personnel and Training

Organizations that undertake a transition need to develop a systematic training program to provide the new skills needed for developing e-business applications. Initially, training will need to be provided for the team selected to undertake the pilot project. Later, as additional pilot projects are added and then as large-scale conversion is undertaken, the training will need to be extended to more and more developers.

Training begins with the first pilot project

We recommend that a combination of consultants and newly hired employees with expertise in distributed component development be used during the early stages of the transition to manage, guide, and mentor the pilot development efforts. The consultants can provide expertise in architecting and designing the pilot projects. They can also assure that the projects occur on schedule.

Hire experienced developers to ease the transition

Their main function during the pilot phase, however, is to transfer expertise to the company's developers. Hiring a few experienced developers from outside can also give this transfer process a boost.

Just-in-time training

We also recommend just-in-time (JIT) training. Employees ought to be given tailored training for what they are about to attempt, just before they actually attempt an activity, and not generic training months in advance of when they will need the new skills. Consultants can provide the training for the pilot teams as needed. Pilot team employees should then provide the same training to other employees during the subsequent phase.

One goal: Gain experience in reusable components

The goal of component-based development is to reduce the time required to develop new applications by reusing components from other projects. Thus, to create an organization that can consistently and quickly generate new e-business applications, a company must first develop a set of reusable components. It's harder to develop reusable components than it is to develop components that will only be used once. Reusable components must be carefully crafted to assure that they are sufficiently generic and can easily be used in multiple applications. Thus, one of the goals of the pilot phase is to gain experience in developing components and then, on subsequent pilot projects, to gain experience in reusing them. (Thus, in planning its initial pilot projects, the management team ought to consider how components might be reused from one project to the next.)

The transition will transform the IT group

Most organizations find that to consistently reuse components, they need a group within IT that specializes in developing and maintaining components for reuse. Thus, in the long run, as an IT organization transforms itself into an e-business software development organization, it will tend to redefine jobs and roles and create new specializations. This kind of organizational change should not begin during the pilot phase, but it should be undertaken during the subsequent phase. During the pilot phase we suggest that all employees be given a chance to try different tasks. It will become obvious to more experienced managers that some are better at creating and maintaining reusable components and that others prefer the process of application development, which will increasingly shift to the rapid assembly of reusable components.

At this point, suffice it to say that a good transition plan should anticipate the changes in job structures and salary structures that will eventually occur and begin to lay the groundwork for it.

A more complex issue that we don't have time to go into here is salary and motivation. Many companies have programs that reward developers, directly or indirectly, for writing lots of lines of code. The whole emphasis in a component-oriented development organization will shift to developing components that can be reused and to assembling components while writing only minimal code. Obviously these new goals will require new ways of thinking about what constitutes success and new reward structures.

The best book to read to obtain a detailed description of the organizational issues that personnel will need to anticipate is Ivar Jacobson, Martin Griss, and Patrik Jonsson's *Software Reuse: Architecture, Process and Organization for Business Success.*

Architecture

In Phase 1, company architects and developers, working with consultants, should develop a tentative application architecture that reflects the company's e-business goals and priorities. In effect, the application architecture describes the set of e-business applications that the company will want to develop. From this overall application architecture, specific applications (or parts of applications) should be selected to serve as pilot projects.

Develop a tentative application architecture

At the same time, the Phase 1 team should define a high-level technical architecture. At this point, this architectural statement is a tentative specification of the technologies to be used. It provides

Develop a high-level technical architecture

a first approximation of the infrastructure that the company will need to develop to support all its distributed component applications. It will be used to guide the developers during the next phase when specific applications are undertaken and will then be revised in light of experience gained in Phase 2.

Figure 8.3 is a slight variation of the architecture overview we described in Chapter 6. It emphasizes that some architectures are independent of actual applications, while some are application specific. In effect, in Phase 1, you review your company or domain needs and develop the more generic architectures. You then use the general and specific architectures in the development of pilot applications and refine the generic architectures in the process.

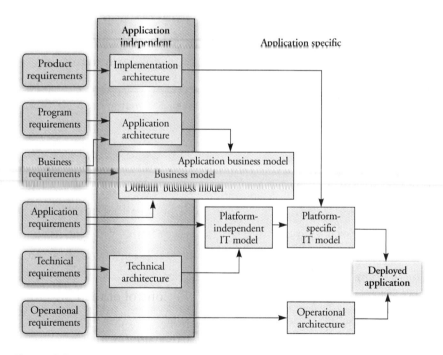

Figure 8.3 The architecture development process.

Components

A few organizations will already have some components that they can reuse. Most will have to begin by developing components for specific applications and then revise them for reuse. In the initiation phase, the transition team should focus on developing a very high level of the company's business model. If a single department is being transitioned, the business model may be a model of a specific domain. The business model will describe the company's or department's key business processes and entities and define how they relate to each other. As specific applications are developed, the business model will be defined more specifically, as components.

Develop a high-level business model

Applications

The application architecture will define a set of applications the company needs to develop. E-business priorities, combined with considerations of which projects will contribute to the development of infrastructure and reusable components, will narrow the field to a few pilot applications that can be developed in the next phase.

Define applications in the application architecture

Tools and Techniques

There will probably be some discussion of tools and specific techniques to be used in applications at this phase, but, in essence, decisions about tools and techniques ought to be left until the next phase and made in the context of specific projects.

Ignore tools and techniques

Management and Control

This task focuses on the management and control of the IT organization and of specific component-based applications. At this point, the priority is to establish an IT team to manage the entire transition process, and to coordinate the IT reengineering effort with the

Create a transition team

company's wider e-business transition efforts. Once it's established, in addition to overseeing all of the other tasks, this team should select employees for the pilot application development teams. The ideal developers for Phase 2 will be those who can learn quickly and who will be able to generalize from what they learn and contribute to the redesign of the IT organization and to the documentation of management and quality control standards during later phases.

Phase 2: Pilot Application Development

The goal

The overall goal of the second phase is to actually begin the transition. This phase is driven by carefully selected pilot application projects. In the course of developing the initial applications, employees are trained, the company's new architecture and infrastructure are initially implemented, and components are developed that can be reused on subsequent projects.

Organization of Phase 2

Undertake the first pilot application

This phase begins when the company starts its first pilot application effort and continues as long as necessary. Some companies will only undertake one or two pilot applications, while others will continue this process for one or more years and develop several different pilot applications. A transition team oversees the entire phase and evaluates the problems and successes of each pilot project. The team determines when the pilot applications have resulted in sufficient experience and the organization is ready to move on to a more extensive conversion.

Individual pilot applications are created by a team of architects and developers. Initially individuals try various tasks, but eventually some tend to specialize in higher-level component design tasks, while others tend to prefer to focus on implementation and systems tasks.

Planning

In this phase the company wants to undertake pilot projects that will produce applications that the company can use immediately, while simultaneously developing the infrastructure, components, and experienced employees needed for subsequent projects. This is perhaps the trickiest part of this whole approach, and it's worth hiring consultants with experience in both distributed component development and e-business application development to obtain advice on what can reasonably be done and what would strain your existing systems and employees to the breaking point.

Produce useful applications with side benefits

Figure 8.4 provides one overview of what you want to do. You can create a table version of this figure and fill in specifics in each of the boxes in the matrix as you plan the pilot phase.

Figure 8.5 provides another overview that you will want to consider. It simply illustrates the fact that companies tend to focus their efforts on customer interfaces, product and service management, and developing supply chains and linking to vendors. The table created by crossing the various tasks we are discussing with the three e-business focuses is another way to think about what kind of pilot projects you might want to consider.

Initial pilot selection

The key is to identify pilot projects that will advance your component architectural development and implementation and the training of personnel in an incremental manner. If the pilot is too complex or comprehensive, and you are forced to develop an extensive architecture, infrastructure, and component framework to support the development of the application, then you lose the advantage of an incremental approach. If you absolutely have to develop a very comprehensive project as your initial effort, then at

Keep pilot efforts limited

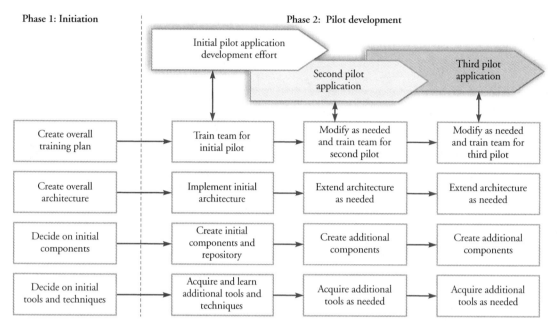

Figure 8.4 The systematic way to develop resources while undertaking pilot application development

least do the project in phases and, in effect, turn each phase into a pilot.

Meetings with the transition task force should be scheduled at intervals during the phase to determine if the pilot projects are on schedule and if the various task objectives are being met.

Communication

Communicate with developers not involved in initial pilots

As the pilots are undertaken, it's important to continue to provide developers not involved in the project with information on what is happening. Stress should be laid on the fact that the company is dedicated to providing training to its existing IT developers so that they will become skilled e-business systems developers.

Personnel and Training

The role of outside consultants

The company will probably use consultants to facilitate the initial pilots, but their role should be structured to assure that they men-

In previous chapters, we've argued that, broadly, a company can think of its e-business architecture as having three interrelated focuses: a customer focus, which is primarily centered on the Web site; a product focus, which concentrates on process efficiencies, tailoring products, and enterprise application integration; and an operational focus, which concentrates on integrating the company's supply chain.

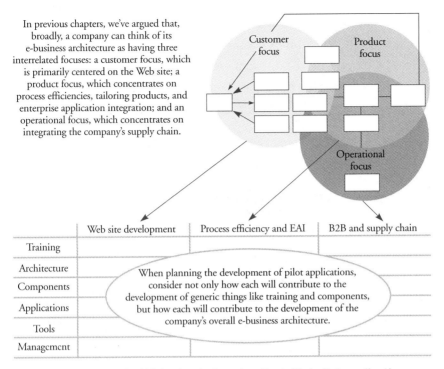

Figure 8.5 One way to think about choosing the initial pilot applications.

tor and advise and that company employees learn to actually develop the applications. (This will vary depending on the size of the pilot selected and the needs of the line organizations for specific applications to support changed business processes.) Most companies also attempt to hire a few new employees with experience in distributed component and Web development to enhance the knowledge transfer process.

Architecture

As we noted when we discussed architectures in Phase 1, some architectures are initially developed as very generic statements of intent, while others are only developed in the context of a specific application. Even those that are initially developed as generic architectures are refined as you begin to develop specific projects.

Improve initial architectures for specific pilots

Phase 2 is organized around pilot application development projects. As each development team tackles a pilot application, they begin by extending the abstract architectures developed in Phase 1 and proceed to expand on specific aspects of the architecture that are needed for that pilot application. This process is illustrated in Figure 8.6.

Components

Introduce component reuse

As described above, during Phase 2, specific applications are developed. Each application has its own component model, and each results in a number of implemented components. The company might acquire business components for use in the development of one or more pilot projects. There are a number of vendors that sell components, and several of the application server products come with some components. Companies that are less familiar with

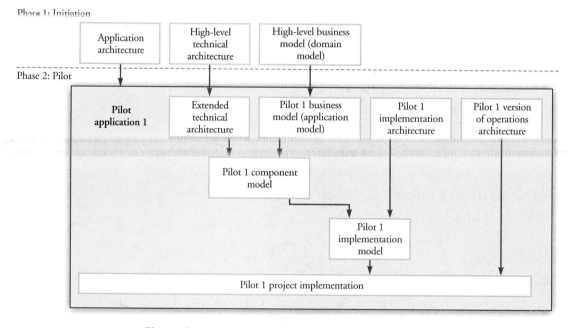

Figure 8.6 How the various architectures and models are extended to create a specific pilot application.

components will probably develop their own components during this phase, simply to learn more about what's involved in the development of components.

Applications

During Phase 2 anywhere from one to a half-dozen pilot projects are undertaken. In most cases two to three pilot applications will be sufficient. Each of these pilot efforts provides a development team with training, generates components, and provides the developers with opportunities to study different software development methodologies, middleware techniques, and tools. The goal is not only to produce applications that can be used immediately, but also to learn about component-based development and the systems problems involved in fielding e-business applications and to create the infrastructure that allows future applications to be developed in less time with less complexity.

Each completed pilot results in more experience

Tools and Techniques

During the pilot phase, the company should resist making firm commitments to specific tools or techniques. Some companies purposely undertake pilot projects that use different tools and techniques in order to learn more about options.

Management and Control

Initially, the transition team and pilot managers can experiment with new modes of managing software development as they explore the uses of architectures and the reuse of components. In most cases a company will adopt a published component development methodology to see how it works. As more projects are completed, they also explore reuse and testing and quality control of the components. This is not the phase for formalizing new

Managers also learn during pilot development

management and methodological practices, but of exploring alternatives to see what works best.

Phase 3: Organizational Conversion

The goal

We won't consider all of the tasks for this phase, but just the most important. In this phase, the organization begins by evaluating what occurred in the pilot phase and making some commitments to architectures and methodologies, based on those experiences. The goal of this phase is to convert the entire IT organization to e-business development and to train the entire IT staff in the techniques and methods already mastered by the teams that took part in the pilot phase.

Organization of Phase 3

Previously trained managers and developers guide the rollout

The organization of this phase is much more complex and varies greatly from company to company. It depends on the number of trained people the company now has, the number to be trained, the number of applications that need to be developed quickly, and a variety of other considerations. This phase involves rolling out distributed computing techniques to the entire IT organization. All of the IT managers will need to take part, and most of the employees will need to be assigned to e-business applications and trained.

Reorganize the IT group to reflect component reuse

During this phase, most companies will reorganize the management hierarchy and groups within IT. The organization will gradually shift so that some developers are primarily focused on the development and maintenance of components for reuse, some are focused on maintaining and enhancing the infrastructure, and others are primarily focused on developing applications and integrating legacy systems. This shift will require the redefinition of management jobs and developer roles, as well as shifts in pay and reward structures.

Planning

As with organization, planning varies greatly from organization to organization, depending on the numbers and how many applications need to be done in what timeframe. The initial plan for this phase will probably be modified by the transition team as a result of what was learned in Phase 2. The ideal plan systematically scales from the teams trained during the pilot phase to the training of the entire IT staff via a series of successively larger application development projects. Obviously this phase will be heavily influenced by the company's overall e-business conversion plan and the demands made by the core business process managers for IT support.

Plans vary with organizations and company goals

Architecture

The basic application architecture and core technical architecture should largely be in place at this point. From now on it should be a matter of gradually extending the architectures as new problems are encountered.

Components

The domain business model should also be largely complete at this point and will only need to be incrementally extended as new applications are undertaken. The main technical work of this phase will be the organization of the company's component resources for reuse. The components developed during the pilot phase are probably not robust enough for widespread reuse. Those components will need to be redesigned with widespread reuse in mind. The group that does this will probably evolve into the group that has long-term responsibility for building and testing reusable components and maintaining those already being used. Some

Components developed for reuse are emphasized

organizations will decide to acquire components from other organizations for reuse, and this group will also probably have the responsibility of testing and otherwise certifying any new components brought into the company.

Applications

Now individuals tend to specialize

The pilot projects may have required integration with legacy systems, but they were probably limited in scope. During the pilot phase the technical architecture gradually evolved into a robust middleware infrastructure that can support companywide application integration. During this phase, as larger e-business applications are begun, one group will probably specialize in developing a robust, scalable middleware system that can integrate all of the company's applications.

Pilot applications may be reimplemented

In some cases, the pilot applications will be reimplemented or expanded and enhanced during Phase 3. This assures that the applications developed during the pilot phase benefit from the experience acquired during that phase and the standards the company settled on at the end of the pilot phase.

Tools and Techniques

Standardize tools and techniques

During the pilot phase, a variety of tools and methods may have been tried. Experimentation will undoubtedly continue in this phase. At some point during this phase, however, the company should begin to standardize on some standards, tools, and methodologies and require these for subsequent application development efforts.

Management and Control

Quality control and testing measures are important

During this phase, managers who worked on the pilot projects during the first phase will probably work with new managers to develop a set of criteria to use in evaluating component development projects and estimate time and costs involved in new application efforts. Similarly, this phase should also focus on the development of testing and quality control measures that are appropriate for the management of the company's ongoing software development activities.

Phase 4: Continuation

We won't describe any of the tasks that occur in this phase in any detail. Suffice it to say that at some point the company's IT group will be converted and able to routinely create distributed component-based applications to support the company's e-business initiatives. From that point on, the company won't be in a transition mode, but will be developing criteria and methods to manage e-business development on a routine basis—and that in essence is the work of the continuation phase. Presumably the architectures will become very mature, components will be available for reuse, and application development will be much more rapid. In other words, component development will become standard, and the organization will be ready to deal with the next software revolutions that undoubtedly will be occurring by then.

Phase 4 involves continuing e-business development and maintenance

Summary

We have described a generic transition strategy that is designed to move a corporate IT organization from where it is today to a point at which it can routinely develop large distributed component-based applications that can be used to support corporate e-business initiatives.

We have not made any time estimates for the various phases. They will vary according to the size of the IT organization, the speed with which the organization needs to convert to e-business

Transition time varies widely

applications, and the existing knowledge and skills possessed by current IT employees. They will also vary according to whether the IT organization decides to rely on its own employees or to rely heavily on experienced consultants to undertake the planning and critical development tasks.

Consider a single task: the initial assessment of where the organization stands today and what it will need to do in order to make the transition. Most companies use outside consultants for this task. An outside assessment can vary from one month to six months, depending on the size of the organization and the detail of the report the consultants prepare. As a very broad generalization, smaller organizations have made the transition in a little under a year, while larger organizations normally take two or more years.

Some executives expect too much from IT

In the past six months we have encountered dozens of corporate software developers who have despaired of the pressure they were under to develop new business applications. A more general complaint was that company executives simply didn't have any idea what kinds of changes were involved in IT processes and methods in order to facilitate the development of large e-business applications. The people we talked to argued that senior managers were calling on their IT groups to develop applications in record time, without realizing that the changes in IT development methods and infrastructure necessarily meant that these first applications would take longer than conventional applications routinely required.

IT managers must explain problems and offer solutions

In part, this is a failure on the part of senior IT managers. They have apparently failed to communicate the need for changes in IT in order to support e-business development. The problem is more complex, however, since senior managers are focused on competitors or fear the entry into their market of a new Internet startup and are unwilling to listen to "excuses" since they feel the survival of the company is at stake. Senior IT managers need to come up with a plan that they can present to senior corporate managers that shows how IT can support the company's need for speed while simultaneously recognizing that the IT process needs to undergo a major reengineering effort. In other words, IT managers need to show the corporate executives how they can "do something quickly that can't be done quickly." They need to propose a transition effort that will generate some applications quickly to satisfy corporate needs while simultaneously using those initial efforts to systematically modify the nature of the corporate IT organization's capabilities. If the senior IT managers fail to be proactive in the current situation, they risk getting forced into an unplanned transition that will call for the development of applications before the IT organization has either the skills or the infrastructure to successfully complete the application—and that's a recipe for disaster.

The transition approach that we've described will not work for every company, but it has worked at many. It offers a generic approach that IT organizations can use as a starting point when they consider how they can support their companies as they transition into e-business organizations.

chapter

9

Retooling for the Internet Age

In this chapter, we want to describe an actual company, *enhansiv,* where the engineering organization has made the transition from supporting a conventional business model with a traditional approach to computing, to an approach more consistent with an Internet company. One of the authors assisted this company throughout its transition and is able to provide the kind of details that only someone intimately involved in the entire process can offer. We could have chosen a large company, with multiple divisions and several different engineering groups, but the details would soon have become overwhelming. *Enhansiv* is a good example, both because it successfully demonstrates the concepts we have been discussing throughout this book, and because the company is small enough to assure that the reader can understand exactly what happened. Most importantly, *enhansiv* is proud of what it has accomplished and is willing to allow others to read about its struggle to reengineer itself.

Most companies have only recently begun to consider the changes they will need to make to their core information systems in order to successfully deploy major applications on the Internet. This is just as true of software vendors as it is of companies selling more conventional products. Many software vendors, like the majority of their clients, are saddled with a large base of legacy code—much of it proprietary—that is hard to retrofit. Many are reluctant to create new products that will compete with their existing products.

Fortunately, that's not a problem at *enhansiv*. *Enhansiv* was formed from the convergence of three companies with years of experience delivering software and services to the Customer Relationship Managment (CRM) industry. Based on their collective experiences and a deep understanding of the far-reaching impact of the Internet on traditional methods of CRM solution delivery, the leadership of each of these companies shared a vision for a new delivery model for e-business CRM (eCRM). While other software and services companies were focused on extending their point solutions and patchwork quilt of software to accommodate the Internet and new delivery mechanisms enabled by the Internet, *enhansiv* saw a tremendous future in the creation of an extensible and flexible *virtual eCRM* solution platform. This vision drove *enhansiv* to create a tightly integrated, channel-independent eCRM application platform that could enable businesses to strategically manage interactions with their customers across the enterprise. *Enhansiv* is now realizing this vision through the deployment of a Web-based, object-oriented eCRM product architecture designed to support

- interaction-based functions such as voice, Computer Telephony Integration (CTI), e-mail, and Web co-browsing
- operational-based processes such as sales force automation, case management, and order management
- enterprise, high-value Customer Value Management (CVM) strategic capabilities such as customer loyalty management, customer complaint management, and customer retention

The result is a family of eCRM solutions that have been designed from the ground up with customer interaction management in mind. Without this customer value-based strategic solution perspective, traditional CRM applications cannot deliver a truly integrated CRM solution. Without a high degree of integration, CRM applications will be unable to deliver on their promise of providing businesses with the ability to consistently manage customer interactions across the enterprise.

In short, *enhansiv*'s vision of integrated, strategically focused, customer-centric eCRM solutions will revolutionize the way eCRM business solutions are created, implemented, and deployed.

Today *enhansiv* stands in sharp contrast to many other software vendors that are struggling to deal with the Internet revolution and the wide variety of new Internet-related development technologies such as Java, CORBA, and EJB. *Enhansiv*'s transition to a Web-based, object-oriented eCRM product architecture will allow the company and its clients to quickly adapt and respond to the accelerating emergence of new technologies and thereby extend its already strong position in the eCRM marketplace.

Enhansiv is in this position because this company made a conscious decision to rearchitect its entire software line and reengineer its engineering organization. They opted to shift to a distributed component-based approach. Luckily, this proved to be exactly the approach needed for large-scale Internet computing. What certainly seemed like a "bleeding-edge" bet several years ago is now paying a handsome dividend. As a result, *enhansiv* has been able to extend and position its component-based software right into the heart of today's Internet-driven software market, and to do so very quickly and efficiently. Moreover, because the companies that formed *enhansiv* began moving in this direction several years before, *enhansiv* has proceeded to quickly take advantage of the Internet and its knowledge of Internet-based computing to develop relationships with Internet companies that complement its own Internet-ready products.

Enhansiv's top management is, of course, delighted with this turn of events. From the beginning, *enhansiv*'s top management supported the engineering group's turn to components and distributed computing. At first, however, nobody fully anticipated just how well that decision would pay off. Today, *enhansiv*'s executives are busy figuring out new ways to exploit the flexible new technology that its engineering group was wise enough to put in place. Today, rather than wondering, like many of its competitors, whether it will shortly be upstaged by some upstart Internet company, *enhansiv* is an Internet upstart itself.

But getting a leg up on the Internet was not the advantage that *enhansiv* originally sought. Back in 1997, the main reason for moving to distributed component-based development was to improve the overall productivity and efficiency of its engineering operations. According to Daniel Riscalla, VP of engineering at *enhansiv*, who over that two years managed this transition to component development, even if the Internet had never assumed the importance it has, they would have been required to make the move, since the move allowed them to realize the following goals:

- Allowing developers to work more closely with business units and customers to precisely specify requirements before and during the development process
- Developing and delivering new applications and customizations much faster, rapidly porting products to new environments, and integrating legacy systems, databases, and system services
- Taking advantage of distributed computing to support high-volume transaction processing, distributed and federated "virtual" interaction centers, and simultaneously processing from/to multiple input and output channels
- Maintaining a clear, traceable trail from requirements through development and customization to better support long-term maintenance and evolution
- Establishing a strong architecture that can provide the levels of scalability, sustainability, and multitenancy required by the virtual eCRM model
- Allowing the business components to take advantage of newer technologies at the infrastructure level, such as moving to J2EE and EJB
- Increasing the quality of the product by leveraging a traceable process and reusing previously tested components
- Attracting, assimilating, and retaining top talent in a tight software labor market, and making more effective use of these scarce resources

The organization's transition to these new technologies was not easy. As we'll discuss, *enhansiv* is still learning, still growing, and still working its way through the transition process. In fact, the overall transition has not so much been from one steady state to another steady state. Instead, as a result of its investment in new technology, *enhansiv* today is able to be both dynamic and experimental, a must for any Internet-based business. In the rest of this chapter, we will examine how *enhansiv* managed to make that transition and the issues raised and answers discovered along the way. We'll also try to paint a picture of where *enhansiv* is today in its transition process and where it expects to go in the future.

The Business Challenge

Traditionally, most of *enhansiv's* customers relied on customer interaction center agents fielding customer phone calls. Legacy software products were originally designed to facilitate only the narrowly focused phone-based customer interaction. However, as *enhansiv's* management team examined business trends in 1997, they realized that this simple paradigm was already starting to break down. By 1997 the traffic load at call centers was increasingly controlled by sophisticated software that preprocessed inbound calls, filled in traffic gaps with outbound predictive dialing, and enhanced sales volume through scripted cross-selling. In the intervening years, the traditional paradigm has been further eroded by new electronic channels such as email, chat groups, and the Web. These channels are already generating large amounts of new traffic and changing the mix of activities at customer interaction centers. *Enhansiv* and others project that electronic traffic volumes could jump by an order of magnitude as customers employ the Internet to contact companies for information and support. Some of the inquiries, of course, can be handled by automated systems. However, many still require human intervention, and some may even require more complex human interaction, as, for example, responding to a complex bid. Vendors like *enhansiv* must be ready to deliver these new capabilities before these new requirements and higher volumes overwhelm their customers.

Changing Software Strategies

While the senior management team was refocusing its business, the engineering group focused on how to change its strategy, processes, and tools to produce new products. Of course, the engineering group needed to develop new products while continuing to support the existing products and a variety of legacy-based client applications. Juggling these conflicting priorities was a major challenge to the transition effort. One option was simply to freeze the legacy products and development on the legacy products until the new software came online. This would have focused most resources on the new approach, but it would have been a kamikaze move in which the company would give up its revenue stream and "bet the farm" on its new product line and its timely delivery. Another scenario would have split the development team into two, one that supported the old technology and one that supported the new. This is what happened at *enhansiv*. At the beginning, this would have meant dividing available resources and development staff, which in the short run could have crippled the company.

Enhansiv's management compromised by creating an advanced technology group that would segregate itself to create a new vision of software development. In brainstorming with the business experts about the overall approach to this transition, the group ultimately decided to move to components (then called "objects") and open distributed computing.

One major factor in their decision was that customer interaction centers were moving away from centralized, monolithic configurations and toward distributed, federated approaches, with traffic apportioned among various locations. This approach suggested that new software should include a commercial object request broker (ORB), a technology that was rapidly gaining ground on traditional messaging middleware and beginning to dominate PC-based development tools, especially those aimed at graphical user interfaces (GUIs). Since the legacy product had a strong GUI component already, this approach struck a familiar chord. As the advanced technology group continued its research and tool evaluations, its thinking coalesced around the new component-centric software architecture in which almost everything in the computing environment is reduced to some type of component (business processes and entities, system services, GUIs, platforms, etc.), all interacting through a universal bus—the ORB.

If this approach proved successful, the group reasoned, *enhansiv* would gain the long-touted advantages of object-oriented development (reuse, ease of change, faster development, improved quality) in the kind of large-scale distributed environment it had to support. This technology was relatively new, and available commercial tools were still immature, which the group viewed as not necessarily a bad thing. As the technology matured, *enhansiv* would have time to make its own transition and still come out ahead of later entrants, and there were sufficient available tools to support the development of prototypes and even initial products.

To make this happen faster, *enhansiv* decided to look for a consulting company to help the transition and chose Genesis Development Corporation, which had been working exclusively in object technology since 1987 and had already helped on a number of large-scale, distributed computing projects. Genesis, which has since been acquired by Iona Technologies, was active in OMG and helped to develop CORBA, Inter-ORB, and other standards. From its experience, Genesis had developed a methodology, called

Suretrack, for transitioning companies to distributed objects and components and had used it in several previous engagements. This reinforced *enhansiv*'s view that the technology, while still young, was starting to become very viable.

A Journey of a Thousand Miles

With any major initiative, once the preliminary research is done and a decision to proceed has been made, the hardest part is taking the first real step. For *enhansiv* this meant getting, and keeping, its key technology and management resources focused on the main issues of transition. They had to form a strong team to thoroughly digest this new technology, but the obvious team members were at first the same people the older technology group counted on for daily leadership and fire fighting.

This problem was compounded by *enhansiv*'s struggle with its overall transition strategy, as described earlier. The team was highly motivated to "get coding" but avoided the more abstract, yet absolutely critical issues, such as architecture and process, that must be settled prior to hard development. But with objects and components, the team soon learned, this "nuts-and-bolts" approach doesn't work very well, and they had to rethink their entire set of assumptions.

After six months of effort the team was beginning to master the complexities of distributed objects and was planning the deliverables when a sudden, all-hands-on-deck crisis occurred. Key transition team members were forced to focus on the crisis, and their work on the transition nearly halted. Other team members, advanced technology types, were spared, and they continued, with Genesis's help, albeit slowly. They wondered about management's commitment to the transition, and management itself had second thoughts. However, the factors driving the transition had not disappeared, but were growing with increasing rapidity. After about six months (one year total elapsed time), the crisis had abated enough for the full transition team to reassemble and resume serious movement.

In retrospect, this pause may have helped the transition team. The pressure to produce code had largely lifted, the advanced technology types had been able to focus on architecture and process issues, and software industry advances had confirmed the team's choice of object/component technology, producing more mature commercial tools and standards. When the team returned from "internal exile," it was ready to begin real product development and to progressively involve the rest of the company's engineering organization.

Flipping Channels

One of the major changes occurring during this period was the rise of the Internet and related technologies. In many companies this was treated as yet another crisis, forcing R&D groups to scramble for short-term patches to their traditional applications. But at *enhansiv*'s advanced technology group, the rise of the Internet meant a "second coming" for the transition to distributed components. In 1997, the transition team had reanalyzed its approach to software architecture along component lines, resulting in a formal architecture known as the internet Component Architecture (iCA).

In terms of the iCA, the Internet was just another specialized version of a "Channel" component, a handy abstraction, applicable to customer interaction center input or output. Other specializations of Channel included telephone calls, EDI transfers, email, ORB messages, and snail mail. We have seen how the architecture described earlier in Chapters 4 and 6 accounts for multiple channels and device independence. Since the team already understood these other specializations of Channel, adding another (even the much vaunted Internet) was not likely to break the model. As Frank Truyen, one of the iCA's main architects, put it:

> The development of a formal architecture, the iCA, was an essential part of *enhansiv*'s transition. The iCA allows us to manage continuous change effectively at a time when Internet speed has become the rule. One has to deal with rapidly changing business requirements as well as a constantly evolving set of infrastructure technologies. The iCA has been at the core of our reuse strategy, allowing us to isolate and manage any volatile requirements and resulting in improved time to market.

The team was able to provide *enhansiv* with a proactive, rather than reactive, Internet strategy. The plans for what would become the eCRM solution were already on the shelf and, with minimal dusting off, could be applied to the Internet. Not only did this avert a new crisis, it helped *enhansiv* turn the Internet craze into a great business opportunity.

The concepts behind the eCRM solution provided a powerful, compelling combination of business and technology incentives around which the transition, and the company, could be regrouped. The business rationale is that the eCRM solution will support the Internet and integrate with customer systems in more flexible ways than legacy solutions can. The technical rationale is that component technology will reduce not only initial development time but, more importantly, the time necessary to update and customize the eCRM solution for specific client environments.

The second half of 1998 saw the beginning of serious work on the eCRM solution product based on the emerging iCA. It is important to realize that the eCRM solution is a large business component, as opposed to a small GUI-style programming object. The eCRM solution is a complex component made up of at least three other major components. Each of these three components contains several Java objects to provide needed channel management functionality. Also, the current implementations of the eCRM components incorporate other software products, including an implementation of a set of iCA services. In other words, this system is a significant application that just happens to be designed and packaged as a component containing other components.

From a functional point of view, the eCRM component reads a wide variety of forms of messages (voice, text, etc.) and reformats them into a single standard request format. It relies on a rule-based "expert system" to analyze requests and determine if they can be answered by a stock response or need to be assigned to a human or other expert service provider. If necessary, the eCRM solution decides which service provider is best qualified to handle a particular request. Besides the rule-based system, the eCRM solution incorporates an object-oriented database to cache messages. Because the iCA encompasses the technology-independent characteristics of *enhansiv*'s architecture, it automatically incorporates the ability to interface with other CORBA, COM, and Java components (see Figure 9.1).

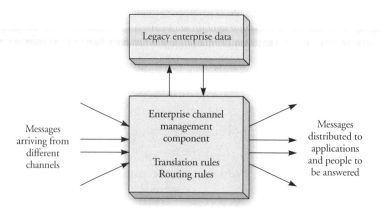

Figure 9.1 An overview of *enhansiv*'s enterprise channel management component.

Expanding the Transition

In mid-1998, the team, having analyzed the requirements and having created an overall design, began to take on new members to help develop the code. Component development requires a different mind-set, and it takes time for developers—even the most savvy—to change to this new perspective. A remark from an original team member, Rich Gibbs, summarizes this important point:

> When I was programming in C, I did all my analysis in my head. I didn't think about it explicitly. I simply thought about how to write the code and then wrote it. My self-image involved how many lines of good code I could write, and how quickly I could do it. When I was first trained in component analysis and design, that was the first time I ever thought about how an application should work without thinking about the code I was going to write. Later, when I started turning my design specifications over to someone else to code, it seemed strange to me. I wasn't sure I was really doing what I should. It requires that you think about problems in a whole new way. And it takes some time to get used to it.

An initial mentoring program was expanded to train the entire development group. The group received a two-week orientation that provided an overview of component technology, the new component architecture, and the new products *enhansiv* planned to develop. In the next phase, the initial advanced technology team organized its colleagues into smaller groups and conducted a systematic training program. Rather than assign individuals to specific tasks, management opted to provide generic training at the outset. Later in the process, the trainees could determine which tasks they preferred to do.

The logic of this approach becomes clear when compared to the previous development process. In the latter, the documentation group created new product documentation only after development was completed, by working backward from end user screens. In contrast, component analysis techniques and the "use cases" that define the functionality of each component provide a completely new model for creating product documentation. The generic training program, which presented all aspects of the component development process, enables the documentation specialists to significantly redefine their jobs. As Ernest Stambouly, a senior member of the development team, put it:

> Capturing analysis and design decisions in separate, non-code artifacts was a difficult process to learn. We were used to making those decisions on the fly while developing code. Our ability to separately capture those decisions has improved the quality of our work and of the product, and it has improved the ability of other departments, like support and documentation, to understand the product without having to read the code.

Enhansiv was also introducing a major change in the organizational structure of the development group. Previously, groups were organized to create specific applications. In 1998, changes were designed to maximize reuse. One group, whose core was the initial team, became component architects. Their job was to maintain the overall architecture and to create components for reuse. The remaining group was divided around specific projects. They were responsible for taking existing components and combining them into new applications. As Jason Matthews, president of Genesis, noted:

> *Enhansiv* really made the full transition to components when it understood that the most important assets to be produced by the development team were the components themselves, not the applications that were subsequently constructed from them. From that point on, *enhansiv* reinvented and reorganized its entire development structure and process around component projects, instead of traditional application projects. The group that is now *enhansiv* came to understand that applications are like yearly car models, changing constantly as the business market moves on. However, core component frameworks are

assets that can be reused across many applications for many years, as long as the basic business model remains the same.

As 1998 went on, more and more members of the engineering group were trained and assigned to work on the new eCRM development. In 1999, the testing and quality assurance group, the last to be transitioned, began the task of testing the eCRM components. The entire group became focused on completing the eCRM product and the supporting iCA infrastructure and tool set. The remaining tasks included testing and packaging, planning for subsequent components, and training others in the company to sell and support the eCRM offering. The transition of the quality assurance group resulted in a unique working relationship with the engineering group. As Daniel Riscalla described it:

> We realized that a component-based development process required an integrated relationship between our quality organization and our engineering group. The challenge was to integrate the quality group as part of the engineering teams to impact quality from the moment requirements are drafted while preserving a separate identity from the engineering group. Today our quality engineers are a core part of the engineering project teams, they participate in all phases of the development process from requirements to implementation, participate in all reviews and lead all quality related activities.

Genesis consultants were on hand to provide advice and specialized training throughout the transition process. However, Genesis's main focus was on training the initial team. That team, and those whom they trained, carried out almost all subsequent education and mentoring efforts. Indeed, most of the developers who helped train their colleagues consider that a significant element in their own transition process.

Although there were some tense periods at the beginning of the transition, by late 1998, enthusiasm was once again very high. It is noteworthy that, during the transition, the engineering group experienced zero turnover. In fact, two employees who had previously left for other jobs asked to be rehired after learning about the transition taking place at *enhansiv*.

The Home Stretch

The *enhansiv* advanced engineering group continued to evolve into a mature component development shop. The organization expanded from 23 largely traditional developers to 65 increasingly skilled component developers trained on OO analysis and design, Java development, J2EE, business modeling, and architectural services. Meanwhile, the group has continued to address the remaining tasks of this transition. A new product launch team was formed to work with product managers, salespeople, and professional service representatives to instruct them about components and the benefits of the new products to clients. The group also planned training courses for original equipment manufacturers who wanted to incorporate the eCRM component into their own packages.

The *enhansiv* management team became increasingly excited by the successful transition of its advanced technology, particularly by the promise of a new line of powerful, component-based products. The engineering managers were happy to have finished their first major new product, and they became confident in their ability to develop future software. By investing in training its existing team of developers, *enhansiv* avoided the high cost of recruitment in today's tough market. Today *enhansiv* has the largest group of skilled component developers in its industry.

Enhansiv also realized that, to be successful with this new technology, it must find ways to help its customers—and its industry—transition to component technology. This includes not only technical issues but also management issues, such as how to price and position components in a still mainly traditional, application-centric marketplace. As a result, *enhansiv* became involved in forums such as OMG. Through the OMG, *enhansiv* was able to talk directly to vendors and end users about their component technology plans and strategies and participate in industry-specific task forces to establish standards. *Enhansiv* even assumed leadership in organizing a group to work on customer interaction center problems. It is working with other interested members to develop common interface standards to facilitate easy integration between software components that will soon be deployed.

Ultimately, however, the tremendous success of the engineering group actually brought the whole of *enhansiv* to a crossroads. Originally, the intent was for the group to develop a new line of call center software products. However, with the rise of the Internet, it became increasingly clear that the new software could be applied to a much wider range of problems than call center management.

Summary

Enhansiv isn't a large firm, but it is already a leader in a brand-new industry. It's a good example of how an existing firm can look at a rapidly evolving market and decide to make changes rather than become obsolete. *Enhansiv* made exactly that decision. Since it's a software vendor, its reengineering effort is slightly different than an average company's. It began by examining how its clients were, or would soon be, reengineering their own business processes to accommodate the new communication channels their customers were using. As a result of this analysis, *enhansiv* decided how it would need to change its core product to make it useful for the new business processes of what are now *enhansiv's* clients.

Having decided on a new product, *enhansiv* then proceeded to reengineer its software development process to support the development and maintenance of its new software product—

ChannelManager. The advanced technology group could have opted for minor changes in an attempt to move quickly. Instead, they chose to undertake a major transition. They began by creating a small advanced software group that worked out what the new engineering group would do. Among other things, this group worked with consultants to design a new corporate software architecture and installed a new software infrastructure, based on Internet technologies. The advanced engineering group took training and eventually designed the new components that would form the heart of the new product.

At this point the group began to transfer their training to the company's overall engineering group, gradually converting the entire engineering team to distributed component-based development techniques. The change process that the advanced engineering group went through reenergized a key, core asset of *enhansiv* and has led to the creation of not only a well-trained group of developers who can support the rapid introduction of new products but also a strategic technological weapon designed to easily adapt to new business and technical challenges spurred on by its clients and the Internet.

Afterword, Surviving the Transition

We've come to the end of a short book designed to help managers think through the implications of the Internet and the Web on the way their companies do business.

The transition that we are witnessing has generated lots of activity and dozens of different predictions. In 1999, when the stock market was awarding extraordinary value to new e-business startups, it seemed as if any Internet strategy was better than none at all. It also looked as if the market was convinced that all conventional retail companies were doomed, soon to be replaced by Web-based retailers. In a magazine article, Peter Drucker, the well-known management guru, suggested that all Fortune 500 companies would eventually be replaced by newer, more flexible e-business companies. A few large corporations launched massive transition programs to assure that they would be among the survivors.

In spite of all the articles that suggest otherwise, most of the largest corporations have made only modest inroads into the world of e-business. They developed Web sites, explored some modest online selling efforts, and studied how they might do something more elaborate. In effect, most large IT organizations looked at the kind of software required for a comprehensive, scalable Internet response that could integrate existing legacy applications and bring the company's existing resources to bear on the Internet challenge and realized that the transition was going to take time and planning.

Luckily for these companies, by mid-2000 the market had come to agree with them. The value of new e-business startup stock was sharply reduced as everyone took a deep breath and realized that most of these companies would fail. Too many companies with vague plans had entered, and if even half of them succeeded, they would be selling more goods and services than the world could possibly absorb. Several entrepreneurs, the market decided, had been a little too ambitious in describing their business plans. On a more technical level, corporate IT managers pointed out that most of the new e-business startups had entered the market at Internet speed and produced lightweight architectures that couldn't possibly scale up.

Some of the same pundits who had proclaimed that the new e-business startups would sweep all the old companies away now switched and claimed that the e-business revolution was much less important than it had been made out to be. This conservatism is just as invalid as the previous supposition that everything would change in six months, led by new startups.

The willingness of customers to buy over the Web has initiated profound changes that will continue to affect the way business is done from now on. Similarly, the cost savings that large companies can realize from integrating and coordinating their business processes with the Internet will gradually drive every company that wants to survive to embrace the Internet. The transition is based on a fundamental change in consumer habits and similar changes in technology that, once begun, is irreversible. Companies can no more afford to ignore the implications of the Web and the Internet than early companies could afford to avoid the implications of trains, electricity, or the telephone.

What has changed is the idea that the transition has to take place in six months. Instead, it will take place over a longer period of time, varying according to industry and customer base. The good news is that this new reality will give large companies more time to get organized for the change. It will not, however, allow them to relax or to wait. Some companies in each industry will plunge ahead. Other companies will either follow or soon find themselves obsolete.

The approach we have outlined in this book is designed for large companies that cannot change overnight. It assumes that a transition will take time. The kinds of system changes required are difficult, and they cannot be completed quickly. Corporate IT organizations need to be reengineered. New technologies need to be mastered, and even harder, new ways of thinking about application development and integration need to be understood. Similarly, new business models need to be adopted. The value of everything the company produces needs to be reconsidered, and new types of products and services need to be developed. Moreover, new core business processes need to be designed to generate the new products and services in the most efficient manner. Corporate leaders need to drive the transition against the resistance of entrenched interests. Nothing less than a major effort will allow a large corporation to transition into a successful e-business organization.

We have argued in this book that change must take place along two parallel tracks. First, business analysts must redefine business processes to take advantage of the new realities—customers that want to buy online and the ability of the Internet to allow a previously unknown degree of coordination between business elements and companies. This Internet-based integration will allow new levels of efficiency and will drive costs down. Second, at the same time that business analysts are reengineering company business processes, IT managers must reengineer the corporate IT organization. Old methods of developing and maintaining software won't work in the Internet era. E-business applications designed for the Internet and Web will necessarily be distributed component-based systems. New applications will not only have to integrate with existing legacy systems, but will also have to work together at an enterprise level. To build such systems, IT organizations must make major changes. They must learn new technologies and skills, acquire new tools, and gain experience in component-based development.

To succeed in changing both business processes and the IT organization will require that companies develop a systematic transition plan that coordinates changes in IT and in corporate business processes. It can be done, but it isn't simple. It will require the support and drive of senior managers and the skill of middle-level managers.

We have described some of the technologies that IT managers and developers will need to master to change their IT organizations. We have also offered a generic transition plan derived from consulting work we have done with companies that have already made a similar transition. The plan we offer won't be right for every company in its specific details, but it should certainly provide ideas and a general sense of direction to anyone who is trying to figure out how their company should approach the e-business transition. If it does, we will have satisfied the goal we set for ourselves when we sat down to create this book.

Glossary

ActiveX A component model. Specifically, a subset of Microsoft's COM model that was especially designed for the Internet.

Applications architecture A subset or viewpoint that describes one aspect of a component architecture. Specifically, an applications architecture describes the set of applications that a company supports or is developing at one point in time and defines the basic relationships between the different applications.

Architecture (software architecture) The basic elements and relationships that will be required or used to solve a problem. There are many different types of architectures. There are hardware as well as software architectures, although in this book we only focus on the latter. Among the high-level or corporate software architectures, the distributed or enterprise component architecture is widely considered the best approach for the development of e-business systems. The enterprise component architecture can be broken down into subarchitectures that specify particular aspects or viewpoints involved in the development of an application. In this book, we break a component architecture down into five subarchitectures or viewpoints: an applications architecture, a technical architecture, a business model, an implementation architecture, and an operations architecture.

Business component (business object) A large-scale component designed to function as a module that can be used in the assembly of an enterprise application. Business components usually contain other smaller components, are often distributed across multiple platforms, and form the basis of serious software reuse.

Business entity A business concept that represents a "thing" (as opposed to a process) in the business. For example, a customer or an order are entities. Usually, business entities are stored in databases and acted on by business processes.

Business model (component business model) In software, a business model is a diagram or definition of how components will fit together to realize a set of business requirements. As we use the term, a business model is a subset or viewpoint that describes one aspect of a component architecture. In effect, business managers develop a "business model" or strategy that defines the goals for a business process, and then software developers define how a set of components will be used to help realize those goals. In the context of a software architecture, there are usually two versions of a business model—an abstract business model, referred to as the domain business model, and a more concrete, application-specific model, referred to as the application business model. The former defines the way a set of components would interact to solve a general type of application, while the latter defines a specific solution to be implemented.

Business process Broadly, a business process is an ongoing set of activities and tasks that are stimulated by customer requests for products or services and result in the production of those products or services. Early BPR theorists sought to divide companies into a few large business processes that cut across departmental lines. These processes are often called core business processes. As time has passed, the term "business process" has often been used more narrowly to refer to any set of related activities that a company is trying to automate or improve.

Business process reengineering/redesign (BPR) The overall process of identifying company processes and reviewing and revising each process to make it more efficient. BPR is postulated on the idea that software technologies were not fully utilized but incorporated in a haphazard way in most pre-1990s companies and that major gains can be made by starting from scratch and deciding how a business process ought best be done in the light of current software technologies. The new emphasis on e-business has reemphasized the need for BPR and for fundamental business process redesign.

Business strategy (business model) A business strategy considers a company's goals and policies, the environment, and competitors and decides how the company should compete to maximize its chances for success. The result of the process is a management consensus, usually documented, that describes the company's strengths and weaknesses, looks at how the environment and competitors are changing, and defines how the company will function to succeed in the changing environment.

Business-to-business (B2B) systems A vague subset of e-business applications that focus on supply chain integration or on businesses selling to other businesses.

Business-to-customer (B2C) systems A vague subset of e-business applications that focus on e-commerce or other applications that sell products or services over the Web or the Internet.

Client components Components are sometimes divided into client and server components. Client components include GUI and utility components that are placed on client machines—desktop personal computers, workstations, wireless phones—and facilitate the interaction between the user and the application.

COM/DNA (Component Object Model/Distributed interNet Application architecture) Microsoft has been systematically developing an approach to component-based development that relies on its COM model and its DNA architecture. Unlike other approaches that provide specifications that multiple vendors can implement, Microsoft incorporates its model directly into the code of its Windows operating systems.

Competitive strategies In classic business strategy theory, there are three leading generic strategies that a company can adopt: offering the lowest price, offering the product with the best general feature set, or offering the product that is best tailored for a specific market segment. In e-business, to date, companies seem to be focusing on one of three new strategies: offering the best consumer access and support, offering the best tailoring, or offering the most efficient process.

Component A software component is an independent module or package of code that can be inserted or removed from an application without requiring other changes in the application. Components hide their internal workings from other components to maintain this independence but offer an interface that other components can use to request services from the component. A component is composed of two things: behavior (the functions it can perform) and state (the business data to which the business functions are being applied). Components are often divided by size and function into GUI components, utility components that serve middleware and service functions, and business components that contain business logic.

Component-based development (CBD) An approach to software application and systems development in which software components play the key role. Components, and hence a CBD approach, are necessary to be agile and competitive in e-business. The focus on the component requires fundamental changes from traditional development processes.

Component container or environment To function, a component must be placed in a run-time environment or container that understands the interface of the component, keeps track of where all the components are located, and manages communications between the components when one component seeks to send information to another. An abstract description of a component container or environment is often called a model or standard (e.g., COM, CORBA). A concrete implementation of a component container or environment is often a product (e.g., the Java language environment, the Windows operating system, IONA's EJB application server product, iPortal).

Component factory An approach to component-based development that simplifies complexity, reduces development time, and enhances reuse. A component factory is a standardization of an enterprise architecture and an implementation of a portion of the component architecture, and specifically of the technical and implementation architectures. In effect, by using a standard software platform or factory, developers can focus on implementing business functionality and avoid re-creating the infrastructure needed for the development of component applications.

Component system or model In order for components to interoperate, there must be a common environment or container that specifies the way interfaces will be described and that manages communications between components making up an application. There are three popular component systems or models in general use: the Object Management Group's CORBA model, Sun's Enterprise JavaBeans/Java 2 Enterprise Edition environment (EJB/J2EE), and Microsoft's Component Object Model/Distributed interNet Application architecture (COM/DNA).

Coordinator or controller Software components that play a specific role in the overall execution of a business process or application. They manage the execution of the business process over one or more business entities and/or coordinate between multiple processes and entities in complex operations.

CORBA (Common Object Request Broker Architecture) A generic term for the middleware architecture and component model being developed by the Object Management Group (OMG), a standards organization with 800 members worldwide. CORBA standards are published documents that different vendors can implement. The OMG always creates standards that are independent of any specific operating system or language and thus able to be used to integrate applications in distributed, heterogeneous enterprise environments.

Customer focus (or customer power) The Web increases a customer's power. The customer can use the Web to examine more options, quickly compare prices and features, and, if appropriate, bargain more effectively with suppliers. The Web is forcing companies to become more customer focused and to increase value and reduce costs in order to compete with competitors that the customer will likely encounter on the Web.

Distributed application (distributed computing) A distributed system is made up of components that reside on a number of different platforms, on desktop machines, on application servers, and on database servers. Large or enterprise systems usually rely on components located on hardware spread throughout the world. Since there is no core or central application, the essence of the application is the middleware that keeps track of the locations of all the components and routes messages from one component to another, wherever they are located.

E-business Businesses that rely on the Internet and the Web to facilitate their core business processes. The transition to e-business is being driven by the willingness of customers to shop on the Web and by the processing efficiencies that companies can obtain by passing information internally and between suppliers. E-business is a broad term that includes specific uses of Internet technologies to facilitate business. E-commerce describes selling products and services over the Web. Supply chain integration describes using the Internet to link a company and its suppliers.

E-business application development E-business application development requires different techniques than those used for conventional development. Specifically, e-business applications require the use of distributed component architectures and techniques. That, in turn, requires that companies reorganize and retrain their IT organizations to produce effective applications.

E-business enterprise applications Large, corporatewide applications that rely on the Internet or Web to link the company to customers and suppliers. This is contrasted to Web applications, which simply support a Web site that customers can use to learn about the company or to communicate with the company. Serious e-business applications require that the company integrate existing legacy applications to provide the customer or supplier with information that resides in major corporate databases, or incorporate major internal or external legacy applications to provide the business logic to process customer or supplier requests.

E-business strategy The development of a business strategy that incorporates an understanding of how the Internet and Web have changed the environment that the business operates in, and indicates how the company will adapt to take advantage of Internet and Web technologies.

E-business transition The process a company or division goes through when it shifts from a conventional approach to sales, manufacturing, and coordination to an approach that relies on the Internet and the Web. This shift requires that business processes be redesigned and that the IT organization learn how to develop enterprise e-business applications.

Enterprise application integration (EAI) Popular current term for methodologies and tools that can be used to integrate new and legacy applications into a single system. EAI is a key element of any major e-business application development effort. Narrowly, EAI is sometimes used to refer to integration of some specific set of applications, like prepackaged SAP and PeopleSoft applications, but increasingly it is used to refer to component- and middleware-based approaches to enterprisewide systems integration.

Enterprise architecture (enterprise component architecture) A type of software architecture that is intended to address enterprisewide e-business requirements. The enterprise architecture is intended to apply to many applications within an enterprise. The enterprise component architecture can be broken down into subarchitectures that specify particular aspects or viewpoints involved in the development of an application. In this book, we break the enterprise component architecture down into five subarchitectures or viewpoints: an applications architecture, a technical architecture, a business model, an implementation architecture, and an operations architecture

Framework (component framework, development framework) A set of established interaction patterns that can be customized to provide a specific solution to a common problem. A component framework is a partial or incomplete component application. Thus, specific frameworks are always described in terms of the set of applications they are designed to facilitate. A bookstore inventory framework would be a set of components designed to facilitate the development of bookstore inventory applications. A development framework is a partial implementation of a development activity. A GUI development framework would be used to provide a common look and feel for all user interfaces.

Functional layers See Tiers.

GUI (graphical user interface) A general term for the code that operates the user interface screens on a computer platform.

IIOP (Internet Inter-ORB Protocol) The OMG's protocol used by those who want to transfer information over the Internet in a language- and platform-neutral way. Originally developed to allow different CORBA implementations to talk to each other and now widely embedded in other systems, including Sun's EJB standard, to facilitate links between Java and non-Java components.

Implementation architecture A subset or viewpoint that describes one particular aspect of a component architecture. Specifically, an implementation architecture describes the way an application will be implemented on a particular product and technology. The use of a specific implementation architecture allows the components to be specified independently of any single technology and to be implemented on multiple different technologies. Thus the use of IONA's EJB application server product will necessitate a different implementation than the use of Microsoft's MTS model running in Windows.

Information In business strategy considerations, information is contrasted with material products. The economics of information is different from material products. You can only sell a single material product once. You can sell the same information many different times. Many companies have embedded information in material products and developed cost models that don't adequately evaluate the real value of each. The Internet and e-business in general are providing huge rewards for companies that can pull information out of a material context and provide it more rapidly and cheaply.

IT organization (information technology organization or IT group or information systems organization) The department or group within a company or division that is charged with creating and maintaining software applications.

Java An object-oriented software language that is especially designed for the development of distributed Web applications. The Java language environment includes support for component models, including JavaBeans and Enterprise JavaBeans. Java was developed and is owned by Sun Microsystems, Inc.

Legacy applications All of the large applications that companies currently rely upon to do business (e.g., accounting, customer information system, inventory, payroll). Most were developed before current languages and techniques were available. Many are poorly documented and difficult to maintain. But all important legacy applications are valuable and can't be shut down, so any new development must be done in such a way that it assures that the legacy applications will be integrated with the new systems being developed.

MTS or COM+ A component model. A subset or variety of Microsoft's COM model. A server-side component model.

Object A self-contained code module, like a component, that is used as the basis for creating software applications. Object technology is the more generic technology. Components are typically constructed using objects and object-oriented techniques. Objects are often associated with, and run in, environments created by languages, like Java, Smalltalk, and C++. From a development perspective, most of the techniques developed for object-oriented development apply, with only slight modifications, to component-based development. However, additional development and organizational techniques are necessary to take maximum advantage of components.

OMG (Object Management Group) The major consortium that sets open standards for object and component technologies. For more information, check *www.omg.com.*

Operations architecture A subset or viewpoint that describes one aspect of a component architecture. Specifically, an operations architecture describes the hardware and software configuration of the deployed system and other parameters required to keep it operational. Additionally, it describes performance that the application must evidence to satisfy a company's requirements and the technologies or processes that will be used to assure that the performance is obtained.

Pattern In software engineering, a proven way of handling a specific design or programming problem. Software developers record recurring patterns and share them so that new developers won't have to solve routine problems from scratch. By consulting a book with specific types of software patterns, a developer can often find a description of a proven way to approach a given type of problem.

Portal A Web site that provides the customer with access to a variety of other Web sites or services. In this sense, a large company might refer to its most generic Web site as the company portal. Another example is a Web site, like Yahoo or AOL, that provides customers with a place to go initially when they sign on the Web to get information like the news, stock reports, and so on. Companies may want to advertise on portals that are popular, since they get lots of traffic.

Porter's model of competition A general model of competition developed in Michael E. Porter's book *Competitive Strategy*. The model postulates that there are five major elements that must be examined to predict the competition in a given market: industry competitors, potential new entrants, changes in the power of suppliers, changes in the power of buyers, and the possibility of new products that could be substituted for the existing product that the company sells.

Reengineering (or business process reengineering or BPR) A process that requires that company managers and employees review how existing business processes work and then redesign those processes, incorporating the latest software technologies and changing how employees function to provide better value to customers.

Scalability In software development, this refers to the ability of an application to quickly and effectively adjust to handling more users. It may refer to the fact that the system was originally designed to provide service for a small number of customers and now needs to be changed to provide service for a much larger number of customers. Increasingly, it refers to e-business systems that must dynamically scale from interacting with a few dozen customers at, for example, 3 PM, to handling inquires from thousands of customers, simultaneously, at 4:30 PM. If applications are to successfully scale dynamically, they must be designed with that in mind. Conventional systems don't scale well.

Scenarios In business strategy planning, a high-level description of several different ways a company could respond to the challenges it faces. Some companies develop several scenarios and then choose one, while others develop several strategies and then pursue two or more at the same time so that they will have options no matter how the market evolves. In BPR, one of several alternative ways that a business process could be organized. In component-based development, one of the multiple ways that a client might interact with a component. Software developers explore different scenarios to assure that their software can respond to all of the different uses that users might want to make of it. This is one of the trickiest aspects of software development. The business environment is changing very fast, and it's very hard to anticipate how software will be used once it is fielded.

Server or server-side components Components are sometimes divided between client and server components. Server components reside on servers. Server component models are newer and more complex than client component models. They usually divide the control of the component between the component interface that provides the ultimate access to the component's functionality and a container interface that interposes system controls on the component's functionality. Thus, if a container is set up to support it, a server component can be used as part of a transaction processing application or can be used within a secure process of one kind or another. Most distributed enterprise applications that process important company data require the use of server-side components. Most business components are implemented as server-side components.

State management "State" refers to data values at a particular point in time. Objects and components have state. "State management" refers to techniques that assure that the application keeps track of data values. Effective state management is critical to scalability.

Supply chain applications Another subset of e-business applications. Applications that link a company to its suppliers. The applications may provide direct links or may link through a brokerage or electronic marketplace that facilitates the distribution of information about purchase requirements, prices, bids, contract terms, and so forth. Supply chain applications may simply involve passing information about needed parts or materials or may include billing and payment subsystems, inventory systems, and so forth.

Technical architecture A subset or viewpoint that describes one aspect of a component architecture. Specifically, a technical architecture describes the technical resources that the company will use and any constraints that the company has agreed upon. The technical architecture describes how IT systems are constructed using components. In general, a technical architecture is an abstraction that applies to a large number of different applications.

Tiers (two-tiered, three-tiered, multitiered) A tier describes a portion of an application. Client-server applications are divided into two parts: a client tier running on client computers and a server tier running on a database server. Distributed applications tend to be three-tiered or multitiered applications. A three-tiered application divides the application into three major parts: one part running on client computers (i.e., the presentation tier), one running on server computers (i.e., the enterprise tier), and a third running on computers with databases (i.e., the resource tier). The multitiered architecture described in this book further divides the presentation tier into a user tier and a workspace tier. This additional tier enhances systems capability to respond to e-business requirements such as multiple different devices and B2B integration.

Transaction processing A transaction, as used in software engineering, is a process that involves modifications to important data and techniques that assure that the process is completed accurately. In effect, a transaction process arranges to make a change and then double-checks to be sure the change was made properly. If it wasn't, for any reason, the data is immediately set back to its state before the transaction was begun.

UML (Unified Modeling Language) An industry-standard language for modeling software systems. UML is supported by all major tools and used to create design artifacts as part of most software development processes.

Use case A software technique for analyzing business requirements. A way of describing what a software application will need to do to satisfy a given set of business requirements.

Value proposition In business strategy, a value proposition describes what value a product or service has to a customer in the most general possible way. A well-defined value proposition suggests all of the products that a customer might consider when deciding what product to buy to fulfill a need. In effect, a value proposition defines a market niche and all of the various kinds of products that are potentially competing with each other in the customer's mind when a purchasing decision is being considered.

XML (eXtended Markup Language) A generic version of the HTML document protocol that allows the developer to specify a unique and extensible syntax (referred to as a tag set) for a document. Using HTML, you were forced to design Web interfaces using the tags specified by the protocol. Using XML, you can specify and use any data tags you wish. Thus, if you want to create unique documents to describe auto loans or pet ownership certificates, you can do it. Whereas HTML is focused on presenting information in a Web browser environment, XML is focused on the transfer of data, independently of how that data will be used. This means that developers can use the XML protocol to easily pass data around the Internet. In the near future, once companies and organizations agree on standard tag sets, XML documents will become the most popular way to pass data files between Internet users.

Notes and References

Chapter 1 The E-Business Challenge

Lapidus, Gary. *E-Automotive Report.* Goldman Sachs Investment Research, 1999.

Chapter 2 Developing an E-Business Strategy

Evans, Philip, and Thomas S. Wurster. *Blown to Bits: How the New Economics of Information Transforms Strategy.* Harvard Business School Press, 2000. ISBN 0-87584-877-X. Referenced in the text. Read this book for insight into how e-business is changing the nature of products by changing the economic balance between selling things and selling information about things.

Kalakota, Ravi, and Marcia Robinson. *E-Business: Roadmap for Success.* Addison-Wesley, 1999. ISBN 0-201-60480-9. Referenced in the text. A great introduction to the nature of e-business applications and some of the problems involved in developing them. It describes a general approach and then has chapters on each different type of application, including e-commerce, B2B, and supply chain applications.

Moore, Geoffrey A. *Crossing the Chasm: Marketing and Selling High-Tech Products to Mainstream Customers.* HarperBusiness, 1991. ISBN 0-88730-717-5. The classic introduction to how new products or technologies go through an adoption life cycle and the kinds of things various types of companies are looking for when they think about acquiring new technologies.

Porter, Michael E. *Competitive Strategy: Techniques for Analyzing Industries and Competitors.* The Free Press, 1980. ISBN 0-02-925360-8. Referenced in the text. The best general introduction to the development of business strategy.

Chapter 3 Redesigning Business Processes for E-Business

Fischer, Layna (Ed.). *The Workflow Paradigm: The Impact of Information Technology on Business Process Reengineering* (second ed.). Future Strategies, Inc., 1995. ISBN 0-9640233-2-6. Provides a discussion of the various ways workflow techniques are used in the analysis of business processes.

Grover, Varun, and William J. Kettinger. *Business Process Change: Reengineering Concepts, Methods and Technologies.* Idea Group Publishing, 1995. ISBN 1-878289-29-2. A collection of articles that provide insights into how BPR developed and how it was used in the mid-1990s.

Hammer, Michael, and James Champy. *Reengineering the Corporation: A Manifesto for Business Revolution.* HarperBusiness, 1993. ISBN 0-88730-687-X. The classic introduction to BPR. In spite of lots of bombast, this book provides the rationale for why businesses need to redesign their business processes in order to take advantage of the latest software technologies.

Kalakota, Ravi, and Marcia Robinson. *E-Business: Roadmap for Success.* Addison-Wesley, 1999. ISBN 0-201-60480-9. Referenced in the text. Describes the major types of e-business applications being developed.

Kilov, Haim, and James Ross. *Information Modeling: An Object-Oriented Approach.* Prentice Hall, 1994. ISBN 0-13-083033-X. This book by Genesis's leading authority on business modeling is a very technical description of a formal approach for aligning business requirements with business models.

Rummler, Geary A., and Alan P. Brache. *Improving Performance: How to Manage the White Space on the Organization Chart* (second ed.). Jossey-Bass Publishers, 1995. ISBN 0-7879-0090-7. If you actually have to analyze a business organization or process, this practical book provides a detailed approach to the mechanics of business process analysis.

Chapter 4 E-Business Applications

Rosenfeld, Louis, and Peter Morville. *Information Architecture for the World Wide Web: Designing Large-Scale Web Sites.* O'Reilly, 1998. ISBN 1-56592-282-4. In spite of its confusing name, this book focuses on how to design good Web sites to support large e-business applications. It doesn't provide help with overall e-business architectures, but it does help managers see how all of the company's capabilities must be integrated to provide the customer with reasonable access to the company's services.

Seybold, Patricia B. *Customers.com.* TimeBooks, 1998. ISBN 0-8129-3037-1. This general introduction to how the Internet and Web are changing the world emphasizes how customers are adapting to the Web and what that means for companies.

Chapter 5 Components

Allen, Paul. *Realizing E-Business with Components.* Addison-Wesley, 2000. ISBN 0-201-67520-X. If you read this book and wished the authors had gone into more technical detail, this is the book to turn to next.

Allen, Paul, and Stuart Frost. *Component-Based Development for Enterprise Systems.* Cambridge University Press, 1998. ISBN 0-521-64999-4. Probably the best book to turn to for a general methodology for component development.

Chappell, David. *Understanding Microsoft Windows 2000 Distributed Services: A Guide for Developers and Managers.* Microsoft Press, 2000. ISBN 1-57231-687-X. The best introduction to Microsoft's COM component model.

Eeles, Peter, and Oliver Sims. *Building Business Objects.* John Wiley & Sons, 1998. ISBN 0-471-19176-0. This book provides an introduction to the idea that large-scale business components can be used to organize enterprise applications.

Fowler, Martin, and Kendall Scott. *UML Distilled: Applying the Standard Object Modeling Language* (second ed.). Addison-Wesley, 1998. ISBN 0-201-65783-X. The best introduction to the Unified Modeling Language notation.

Herzum, Peter, and Oliver Sims. *Business Component Factory: A Comprehensive Overview of Component-Based Development for the Enterprise.* John Wiley & Sons, 1999. ISBN 0-471-32760-3. This is probably the best book on large-scale component design and development currently available. Sims is a member of the technical staff at Genesis (Iona).

Orfali, Robert, Dan Harkey, and Jeri Edwards. *The Essential Distributed Objects: Survival Guide.* John Wiley & Sons, 1996. ISBN 0-471-12993-3. It's hard at this point to recommend a good introduction to object technology. There is so much, and increasingly object techniques and component techniques are confused. This book, written in 1996, is probably the best general description of object technology and how it could be used to build distributed systems before everyone started emphasizing components.

Roman, Ed. *Mastering Enterprise JavaBeans and the Java 2 Platform, Enterprise Edition.* John Wiley & Sons, 1999. ISBN 0-471-33229-1 The EJB specification keeps changing, and we know of no gentle introduction we can recommend. This book seems to provide the best detailed look at what's involved in developing EJB applications.

Siegel, Jon. *CORBA 3: Fundamentals and Programming* (second ed.). John Wiley & Sons, 2000. ISBN 0-471-29518-3. A detailed description of all of the elements in the Object Management Group's component model and associated middleware services and of how they are implemented in various CORBA products.

Chapter 6 An Enterprise Component Architecture

Bass, Len, Paul Clements, and Rick Kazman. *Software Architecture in Practice.* Addison-Wesley, 1998. ISBN 0-201-19930-0. An academic description of software architectures providing a high-level overview of all of the kinds of architectures there are.

Buschmann, Frank, et al. *Pattern Oriented Software Architecture.* John Wiley & Sons, 1996. ISBN 0-471-95869-7. A description of architectural patterns that are used for a variety of different software applications.

Chapter 7 Implementing a Component Architecture

Bernstein, Philip, and Eric Newcomer. *Principles of Transaction Processing.* Morgan Kaufmann, 1997. ISBN 1-55860-415-4. The best overall description of transaction processing for the average developer or manager.

Conallen, Jim. *Building Web Applications with UML.* Addison-Wesley, 1999. ISBN 0-201-61577-0. This book provides a detailed look at building the presentation layers of Web-based systems and provides UML models for various designs.

Rosenberg, Doug, and Kendall Scott. *Use Case Driven Object Modeling with UML.* Addison-Wesley, 1999. ISBN 0-201-43289-7. This book provides a step-by-step process for going from use case business models down to detailed implementation models.

Zahavi, Ron. *Enterprise Application Integration with CORBA.* John Wiley & Sons, 2000. ISBN 0-471-32720-4. A good description of how to use CORBA for integration of legacy systems.

Chapter 8 Managing the Transition to an E-Business

Jacobson, Ivar, Martin Griss, and Patrik Jonsson. *Software Reuse: Architecture, Process and Organization for Business Success.* Addison-Wesley, 1997. ISBN 0-201-92476-5. This book is still the best available book if you want to understand the value of component reuse and the IT organizational changes necessary to implement a component reuse system.

Bibliography

We have included all the books that are specifically referred to in chapters of this book or that are especially relevant to a particular topic discussed in a specific chapter in the "Notes and References" section. All are repeated here, listed in order based on the lead author's name. This bibliography is not intended to be extensive. Instead, it is designed to help interested readers find a few good books that will extend their knowledge of subjects discussed in this book.

Allen, Paul. *Realizing E-Business with Components.* Addison-Wesley, 2000. ISBN 0-201-67520-X.

Allen, Paul, and Stuart Frost. *Component-Based Development for Enterprise Systems.* Cambridge University Press, 1998. ISBN 0-521-64999-4.

Ambler, Scott. *Building Object Applications That Work.* Sigs Books, 1998. ISBN 0-521-64826-2.

Bass, Len, Paul Clements, and Rick Kazman. *Software Architecture in Practice.* Addison-Wesley, 1998. ISBN 0-201-19930-0.

Bernstein, Philip, and Eric Newcomer. *Principles of Transaction Processing.* Morgan Kaufmann, 1997. ISBN 1-55860-415-4.

Booch, Grady, James Rumbaugh, and Ivar Jacobson. *The Unified Modeling Language Users Guide.* Addison-Wesley, 1999. ISBN 0-201-57168-4.

Buschmann, Frank, et al. *Pattern Oriented Software Architecture.* John Wiley & Sons, 1996. ISBN 0-471-95869-7.

Chappell, David. *Understanding ActiveX and OLE: A Guide for Developers & Managers.* Microsoft Press, 1996. ISBN 1-57231-216-5.

Chappell, David. *Understanding Microsoft Windows 2000 Distributed Services: A Guide for Developers and Managers.* Microsoft Press, 2000. ISBN 1-57231-687-X.

Conallen, Jim. *Building Web Applications with UML.* Addison-Wesley, 1999. ISBN 0-201-61577-0.

D'Souza, Desmond F., and Alan Cameron Wills. *Objects, Components, and Frameworks with UML: The Catalysis Approach.* Addison-Wesley, 1999. ISBN 0-201-31012-0.

Eeles, Peter, and Oliver Sims. *Building Business Objects.* John Wiley & Sons, 1998. ISBN 0-471-19176-0.

Evans, Philip, and Thomas S. Wurster. *Blown to Bits: How the New Economics of Information Transforms Strategy.* Harvard Business School Press, 2000. ISBN 0-87584-877-X.

Fischer, Layna (Ed.). *The Workflow Paradigm: The Impact of Information Technology on Business Process Reengineering* (second ed.). Future Strategies, Inc., 1995. ISBN 0-9640233-2-6.

Fowler, Martin. *Analysis Patterns: Reusable Object Models.* Addison-Wesley, 1997. ISBN 0-201-89542-0.

Fowler, Martin, and Kendall Scott. *UML Distilled: Applying the Standard Object Modeling Language* (second ed.). Addison-Wesley, 1998. ISBN 0-201-65783-X.

Gamma, Erich, et al. *Design Patterns: Elements of Reusable Object Oriented Software.* Addison-Wesley, 1995. ISBN 0-201-63361-2.

Grover, Varun, and William J. Kettinger. *Business Process Change: Reengineering Concepts, Methods and Technologies.* Idea Group Publishing, 1995. ISBN 1-878289-29-2.

Guttman, Michael, and Jason R. Matthews. *The Object Technology Revolution.* John Wiley & Sons, 1995. ISBN 0-471-60679-0.

Hammer, Michael, and James Champy. *Reengineering the Corporation: A Manifesto for Business Revolution.* HarperBusiness, 1993. ISBN 0-88730-687-X.

Herzum, Peter, and Oliver Sims. *Business Component Factory: A Comprehensive Overview of Component-Based Development for the Enterprise.* John Wiley & Sons, 1999. ISBN 0-471-32760-3.

Jacobson, Ivar, Grady Booch, and James Rumbaugh. *The Unified Software Development Process.* Addison-Wesley, 1999. ISBN 0-201-57169-2.

Jacobson, Ivar, Martin Griss, and Patrik Jonsson. *Software Reuse: Architecture, Process and Organization for Business Success.* Addison-Wesley, 1997. ISBN 0-201-92476-5.

Kalakota, Ravi, and Marcia Robinson. *E-Business: Roadmap for Success.* Addison-Wesley, 1999. ISBN 0-201-60480-9.

Kilov, Haim, and James Ross. *Information Modeling: An Object-Oriented Approach*. Prentice Hall, 1994. ISBN 0-13-083033-X.

Maruyama, Hiroshi, Kent Tamura, and Naohiko Uramoto. *XML and Java: Developing Web Applications*. Addison-Wesley, 1999. ISBN 0-201-48543-5.

McKenna, Regis. *Real Time: Preparing for the Age of the Never Satisfied Customer*. Harvard Business School Press, 1999. ISBN 0-87584-934-2.

Monday, Paul, James Carey, and Mary Dangler. *San Francisco Component Framework: An Introduction*. Addison-Wesley, 2000. ISBN 0-201-61587-8.

Moore, Geoffrey A. *Crossing the Chasm: Marketing and Selling High-Tech Products to Mainstream Customers*. HarperBusiness, 1991. ISBN 0-88730-717-5.

Mowbray, Thomas J., and William A. Ruh. *Inside CORBA: Distributed Object Standards and Applications*. Addison-Wesley, 1997. ISBN 0-201-89540-4.

Orfali, Robert, Dan Harkey, and Jeri Edwards. *The Essential Distributed Objects: Survival Guide*. John Wiley & Sons, 1996. ISBN 0-471-12993-3.

Porter, Michael E. *Competitive Strategy: Techniques for Analyzing Industries and Competitors*. The Free Press, 1980. ISBN 0-02-925360-8.

Roman, Ed. *Mastering Enterprise JavaBeans and the Java 2 Platform, Enterprise Edition*. John Wiley & Sons, 1999. ISBN 0-471-33229-1.

Rosenberg, Doug, and Scott Kendall. *Use Case Driven Object Modeling with UML*. Addison-Wesley, 1999. ISBN 0-201-43289-7.

Rosenfeld, Louis, and Peter Morville. *Information Architecture for the World Wide Web: Designing Large-Scale Web Sites*. O'Reilly, 1998. ISBN 1-56592-282-4.

Ruh, William, Thomas Herron, and Paul Klinker. *IIOP Complete: Understanding CORBA and Middleware Interoperability*. Addison-Wesley, 2000. ISBN 0-201-37925-2.

Rumbaugh, James, Ivar Jacobson, and Grady Booch. *The Unified Modeling Language Reference Guide*. Addison-Wesley, 1999. ISBN 0-201-30990-8.

Rummler, Geary A., and Alan P. Brache. *Improving Performance: How to Manage the White Space on the Organization Chart* (second ed.). Jossey-Bass Publishers, 1995. ISBN 0-7879-0090-7.

Seybold, Patricia B. *Customers.com*. TimesBooks, 1998. ISBN 0-8129-3037-1.

Siegel, Jon. *CORBA 3: Fundamentals and Programming* (second ed.). John Wiley & Sons, 2000. ISBN 0-471-29518-3.

Zahavi, Ron. *Enterprise Application Integration with CORBA*. John Wiley & Sons, 2000. ISBN 0-471-32720-4.

Index

abstract component models, 139
abstraction layer, 147
access types for customers, 85–86
acquiring companies for needed technologies, 63–64
ActiveX
    container support, 125
    impact on visual programming, 120
    for interface components, 121
    security model, 123–124
    as sticky components, 123
    Windows platform dependence, 124
activity controller, 164–165, 191–193
Amazon.com, 105
AOL, 29, 85
application adapters, 166
application controlled state management model, 180
application management
    configurability issues, 99
    defined, 98, 99
    monitoring applications, 99
    need for, 98–99
    system integration, 99–100
application servers
    application integration, 130–131
    as containers, 129–132
    enterprise class infrastructure, 130
    selecting, 129–131
    server platform environment, 131–132
    types of, 129–130
applications, 83–108
    architecture, 144, 211, 213
    building simplified by architecture, 148
    business-to-business (B2B), 103–104
    business-to-customer (B2C), 105–106
    component factory patterns and, 172
    component-based development, 88–91, 110, 115–116, 170–172

constituents, 94
customer expectations and, 86–88
deployment, 100–101
ease-of-use issues, 87
e-business challenges, 84–94
e-marketplaces, 106
enterprise application requirements, 94–101
first-generation vs. second-generation, 49
increased competition and, 88
for information access and information-sharing, 103
integration by technical architecture, 155
intermediaries, 106–107
interoperability issues, 93–94
large-scale application challenges, 94–95
legacy integration, 91–93, 193–195
management, 98–100
multiple version support, 100–101
new usage patterns and, 84–86
patterns for design, 153, 161
performance issues, 87, 173
pilot application development phase, 214–220
portals, 107
scenarios, 188–195
shortened product life cycle and, 88
simple Web site applications, 102
state management, 96–98
supply chain integration, 104–105
transition plan and, 37, 49
transition task, 206, 213, 219, 222
Web applications vs. second-generation e-business, 49
    See also e-business challenges; pilot application development phase; software
applications transition task
    initiation phase, 213
    organizational conversion phase, 222

applications transition task *(continued)*
    overview, 206
    pilot application development phase, 219
architecture
    application architecture, 144, 211, 213
    defined, 142
    development process, 148–152, 211–
        212
    e-business architectures, 143
    eCRM product architecture, 229
    software architectures, 142–143
    technical architecture, 152–167
    transition task, 206, 211–212, 217–218,
        221
    See also enterprise component architecture;
        technical architecture
architecture transition task
    initiation phase, 211–212
    organizational conversion phase, 221
    overview, 206
    pilot application development phase, 217–
        218
ATMs
    availability challenges, 85–86
    Citibank innovation in California, 11
auction systems. *See* exchanges
authentication in ActiveX, 123–124
automakers, 13–17
    custom car creation, 13–14
    e-business strategy examples, 31–32
    globalization and, 28
    joint exchange system announced, 15
    online parts exchanges, 13, 14–15, 16, 66–
        67
    strategies for competing, 31–32
    Web site efforts announced, 13
    See also specific automakers
AutoXchange system (Ford), 14–15, 16
availability challenges, 84–86

B2B applications. *See* business-to-business
    (B2B) applications
B2B controllers, 163–164
B2C (business-to-customer) applications, 102,
    105–106
Barnes & Noble, Internet rivals, 3
barriers to entry
    capital investment, 27, 39–40
    globalization and, 28
    in Porter's model of competition, 27–28
    stores and distribution system, 27–28, 39–
        40, 62–63
bean-managed persistence, 133–134
Benchmark Capital, 5
Blown to Bits, 40, 41
booksellers, value proposition for, 29
BPI (business process improvement), 52

See also business process reengineering
    (BPR)
BPR. *See* business process reengineering (BPR)
brand names, as barrier to entry, 27
brochureware, 102, 198
business components, 111–118
    as application building blocks, 110, 115–
        116
    basic models, 115
    business functions exposed by, 112
    changes localized by, 112
    containers, 117–118
    defined, 111
    e-business components, 116
    events published and subscribed by, 112–
        113
    interfaces and connection points, 111–112
    large-scale, 114
    second-generation models, 115
    server platform environment, 131–132
    types of, 113–117
    See also components
business model. *See* strategy development
business process improvement (BPI), 52
    See also business process reengineering
        (BPR)
business process reengineering (BPR)
    acquiring companies for technologies, 63–
        64
    analysis of business processes, 52
    basic terms, 50–58
    change process management, 57
    converting to an e-business, 60–64
    customer role in e-businesses, 64–68
    for e-business, 58–59
    e-business focuses, 58–59
    focus on customers, 58, 60–61, 67–68
    horizontal vs. vertical integration, 52
    identification of business processes, 52
    Internet impact on, 57–58
    IT process reengineering, 59, 198–199,
        202–204
    large gains from small changes, 55–56
    management of change process, 57
    new company creation vs., 63
    order fulfillment process example, 68–81
    overview of generic phases, 53
    Phase 1: creating enterprise model, 52, 53
    Phase 2: documenting existing processes,
        53
    Phase 3: redesigning business process, 54–
        56
    Phase 4: make necessary changes, 56
    Phase 5: implement changed process, 56
    resistance to, 70–71, 198–199
    Stereos-R-Us example, 68–81
    time and planning required for, 59

in transition plan, 48–50
See also Stereos-R-Us example
business processes
    activity controller and, 193
    defined, 50
    entities operated on, 166
    external vs. internal, 50
    horizontal integration in, 50–51
    identification and analysis of, 52
    rules service, 166
    technical architecture, 165–166
business viewpoint, 132–134
    component creation by, 132
    component described by, 132
    as component's primary purpose, 132
    described, 125, 126
    persistence management, 132–134
business-to-business (B2B) applications
    B2B controllers, 163–164
    market-based allocation in, 104
    overview, 103–104
    requirements for, 102, 103
    supply-chain integration applications, 104–105
business-to-customer (B2C) applications, 102, 105–106
buyers
    in Porter's model of competition, 26
    Web opportunities for, 42–43
    See also customers

capital investment
    as barrier to entry, 27, 39–40
    venture money in future, 40
CCM. *See* CORBA Component Model (CCM)
challenges. *See* e-business challenges
Channel component, 236–238
Charles Schwab, 8–10
    CEO behind Internet innovation, 9
    continuing innovations of, 9–10
    outside developers hired by, 9
    pre-Web innovations, 9
    quick reaction to Internet challenge, 8–9
    wireless trading supported by, 10
chemical exchange, 14
CIO magazine, 197
Citigroup, 10–13
    1 billion customers goal, 10, 12
    ATM card innovation in California, 11
    eCiti subsidiary, 12–13
    U.S. dollar accounts sold by, 10–11
    worldwide Internet service plans, 11–12
client components, 118–125
    characteristics or capabilities, 118–119
    container support, 125
    downloadable, 121–122
    enterprise considerations, 121–123

    JavaBeans vs. ActiveX, 122–125
    platform independence and, 124
    security, 123–124
    sticky vs. nonsticky, 122–123
    technologies, 120–121
    user interface tasks managed by, 117–119
    See also components
clients
    as application components, 94, 95
    client components, 118–125
    component containers for, 117–118
    resource management, 95–96
    "rich," 100
    servers as, 96
    thin, 100, 121
    transaction control and, 181
CMP (container-managed persistence), 133
COM, 120, 136–137
COM+, 111, 125, 136–137
Commerce One, 15
commercial-off-the-shelf (COTS) software, 92
communication transition task
    initiation phase, 208–209
    overview, 206
    pilot application development phase, 216
competition model, Porter's. *See* Porter's model of competition
competition with existing systems. *See* self-competition
competitive pressures
    barriers to entry and, 27–28, 39–40
    customer expectations and, 88
    for employees, 44
    globalization and, 28
    See also Porter's model of competition
Competitive Strategy, 22, 25
component architectures
    abstraction layer, 147
    application building simplified by, 148
    business model, 143–144, 150, 172–173, 213
    changes accommodated by, 147
    development process, 148–152
    implementation architecture, 143, 150
    implementation independence, 147–148, 151–152
    implementing, 169–196
    infrastructure vs., 149
    IT model, 150–151
    models vs., 148–149
    operational architecture, 144, 151
    overview, 142–148
    phased implementation process, 148
    platform specific IT model, 150–151
    separation of software concerns by, 146–147
    software system concerns, 145
    subarchitectures, 143

component architectures *(continued)*
system described by, 144–145
technical architecture, 150, 152–167
transaction models, 180–182
viewpoints, 146–147
See also enterprise component architecture;
implementing a component architecture; technical architecture
component factory, 170–172
applications and, 172
defined, 170
infrastructure concerns and, 170–171
interface design pattern, 187–188
iterative development of, 171
as standard platform, 170
component factory pattern, 187–188
component-based application development, 88–
91
component factory and, 170–172
connecting components, 115–116
enterprise application requirements, 94–101
enterprise component architecture and, 90
need for, 88–89
productivity increased by, 90–91
programming tasks simplified by, 90
reaction times quickened by, 89–90
traditional application development vs., 90
component-managed persistence, 133–134
components
abstract component models, 139
application servers as containers, 129–132
assemblies, 136, 137
basic models, 115
business components, 110, 111–118
business viewpoint, 125, 126, 132–134
Channel component, 236–238
client components, 118–125
component factory, 170–172
component model, 172–173
component-managed persistence, 133–134
container overview, 117–118, 125
container viewpoint, 125, 126, 127–129
deployment descriptors, 135–136
e-business components, 116
enhansiv's enterprise channel management
component, 237–238
enterprise component architecture, 141–167
identity policies, 177, 184
implementation component models, 139
instance creation, 132
IT groups and, 110
large-scale, 114
location independence, 176–177
need for component infrastructures, 110
packaging viewpoint, 125–126, 127, 134–
136
persistence management by, 132–134

relationships between, 114
reuse potential for, 115–116, 135, 218–219,
220, 221–222
second-generation models, 115
server component models, 136–138
server components, 125–127
standards for, 111
state management, 96–98
stateful vs. stateless, 178, 179
transaction models, 180–182
transactional policy, 135
transition task, 206, 213, 218–219, 221–
222
types of, 113–117
usage models, 183–184
See also business components; client components; containers; enterprise component
architecture; server components
components transition task
initiation phase, 213
organizational conversion phase, 221–222
overview, 206
pilot application development phase, 218–
219
conceptual model of technical architecture,
153–159
described, 152
distribution tiers, 152, 155–158
functional layers, 152, 154–155, 161–167
nontechnical communication by, 153
concurrency
application issues, 96–97
component architecture implementation,
176, 177–178
transaction models and, 183–184
configuration
defined, 99
dynamic changes, 99
enterprise application configuration, 157
workgroup application configuration, 156
consultants
for initiation phase, 207, 208
for pilot application development phase,
216–217
Schwab's use of, 9, 10
container viewpoint, 127–129
described, 125, 126
distribution services, 127–128
security and transaction services, 128
services provided, 127
state management, 129
container-managed persistence (CMP), 133
containers
application servers as, 129–132
client component support, 125
client platform, 117–118, 125
container-managed persistence, 133

overview, 117–118
relationship with components, 117
server platform, 117, 118, 131–132
viewpoint, 125, 126, 127–129
Web browsers as, 117
See also components
continuation phase of transition plan, 205, 223
control transition task. *See* management and
control transition task
controller/process pattern, 185–186
converting to an e-business, 60–64
focus on Web-oriented customers, 60–61
questions to consider, 61–64
radical reevaluation needed, 64
vulnerability to Internet startups, 62–63
See also transition plan
CORBA Component Model (CCM)
as component container, 117
as distributed component middleware, 111
as server component, 125
as server component model, 138
cost leadership strategy, 31–32
COTS (commercial-off-the-shelf) software, 92
CRM (Customer Relationship Management),
228–229
current position, strategy definition and, 23–24
custom tailoring. *See* personalization
Customer Relationship Management (CRM),
228–229
customer service
online support, 74–75
Web and expectations for, 65, 66–67
customers
24 X 7 availability expected by, 84–86
access types for, 85–86
business-to-customer (B2C) applications,
105–106
company interaction with, 62
e-business focus on, 58, 60–61, 67–68
expectations changed by the Web, 65–66,
86–88
infomediaries for, 42–43, 106–107
online vs. in-store shopping, 64
role in e-businesses, 64–68
in Stereos-R-Us example, 73–76
strategic analysis starting with, 30, 46
"touch and feel" needs of, 65
transition of business processes and, 60–61
usage patterns changed by the Web, 84–86
See also buyers
cyclical approach to strategy development, 34–
38
company evaluation, 36
environmental monitoring, 35
implementation, 38
strategy creation, 36
transition plan creation, 36–38

DaimlerChrylser, 13
See also automakers
data, as application component, 94
databases
abstraction layer, 147
managing server connections, 96
servers as clients, 96
defining a strategy
changing business environment and, 24–25
Phase 1: current position, 23–24
Phase 2: environmental conditions, 24
Phase 3: new strategy, 24
delivery process for Stereos-R-Us, 69, 77
deployment of applications, 100–101
client components for, 121–122
components as deployment units, 134,
135–136
deployment descriptors, 135–136
multiple version support, 100–101
security issues, 101
tools for "rich" clients, 100
deployment of distribution tiers, 156
device independence of technical architecture,
155
differentiation strategy, 31, 32
discounted prices, Web and customer expectations for, 65–67
distribution
access as barrier to entry, 27–28
as functional layer concern, 154
services, 127–128
distribution tiers of technical architecture, 155–
158
deployment over physical nodes, 156–157
described, 152
enterprise application configuration, 157
enterprise tier, 158, 191–193
functional layers assigned to, 156
implementation samples, 188–195
presentation tiers, 157–158, 189–191
resource tier, 158, 193–195
scalability concerns, 155
user tiers, 157–158, 189–191
workgroup application configuration, 156
workspace tiers, 158, 189–191
documenting existing business process, 54
domain components, 114
Drucker, Peter, 245
dynamic configuration changes, 99

EAI (enterprise application integration), 91–93,
203
ease-of-use issues for applications, 87
e-business challenges
24 X 7 availability, 84–86
automakers and parts suppliers example,
13–17

e-business challenges *(continued)*
   Charles Schwab example, 8–10
   Citigroup example, 10–13
   competition increased, 88
   component-based development, 88–91
   for *enhansiv,* 232–233
   integration and interoperability, 91–94
   as management challenge, 19–20
   new customer expectations, 86–88
   new generation of applications needed, 84
   new usage patterns, 84–86
   other challenges, 18
   product life cycle shortened, 88
   reconceptualization needed to meet, 19
   software and computer systems needed to
      meet, 19
   Toys R Us example, 2–8
   Web impact on business systems, 84
eCRM (e-business Customer Relationship Management), 228–229, 237–238, 241
   See also enhansiv
EJB. *See* Enterprise JavaBeans
Electronic Data Interchange (EDI) systems, 43
e-marketplaces, 105, 106
   See also exchanges
embedded functions in technical architecture,
   162
employees, competition for, 44
enhancements as technical architecture concern,
   155
enhansiv
   business challenge, 232–233
   changing software strategies, 233–235
   eCRM vision, 228–229
   enterprise channel management component,
      237–238
   expanding the transition, 239–242
   first steps and delays, 235–236
   goals, 231
   Internet Component Architecture (iCA),
      236–238
   overview, 227–232
   success of new technology, 242–243
enterprise application integration (EAI), 91–93,
   203
enterprise application requirements, 94–101
   application deployment, 100–101
   application management, 98–100
   client resources, 95–96
   multiple version support, 100–101
   resource utilization challenges, 94–95
   security, 101
   state management, 96–98
enterprise channel management component of
   enhansiv, 237–238
enterprise component architecture, 141–167
   abstraction layer, 147

   application building simplified by, 148
   architecture defined, 142
   business model, 143–144, 150, 172–173,
      213
   changes accommodated by, 147
   development process, 148–152
   e-business architectures, 143
   implementation architecture, 143, 150
   implementation independence, 147–148,
      151–152
   implementing, 169–196
   infrastructure vs., 149
   IT model, 150–151
   models vs., 148–149
   operational architecture, 144, 151
   overview, 142–148
   phased implementation process, 148
   platform specific IT model, 150–151
   separation of software concerns by, 146–147
   software architectures, 142–143
   software system concerns, 145
   subarchitectures, 143
   system described by, 144–145
   technical architecture, 150, 152–167
   transaction models, 180–182
   viewpoints, 146–147
   See also implementing a component archi-
      tecture; technical architecture
enterprise distribution tier, 158, 191–193
Enterprise JavaBeans
   activity controller implementation, 191–
      193
   application servers, 111
   bean-managed persistence, 133–134
   as component containers, 117
   as server component model, 137–138
enterprise model, creating, 52, 54
entities
   for business processes, 166
   model for component usage, 184
   process use of, 193
entrants
   barriers to entry, 27–28, 39–40, 62–63
   in Porter's model of competition, 27–28
environmental conditions
   monitoring continuously, 35–36
   in Porter's model of competition, 26–28
   strategy definition and, 24
established companies' resistance to change, 6–
   7, 197–199
eToys
   market capitalization, 3–4, 6
   success of, 105–106
   Toys R Us challenged by, 2–6
Evans, Philip, 40
events, publish and subscribe function for, 112–
   113

exchanges
        for automakers, 13, 14–18, 66–67
        AutoXchange system (Ford), 14–15, 16
        e-marketplaces, 105, 106
        joint system for automakers, 15–16
        monopoly issues, 15
        popularity of, 14
        quality issues, 17
        reengineering required for suppliers, 15, 17–18
        as second-generation e-businesses, 17, 18
        survey results, 198
        TradeXchange system (GM), 14, 15, 16
external processes, 50

facade/mediator pattern, 185
Federal Express, 2, 15
flexibility, 33, 203–204
Ford, Henry, 31
Ford Motor Company
        cost leadership strategy of, 31–32
        custom car creation by, 13–14
        online parts exchange, 14–15, 16, 66–67
        Oracle partnership with, 15
        Web site efforts announced, 13
        See also automakers
functional layers of technical architecture, 161–167
        activity controller, 164–165, 191–193
        application adapters, 166
        B2B controllers, 163–164
        business processes, 165–166
        concerns of, 154–155
        described, 152
        distribution tier assignments, 156
        embedded functions, 162
        enterprise application configuration, 157
        presentation layer, 161–162
        resource adapters, 166, 167
        user profiles, 163
        view controller, 162, 189–190
        work coordinator, 163, 164–165, 190
        workflow implementation, 165
        workgroup application configuration, 156

gazoo.com, 13
General Motors
        Commerce One partnership with, 15
        custom car creation by, 13–14
        differentiation strategy of, 32
        online parts exchange, 14, 15, 16, 66–67
        Web site efforts announced, 13
        See also automakers
Genesis Development Corporation, 199, 234
Gibbs, Rich, 239
globalization and increased competition, 28
GM. See General Motors

goals
        defined by strategy, 22
        of enhansiv, 231
        of initiation phase, 207, 210
        of organizational conversion phase, 220
        of pilot application development phase, 214
Goldman Sachs, 13, 14
government policies as barrier to entry, 28
granularity, increasing for requests, 174, 175
graphical user interface (GUI) components, 113
Greenspan, Alan, 4
Griss, Martin, 211
GUI components, 113

hardware, business process improvement from, 55–56
Harvard Business School, 22
high-touch items, 65

iCA (Internet Component Architecture), 236–238
identity policies, 177, 184
IDEs (integrated development environments), 126, 127
implementation
        architecture, 143, 150
        of business components, 112
        of changed business process, 56–57
        of component architecture, 169–196
        component models, 139
        in cyclical approach to strategy development, 38
        independence of architecture, 147–148, 151–152
        organizational conversion phase, 220–223
        phased process for architecture, 148
        See also implementing a component architecture; organizational conversion phase
implementing a component architecture, 169–196
        application scenarios, 188–195
        component factory, 170–172
        component model, 172–173
        component usage models, 183–184
        concurrency control, 176, 177–178
        enterprise tier sample, 191–193
        identity policies, 177
        interface design considerations, 173–176
        interface design patterns, 185–188
        location independence issues, 176–177
        presentation tier sample, 189–191
        resource tier sample, 193–195
        scalability issues, 176, 178
        state management, 179–180
        stateful vs. stateless components, 178, 179
        transaction models, 180–182

infomediaries, 42–43, 106–107
information
    independent product flow for, 41–42, 45
    infomediaries, 42–43, 106–107
    materials vs., 40, 41
    in product mix, 40–41
    role in e-business strategy, 40–42
    in value propositions, 40
information access applications, 103
information-sharing applications, 103
infrastructure
    architecture vs., 149
    component factory and, 170–171
infrastructure viewpoint, 159–161
    application services, 152, 160–161
    component factory and, 170–171
    described, 152–153
    frameworks, 152
    patterns, 153, 161
    programming environment provided by,
        159–160
    programming guidelines and productivity,
        160
initiation phase, 207–214
    applications task, 213
    architecture task, 211–212
    communication task, 208–209
    components task, 213
    goal, 207
    IT response, 209
    management and control task, 213–214
    organization, 207
    outside help needed for, 207, 208
    overview, 205
    personnel and training task, 209–211
    planning task, 207–208
    tools and techniques task, 213
    transition team, 207, 213–214
integrated development environments (IDEs),
    126, 127
integration
    with COTS software, 92
    e-business demand for, 93
    interoperability vs., 93
    with legacy systems, 91–92, 193–195
    with other systems, 92–93
    by technical architecture, 155
interface design
    component architecture implementation
        considerations, 173–176
    grouping related objects, 175
    increasing request granularity, 174, 175
    local objects, 175
    OO design conflicts, 174
    patterns, 185–188
    remote vs. local invocations, 174
    rules of thumb for, 173–174

    separating business logic decisions, 176
    single attribute distribution and, 176
interfaces for business components, 111–112
intermediaries (infomediaries), 42–43, 106–107
Internet Component Architecture (iCA), 236–
    238
Internet startups
    BPR vs. new company creation, 63
    drop in value (March 2000), 6, 246
    market capitalizations assigned to, 3–4
    predictions regarding, 245–246
    technology advantages of, 4–5
    vulnerability to, 62–63
interoperation
    integration vs., 93
    need for, 92–94
intranets, sticky components for, 122
IT model for component architectures, 150–
    151
IT process reengineering, 59, 202–204
    resistance to, 198–199

Jacobson, Ivar, 211
Java
    described, 120–121
    servlets, 189–190
Java Server Pages (JSPs), 190
Java Virtual Machine (JVM), 123
JavaBeans
    container support, 125
    described, 121
    as distributed component middleware, 111
    as nonsticky components, 123
    platform independence, 124
    security model, 123
JIT (just-in-time) training, 210
Jonsson, Patrik, 211
JSPs (Java Server Pages), 190
just-in-time (JIT) training, 210
JVM (Java Virtual Machine), 123

large-scale components, 114
legacy integration, 91–93, 193–195
legacy systems, outsourced, 200
local vs. remote invocations, 174
location independence, 176–177
low-touch items, 65

management
    of BPR change process, 57
    commitment required for e-business, 49
    IT managers, 224–225
    large gains from small changes, 55–56
    of rollout, 220
    as transition drivers, 38
    transition team, 207, 213–214
    See also transition plan

management and control transition task
    initiation phase, 213–214
    organizational conversion phase, 222–223
    overview, 206
    pilot application development phase, 219–220
managing applications, 90–100
Mandatory transaction model, 182
manufacturing process for Stereos-R-Us, 69, 75–76
market capitalization
    drop in value for e-businesses (March 2000), 6, 246
    of eToys, 3–4, 6
    physical commerce vs. e-commerce and, 3–4
    of Toys R Us, 3–4, 6
marketing and sales for Stereos-R-Us, 69, 73–75
materials vs. information, 40, 41
Matthews, Jason, 240
McCreary, Bill, 15
memory
    state management for, 179–180
    stateful vs. stateless components and, 179
Merrill Lynch, 3, 8, 16–17
metadata repository for legacy system interface, 195
methods transition task. See tools and techniques transition task
migrations as technical architecture concern, 155
monitoring
    alternative strategies, 36
    customers' Web practices, 36
    environmental conditions, 35–36
monopoly issues for automaker exchanges, 15
Moog, Bob, 5
Moore, Geoffrey, 198
MTS, 125
music CDs, information vs. material in, 41

Never transaction model, 182
niche specialization strategy, 31, 32
Nickelodeon, 6
nonsticky components, 122
Not Invented Here (NIH) syndrome, 115
Not supported transaction model, 182

OO conflicts with distributed design, 174
operational architecture, 144, 151
Oracle, 15
order fulfillment process example. See Stereos-R-Us example
organizational conversion phase, 220–223
    applications task, 222
    architecture task, 221
    components task, 221–222
    goal, 220

management and control task, 222–223
    organization, 220–221
    overview, 205
    planning task, 221
    tools and techniques task, 222
outsourced legacy systems, 200

packaging viewpoint, 134–136
    component assemblies, 136, 137
    components as deployment units, 134, 135–136
    described, 125–126, 127
    role-based security, 135
    transactional policy, 135
parts suppliers for automakers, 17–18
    online efforts by automakers, 13, 14–15
    price depression by exchange systems, 16, 17
    quality issues for exchange systems, 17
    reengineering required by exchange systems, 15, 17–18
    See also exchanges
patterns
    for interface design, 185–188
    for software design, 153, 161
per method state management model, 180
per process state management model, 180
per transaction state management model, 180
performance
    application issues, 87
    interface design and, 173
    remote vs. local invocations and, 174
    request granularity and, 174, 175
    transaction length and, 181
persistence adapter, 133
persistence management by components, 132–134
    component-managed persistence, 133–134
    container-managed persistence, 133
personalization
    business advantages from, 87–88
    customer expectations for, 66, 87
personnel and training transition task
    initiation phase, 209–211
    overview, 206
    pilot application development phase, 216–217
physical presence vs. Internet presence, 2–3, 62–63
Pilkington Holdings, 15
pilot application development phase, 214–220
    applications task, 219
    architecture task, 217–218
    communication task, 216
    components task, 218–219
    extending architectures and models, 218
    goal, 214

pilot application development phase *(continued)*
  initial pilot selection, 215, 217
  limiting pilot efforts, 215–216
  management and control task, 219–220
  organization, 214–215
  outside consultants' role, 216–217
  overview, 205
  personnel and training task, 216–217
  planning task, 215–216
  systematic resource development during,
      216
  tools and techniques task, 219
planning transition task
  initiation phase, 207–208
  organizational conversion phase, 221
  overview, 206
  pilot application development phase, 215–
      216
portals, 107
Porter, Michael E., 22
Porter's model of competition, 25–28, 38–44
  barriers to entry and, 27–28, 39–40
  buyers in, 26, 42–43
  cost leadership strategy, 31–32
  differentiation strategy, 31, 32
  for e-business relationships, 61
  employees as extension to, 44
  extending as cyclical approach, 34–38
  globalization and increased competition,
      28
  industry changes and, 29
  modified version, 39
  new companies in, 27–28
  niche specialization strategy, 31, 32
  rivalry in, 25–26
  substitutes in, 27, 44
  suppliers in, 26–27, 43
  value propositions and, 29–30, 45–46
presentation distribution tiers
  implementation sample, 189–191
  presentation rules, 190–191
  user tiers, 157–158
  workspace tiers, 158
presentation layer of technical architecture,
      161–162
price pressure
  customer expectations and, 65–67
  Web rivalry and, 42
process model for component usage, 184
productivity
  component-based application development
      and, 90–91
  programming guidelines and, 160
products
  information and materials mix in, 40
  shortened life cycle, 88
  value propositions for, 29–30

programming environment
  patterns for software design, 153, 161
  of technical architecture, 159–160
proprietary knowledge as barrier to entry, 27–28
publish and subscribe function, 112–113

quality control transition task. *See* management
    and control transition task

reconceptualization
  established companies' resistance to, 6–7,
      197–199
  self-competition due to, 3, 5, 7
  turf fights resulting from, 7–8
redesigning the business process, 54–56
  See also business process reengineering
      (BPR)
Reed, John, 12
reengineering business processes. *See* business
    process reengineering (BPR)
remote vs. local invocations, 174
request granularity, increasing, 174, 175
Required transaction model, 182
Requires new transaction model, 182
resource adapters, 166, 167
resource distribution tier, 158, 193–195
resource utilization
  application deployment, 100–101
  application management, 99–100
  in application servers, 95
  client resources, 95–96
  constituents, 94
  servers as system resources, 97–98
  state management, 96–98
reuse of components, 115–116, 135, 218–219,
      220, 221–222
rich clients, 100
Riscalla, Daniel, 230, 241
rivalry
  assessing competitors, 62
  globalization and, 28
  infomediaries and, 42–43
  information as product and, 41–42
  in Porter's model of competition, 25–26
  Web, price pressure and, 42
role-based security, 135
rules service for business processes, 166

sales and marketing for Stereos-R-Us, 69, 73–
      75
scalability
  activity controller requirements, 193
  component architecture implementation,
      176, 178
  distribution tiers and, 155
  as functional layer concern, 154, 157
  process controllers and, 185–186

stateful vs. stateless components and, 178
    transaction models and, 183–184
Schwab, Charles, 9
Schwab (company). *See* Charles Schwab
second-generation component models, 115
second-generation e-businesses
    automakers' exchange initiative as, 17, 18
    Web applications vs., 49
security
    client components, 123–124
    container viewpoint, 128
    enterprise applications, 101
    role-based, 135
self-competition
    challenge of, 7
    at Toys R Us, 3, 5
separation
    of application from infrastructure develop-
        ment, 154–155
    of business logic decisions, 176
    of software concerns by component archi-
        tecture, 146–147
server components, 125–127
    application servers as containers, 129–132
    business functions supported by, 118
    business viewpoint, 125, 126, 132–134
    container viewpoint, 125, 126, 127–129
    models, 136–138
    packaging viewpoint, 125–126, 127, 134–
        136
    See also components
servers
    as application components, 94
    application servers, 129–132
    as clients, 96
    component containers for, 117, 118
    component models, 136–138
    concurrency issues, 97
    database connection management, 96
    resource utilization in, 95, 96–97
    server components, 125–127
    state management, 96–98
    as system resources, 97–98
service model for component usage, 183, 184
services
    application services, 152, 160–161
    distribution services, 127–128
    security and transaction services, 128
    value propositions for, 29–30
session model for component usage, 183, 184
small companies' transition issues, 200
software
    architectures, 142–143
    business process improvement from, 55–56
    competition for employees, 44
    for customers, 64
    enhansiv software strategies, 233–235

IT process reengineering, 59, 202–204
    patterns for design, 153, 161
    Stereos-R-Us example, 78–79
    See also applications
Software Reuse, 211
Stambouly, Ernest, 240
state management, 96–98
    component architecture implementation,
        179–180
    concurrency issues, 96–97
    container viewpoint, 129
    controlling memory resources, 179–180
    defined, 97
    models, 180
    for session state, 191
    transaction models and, 183–184
stateful components, 178, 179
stateless components, 178, 179
steel exchange, 14
Stereos-R-Us example, 68–81
    delivery process changes, 77
    first draft of revised e-business process, 79–
        81
    management disagreements, 72–73
    managing the transition, 77
    manufacturing and delivery functions, 69
    manufacturing process changes, 75–76
    marketing and sales changes, 73–75
    marketing and sales functions, 69
    order fulfillment process overview, 68
    processes already improved, 69–709
    resistance to reengineering, 70–71
    software development process changes, 78–
        79
    Web customer increases, 71
sticky components, 122
strategy development, 21–46
    component architecture business model,
        143–144, 150, 172–173, 213
    cost leadership strategy, 31–32
    customers as starting point, 30, 46
    cyclical approach, 34–38
    defining a strategy, 23–25
    differentiation strategy, 31, 32
    e-business strategy, 32–38
    flexibility requirements, 33
    goals defined by strategy, 22
    industry changes and, 29
    information flow and, 40–43, 45
    niche specialization strategy, 31, 32
    Porter's definition of strategy, 22–25
    Porter's model of competition, 25–28, 38–
        44
    reliance on winning strategies, 32
    schools of, 22
    value propositions for, 29–30, 45–46
subscribe function, 112–113

substitutes
    Internet's effect on, 44
    in Porter's model of competition, 27, 44
suppliers
    company integration with, 43, 56, 104–
        105
    company interaction with, 62
    competition increased by Web, 88
    e-business focus on supply chain, 58–59
    e-marketplaces, 105, 106
    Internet's affect on, 43
    in Porter's model of competition, 26–27,
        43
    supply chain integration applications, 104–
        105
    See also parts suppliers for automakers
supply chain integration applications, 104–105,
    106
Supports transaction model, 182
system components, 114

technical architecture, 152–167
    application services, 152, 160–161
    conceptual model, 152, 153–159
    described, 150
    developing, 211–212
    distribution tiers, 152, 155–158
    e-business architecture, 152
    functional layers, 152, 154–155, 161–167
    infrastructure viewpoint, 152–153, 159–
        161, 170–171
    patterns, 153, 161
    programming environment, 159–160
    See also functional layers of technical archi-
        tecture
techniques transition task. See tools and tech-
    niques transition task
technology independence
    abstract component models and, 139
    client components and, 124
    implementation component models and,
        139
    of technical architecture, 155
thin clients, 100, 121
Time-Warner-AOL, 29, 85
tools and techniques transition task
    initiation phase, 213
    organizational conversion phase, 222
    overview, 206
    pilot application development phase, 219
"touch and feel" purchases, 65
Toyota, 13
    See also automakers
Toys R Us, 2–8
    established presence of, 2
    eToys challenge to, 2–6
    market capitalization, 3–4, 6

resistance to change at, 5–6, 7–8
    technology lag in, 4–5
Toysrus.com
    initial problems, 5–6
    Nickelodeon deal with, 6
    startup, 5
TradeXchange system (GM), 14, 15, 16
training transition task. See personnel and train-
    ing transition task
transaction models, 180–182
transaction services, 128
transactional policy for components, 135
transition plan, 197–225
    commitment required for, 48–49
    in cyclical approach to strategy develop-
        ment, 36–38
    first-generation vs. second-generation appli-
        cations, 49
    outsourced legacy systems and, 200
    overview, 48, 201–204
    Phase 1: initiation, 205, 207–214
    Phase 2: pilot application development,
        205, 214–220
    Phase 3: organizational conversion, 205,
        220–223
    Phase 4: continuation, 205, 223
    resistance to reengineering, 198–199
    survey on transition prevalence, 197–198
    tasks overview, 206
    transition team, 207, 213–214
    types of transitions, 199–201
transition team, 207, 213–214
Truyen, Frank, 237
TRW, 15

Unified Modeling Language (UML), 139,
    195
UPS, 2
usage models for components, 183–184
user distribution tiers, 157–158, 189–191
user profiles in technical architecture, 163
utility components, 113

value object pattern, 187
value propositions
    creating new, 45–46
    defined, 29
    information in, 40
    materials vs., 40
    overview, 29–30
view controller, 162, 189–190
Visual Basic applications, 90–91

Web
    BPR for, 68–81
    focus on customers willing to use, 60–61
    impact on business systems, 84

infomediaries, 42–43
markets not suitable for, 65
price pressure and, 42
Web applications
overview, 102
second-generation e-businesses vs., 49
survey results, 198
third-party tools, 121
Web browsers
as component containers, 117
nonsticky components for, 122–123
See also ActiveX

work coordinator, 163, 164–165, 190
workflow implementation in technical architecture, 165
workflow systems, 56
workspace distribution tiers, 158, 189–191
Wurster, Thomas S., 40

XML
files as deployment descriptors, 136
message formatting by, 194–195
schemas, 195
tags, 194–195

About the Authors

Paul Harmon is a well-known consultant and technology analyst. He is the editor of the *Component Development Strategies* newsletter and the former editor of *BPR Strategies* newsletter. He is a Senior Consultant with Cutter Consortium's Distributed Computing Architecture service. With Cutter and independently, he consults with major corporations on trends in the software industry and on improving business processes for e-business. He has coauthored many books, including *Understanding UML: The Developer's Guide* (1997, Morgan Kaufmann), *The Object Technology Casebook* (1996, John Wiley & Sons), and the international bestseller *Expert Systems: Artificial Intelligence for Business* (1985, John Wiley & Sons).

Michael Rosen is Chief Enterprise Architect at Genesis Development Corporation, (an IONA Technologies' Company), a consulting organization specializing in enterprise component strategies and solutions. He consults with major corporations in the development of e-business enterprise architectures for the current and next generation of applications. He has over 20 years of experience in distributed computing technologies including transaction processing, object systems, DCE, MOM, COM, and CORBA and has been a product architect for a number of commercially available middleware products. He is coauthor of the book *Integrating CORBA and COM Applications* (1998, John Wiley & Sons).

Michael Guttman is Chief Technology Officer and cofounder of Genesis Development Corporation, now an Iona Technologies' Company. He is an expert in enterprise component architectures and in the analysis and design of large-scale distributed applications and services. He has been a long-standing member of the Technical Committee of the Object Management Group (OMG), where he played a key role in the definition and evolution of CORBA (Common Object Request Broker Architecture), OMG's primary standard for distributed object computing. He has also served on the program committee of Object World and the Board of Directors of OMG. He is the author of many articles on component and enterprise computing, as well as coauthor of the book *The Object Technology Revolution* (1995, John Wiley & Sons).